VALCOUR

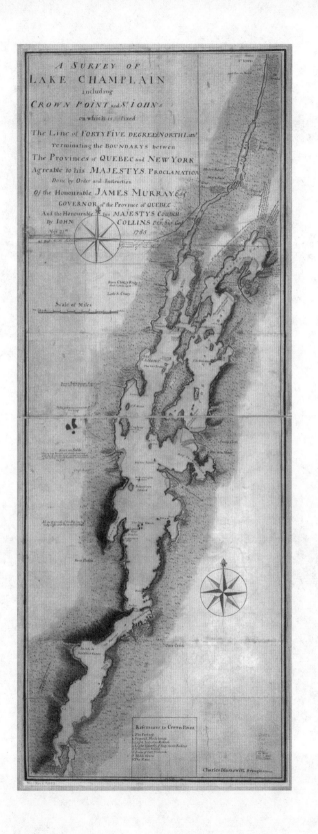

Benedict Arnold

Horatio Gates

Philip Schuyler

Guy Carleton

VALCOUR

The 1776 CAMPAIGN
THAT SAVED
the CAUSE of LIBERTY

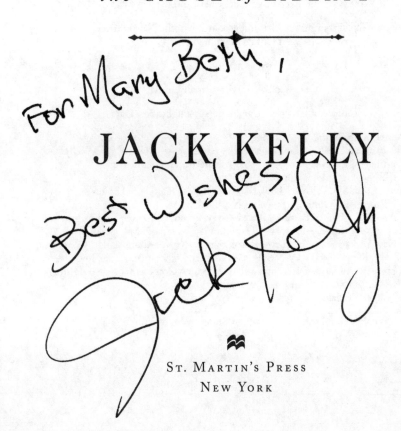

For Mary Beth,

JACK KELLY

Best Wishes

Jack Kelly

ST. MARTIN'S PRESS
NEW YORK

First published in the United States by St. Martin's Press, an imprint of
St. Martin's Publishing Group

VALCOUR. Copyright 2021 by Jack Kelly. All rights reserved. Printed in the
United States of America. For information, address St. Martin's Press, 120
Broadway, New York, NY 10271.

Map page iii and photograph of *Philadelphia II* page 261 courtesy of the
Lake Champlain Maritime Museum

PORTRAITS, PAGE IV:
Benedict Arnold: Copy of engraving by H. B. Hall after John Trumbull,
published 1879. Credit: National Archives and Records Administration.
Horatio Gates: Credit: The Miriam and Ira D. Wallach Division of Art,
Prints and Photographs: Print Collection, The New York Public Library.
Philip Schuyler: Credit: The Miriam and Ira D. Wallach Division of Art,
Prints and Photographs: Print Collection, The New York Public Library.
Guy Carleton: Credit: Library of Congress Prints and Photographs Division.

Maps, pages xi–xv, and drawings of American Champlain Fleet,
pages 257–260—Joy Taylor

Gondola *Philadelphia* photo, page 252, courtesy of The Smithsonian
National Museum of American History

Watercolors page 262, by C. Randle, courtesy of the Naval History and
Heritage Command

www.stmartins.com

Designed by Meryl Sussman Levavi

Library of Congress Cataloging-in-Publication Data

Names: Kelly, Jack, 1949- author.
Title: Valcour : the 1776 campaign that saved the cause of liberty / Jack Kelly.
Identifiers: LCCN 2020045307 | ISBN 9781250247117 (hardcover) |
   ISBN 9781250247124 (ebook)
Subjects: LCSH: Valcour Island, Battle of, N.Y., 1776. | United States—
   History—Revolution, 1775-1783—Naval operations. | Arnold, Benedict,
   1741–1801. | United States--History—Revolution, 1775-1783—Campaigns. |
   New York (State)—History—Revolution, 1775-1783—Naval operations. |
   New York (State)—History—Revolution, 1775-1783—Campaigns. | Champlain,
   Lake, Region—History, Naval—18th century. | Champlain, Lake, Region—
   History, Military—18th century. |United States. Continental Navy—History.
Classification: LCC E241.V14 K45 2021 | DDC 973.3/5—dc23
LC record available at https://lccn.loc.gov/2020045307

First published in the United States by St. Martin's Press

First Edition: 2021
10 9 8 7 6 5 4 3 2 1

Our decks were stain'd with blood.
Our crew behaved with the greatest bravery.

—Lieutenant Isaiah Canfield

Contents

PART TWO

‿

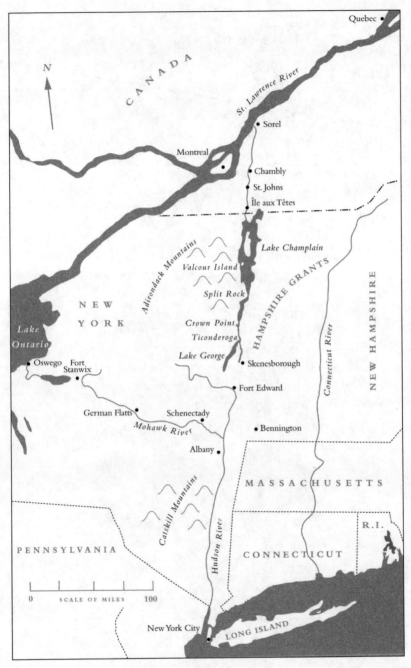

1. The Great Warpath

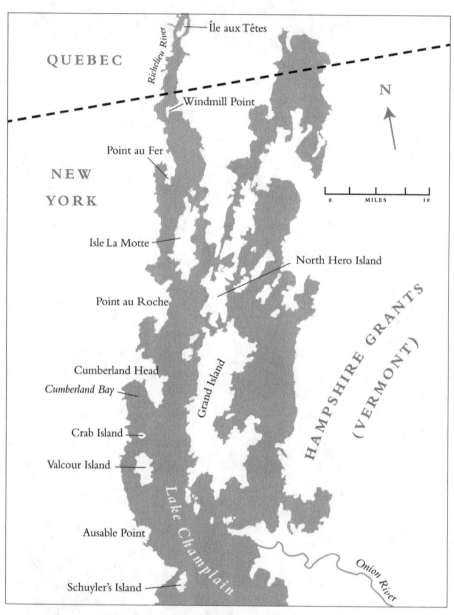

Île aux Têtes

Richelieu River

QUEBEC

Windmill Point

N

Point au Fer

NEW
YORK

0   MILES   10

Isle La Motte

North Hero Island

Point au Roche

HAMPSHIRE GRANTS
(VERMONT)

Cumberland Head

Cumberland Bay

Grand Island

Crab Island

Valcour Island

Lake Champlain

Ausable Point

Onion River

Schuyler's Island

2. Lake Champlain (north)

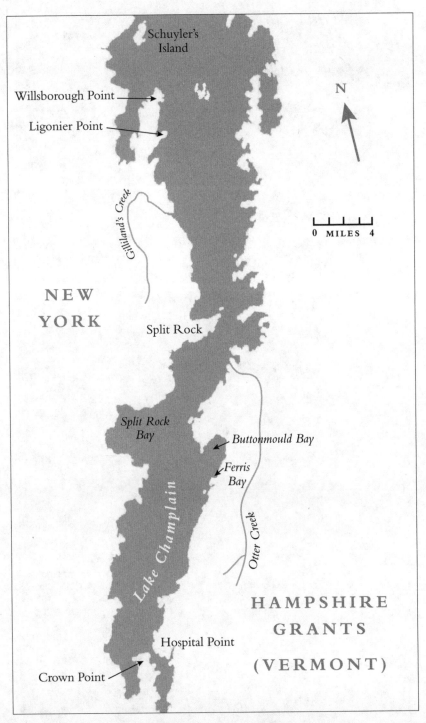

Schuyler's
Island

Willsborough Point

Ligonier Point

N

Gilliland's Creek

NEW
YORK

Split Rock

0 MILES 4

Split Rock
Bay

Buttonmould Bay

Ferris
Bay

Lake Champlain

Otter Creek

HAMPSHIRE
GRANTS
(VERMONT)

Hospital Point

Crown Point

3. Lake Champlain (south)

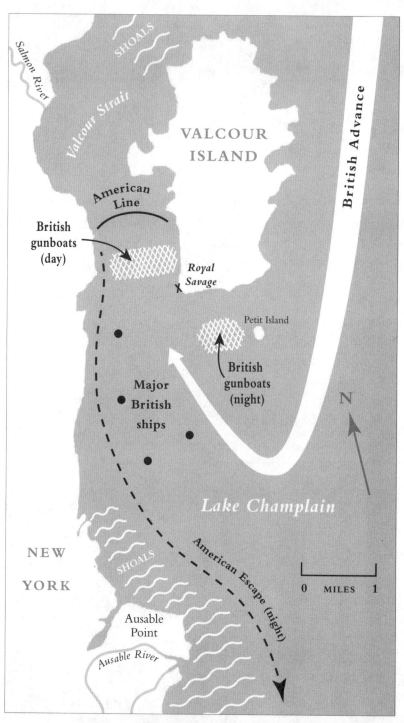

4. Valcour Island (battle scene)

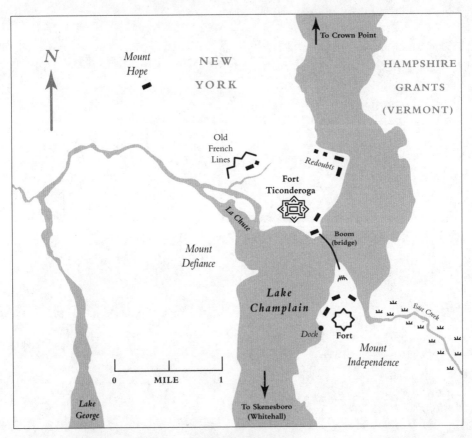

5. *Fort Ticonderoga*

PART ONE

I

---◆---◆---

The Last Man

ON THE MILD EVENING OF ONE OF THE LONGEST DAYS OF
1776, a brigadier general of the rebel army strode the bank of the
Richelieu River. He barked orders and urged on the beleaguered
troops. A soldier, his face a macabre mask of pustules, stumbled toward the broken wharfs of St. Johns, Quebec. Fever had lofted his
mind to nightmare. He peered through crusted lids at the coins of
light winking from the surface of the river. His companion, who
remembered his own bout with the pox, helped him climb over the
gunwale of a flat-bottomed rowboat, where he joined twenty other
men resting on thwarts or slumped between them.

The riverside smelled of desolation, of woodsmoke and smoldering pitch and animal carcasses. Gnats stitched the air. Soldiers
swatted clouds of blood-hungry mosquitoes. The men imagined
the distant tramp of boots, British infantrymen in scarlet coats,
armed grenadiers hurrying forward to kill them. A few civilians
clutching paltry treasures boarded boats bound for the unknown.

The army's commander, thirty-six-year-old New Hampshire
lawyer John Sullivan, had already departed upstream to supervise
the procession of vessels that were ferrying back and forth to withdraw his beaten men. Two weeks earlier in distant Philadelphia,

Richard Henry Lee had proposed to Congress that the colonies declare themselves independent states. His words made the hearts of patriots leap, but the men of the northern army knew only fear and defeat.

The few remaining American soldiers ranged through the demolished settlement with flaming brands, anointing anything that would burn. The patriots, who had lately dreamed of adding Canada to the thirteen colonies, now only prayed they could return to their own country alive.

～

St. Johns lay twenty-five miles north of the border of what was still known as the United Colonies. The town center was dominated by a small bastion, a stone barracks and magazine surrounded by two redoubts of earth and logs. A fetid ditch and a maze of trenches completed the fortification. The village's few dwellings, shops, and warehouses had been burned, its bridges and mills smashed.

Frenchmen had erected Fort St. Jean more than a generation earlier to guard the waterway that led into Canada from the British colonies to the south. The now blasted settlement lay on a stretch of fertile farm fields and wetlands at the top of a series of rapids. The Richelieu flowed northward out of Lake Champlain and down to the St. Lawrence River.

The general directing the retreat at St. Johns was Benedict Arnold, an early hero of the year-old conflict. His leaden jaw, meaty confidence, and agate eyes gave him the aspect of a professional pugilist. Although he walked with a limp, he did not carry himself like a defeated man.

The landscape was familiar to him—not that long ago he had traded here regularly. He had wrangled herds of shaggy Canadian steeds onto ships, selling them for a profit in the West Indies. British lords dismissed him as a "horse jockey." How the devil could such a plebeian, they muttered, have the gall to . . .

Fourteen months, a lifetime, had passed since Arnold left his business in the care of his sister and rushed off to join the wild patriotic response that greeted the violence at Lexington and Concord.

The previous autumn, he had led a band of American soldiers over the Maine mountains to attack Quebec City, gaining a reputation as one of the most audacious of the patriot officers, America's Hannibal. Now he was overseeing the last days of that spent venture.

⌁

Every war starts with enthusiasm, followed by a sober recognition of the reality, the cost, and the horror. In Canada, Benedict Arnold had seen men die and had suffered a serious wound to his left leg. He had endured an extraordinarily brutal winter, with drifts of snow creeping toward the top of Quebec's high walls. He had watched smallpox scythe whole companies, had described his men as "neglected by Congress below; pinched with every want here."

In early May 1776, while Arnold was still recuperating from his injury in Montreal, the first of ten thousand British redcoats had landed at Quebec. Their appearance sparked a disgraceful rout. Fleeing Americans abandoned sick comrades, looted supplies, and ran away "in the most helter skelter manner," leaving behind muskets, ammunition, even clothes.

An orderly retreat in the face of the enemy is one of the most difficult of military maneuvers, and in a prolonged contest, one of the most essential. Arnold had looked on in dismay as the shattered and demoralized American army arrived at Sorel, where the Richelieu joined the St. Lawrence. He vowed to do everything possible to "keep possession of this country, which has cost us so much blood and expense."

In a last-ditch effort to stem the retreat, General Sullivan had boldly sent his men down the St. Lawrence to attack a superior enemy force at Three Rivers. Appointed for his connections rather than his competence, Sullivan had little military experience to draw on. The American attackers were hurled back, losing three hundred men in the process. The disaster made Sullivan conclude that he commanded "a dispirited Army, filled with horror at the thought of seeing their enemy."

Five days later, on June 13, Arnold wrote to Sullivan, advising him to get out of Canada while he still had an army to lead. "The junction of the Canadians with the colonies, an object which brought us into this country is now at an end." His advice, he insisted, was not motivated by fear for his personal safety: "I am content to be the last man who quits this country, and fall, so that my country rise. But let us not fall together."

Events had forced the truth of his words on Sullivan. The British forces, led by Canada's able governor and military leader, General Guy Carleton, soon arrived by ship at Sorel. Sullivan scrambled south to Chambly, a fortified town fifty miles farther south along the Richelieu at the bottom of the rapids. There his men burned gunboats and an army barracks to prevent their use by the enemy, "leaving nothing but ruin behind."

A rumor of approaching redcoats set off a panic that, Sullivan reported, "had the effect of sending great Numbers of officers and Soldiers upon the run." Those who remained struggled to haul boats loaded with arms and supplies up the long rapids. Wading through the icy water, they manned poles and ropes to drag the vessels against the sharp spring current.

A chaplain who accompanied the troops observed: "Our days are days of darkness."

⁓

From his headquarters in Montreal, Arnold sent an aide, nineteen-year-old James Wilkinson, to deliver a message to Sullivan at St. Johns, twenty-five miles to the east. Encountering instead a force of British troops, the young man rushed back to raise the alarm. Arnold immediately mustered Montreal's three-hundred-man garrison. That night he ferried them across the St. Lawrence in a driving rain. "Had not the wind failed," Carleton wrote to Lord Germain, King George's secretary of state for the colonies, "this column might have arrived at Longueuil [on the southern bank of the St. Lawrence] the same night, and about the same time with Mr. Arnold and the remainder of the Rebels."

The Americans rounded up carts and Arnold led his men to St. Johns, destroying bridges and felling trees in their wake. Two days later, on June 17, Sullivan called a council of war. His officers, led by Arnold, urged him to fall back.

Ever on the lookout for his own honor, Sullivan decided to move his remaining men only to Île aux Noix, an island in the river about halfway to the American border. He insisted he would remain in Canada pending a direct order from his superior, Major General Philip Schuyler. That Noix was a soggy, mosquito-infested trap did not deter him.

Soldiers rowed bateaux back and forth along the river that day and the next. They hauled out tons of supplies, including the disassembled frames of several small war vessels that American boatbuilders had been constructing along the wharfs. By June 18 only a few men remained at St. Johns, including Arnold, Wilkinson, and forty-four-year-old Jeduthan Baldwin, a Massachusetts farmer and carpenter who had joined the rebels as a military engineer and was just getting over an attack of smallpox.

An umber sun was sinking into the thick air of the midsummer evening. All suspected that the British had already reached Chambly, twelve miles downstream. They waited nervously for the order to push off.

Benedict Arnold had an exceptional ability to envision the narrow and wider pictures simultaneously. He recognized the immediate problem in Canada, but he saw as well the larger situation on the continent. Once the British drove the Americans from the northern province, they would have easy access to Lake Champlain. Only a depleted American garrison up the lake at Fort Ticonderoga, together with a few armed sailing vessels, would stand in their way. If they broke through, they could continue down Lake George and make a quick march to the Hudson River, opening the way to Albany. From there they could continue south, threatening George Washington's army in New York City. A right turn could take redcoats up the Mohawk Valley, already rife with loyalists and Indians potentially hostile to the patriot cause. Veering to the left, they could strike through the undefended heart of New England, crashing on toward Boston, which they had abandoned in March. They had to be stopped before these possibilities became dire threats.

In the thirteen colonies, men were wrestling with the structure of a new order. "The important day is come, or near at hand," an anonymous screed declared, "that America is to assume a form of government for herself." The writer insisted that "there must never be any power like a Kingly power" in the country they were forming. The kingly power of Britain, it was now clear, would do its utmost to prevent the nation from being born.

For the moment, as dusk descended, the immediate danger had to be addressed—saving the men of the northern army, securing supplies, destroying everything that the enemy could put to use. With a creak of leather, the general swung onto his horse. Followed by Wilkinson, he headed north to survey the scene. It was a gesture of defiance characteristic of Arnold.

The men rode only a couple of miles before spotting in the distance the bright red splotches of enemy uniforms. Arnold sat on his horse for a moment, watching and evaluating. He was well known to the British. The soldiers recognized him and began to run forward. Finally he and Wilkinson yanked their horses' heads and spurred back toward St. Johns.

"I am sorry you did not get Arnold," Germain would write in reply to Carleton, "for of all the Americans, he is the most enterprising and dangerous."

Baldwin, a man not impressed by bravado, paced the wharf beside the last serviceable boat left in the region. The two riders soon appeared from up the rutted road, their horses blowing as they clattered to a halt beside the river landing. The sky was silently exhaling the last of its light.

Arnold climbed down, removed his saddle, and heaved it into the boat. Wilkinson did the same. The general pulled out his flintlock pistol. While the others watched, this man who knew and loved horses put the gun's muzzle to the head of his mount and pulled the trigger. A muffled blast; the animal's legs buckled. It collapsed to the ground, gushing blood. A reluctant Wilkinson obeyed the order to dispatch his horse in the same way. Nothing would be left for the enemy. Nothing.

The men climbed into the boat. With the British soldiers approaching in the distance, Arnold shoved the vessel away from the wharf and leapt in, fulfilling his offer to be the "last man" to quit the country. The invasion of Canada was at an end. The danger to the American cause was just beginning.

2

Superiority on the Lakes

"WAS STRUCK WITH AMAZEMENT UPON MY ARRIVAL,"
army doctor Lewis Beebe wrote from Île aux Noix, "to see the vast
crowds of poor distressed Creatures ... Language cannot describe
nor imagination paint, the scenes of misery and distress the Sol-
diery endure."

An hour and a half after leaving his horse dead on the riverbank
at St. Johns, Benedict Arnold arrived at Noix, the Island of Nuts,
to find a hellhole. In the twilight he could see the masses of the
sick, infected, Beebe wrote, "with fluxes, fevers, Small Pox and over
run with legions of lice." Stretched out in barns, lacking blankets,
maggots writhing on their bodies, the men were "calling for relief,
but in vain." The devout Dr. Beebe commented, "God seems to be
greatly angry with us."

General Sullivan was anxious to alert General Schuyler to the
vexing situation and to deflect blame for the Canadian debacle
from himself. He chose to send Arnold and his aide Wilkinson to
Fort Ticonderoga in order to confer with the commander of the
Northern Department.

As he was rowed southward the next day, Arnold looked out on
the great forests that extended beyond sight. The birch and maple

and beech trees were bursting with their summer leaves. The dark stands of hemlock and spruce stood sentinel in the high clefts of rocks. Only widely spaced shorefront farms disturbed nature's ancient face. The remoteness of the wilderness and pioneers' lingering fear of Indian raids discouraged settlement. In addition, both New Hampshire and New York claimed the territory between Lake Champlain and the Connecticut River to the east, land that would become the state of Vermont. The validity of property titles there was uncertain.

The fresh water glistened in the sun. To the west, the foothills of the towering Adirondacks nearly abutted the shore along much of the lake's length. The eastern bank rose more gradually onto a flat plain, beyond which the Green Mountains seemed to float in the blue distance.

Lake Champlain was a ragged carrot-shaped body of water that narrowed to a taproot at its southern end. Its basin had been scoured by glaciers that, it would later be known, had last retreated thirteen thousand years earlier. The melting of the ice dam in the St. Lawrence Valley had allowed seawater to pour in from the north and had for a time turned Champlain into an arm of the ocean. Arnold's boat floated over the skeletons of beluga whales buried in the sediment below.

For eons, the lake had drained south. With the glaciers gone, the unburdened land rebounded and left the valley tipped to the north. The flow of water reversed, seeping down the Richelieu into the St. Lawrence to reach the Atlantic. The south end of the lake, barely wider than a river, now ended in a swampy expanse near Skenesborough, New York, almost 120 miles south of the Canadian border. Because of the direction of flow, "up the lake" meant toward the south, a designation that ran counter to intuition and created confusion then as it does now.

⁓

The lake held many memories for Arnold. During the French and Indian War, the future general, then a sixteen-year-old apothecary apprentice, had tramped north in response to a 1757 attack at Fort

William Henry on Lake George. The young man, proud to serve his king, demonstrated his endurance by marching for a week with a militia contingent from his hometown of Norwich, Connecticut. But the threat was over by the time they arrived, and he returned without seeing action.

As a boy in Norwich, Benedict Arnold occasionally performed a favorite stunt. A large gristmill in town featured an undershot waterwheel. Arnold entertained his friends and horrified onlookers by leaping onto the top of the wheel and "holding on as it made its revolutions," riding it downward into the sluice, knowing if he lost his grip he would die. The water gushing through the race would try to pull him away, but he held his breath and did not let go. He burst into the air still gripping the wheel. His taste for adventure and risk-taking would remain a lifelong trait.

Eighteen years after his brief military experience, having built his own apothecary business into an international trading firm and moved to New Haven, Arnold had again taken up martial affairs. Amid the revolutionary turmoil, he helped to found a militia unit chartered as the Governor's 2nd Company of Foot Guards. On April 21, 1775, news of the clash of patriots with the king's troops at Lexington and Concord electrified the town's population. Arnold, dressed in a fancy military uniform, whipped up the passion of his men, who voted to hurry to the scene of the violence. He recruited a few Yale students eager to join the action.

Arnold had little formal training in war. His facility came from a mind tuned to the right key, poised between reality and imagination, agile, decisive, and able to grasp the dynamics of events in motion.

The people of New Haven cheered—the town fathers hesitated. They wanted to know more about what had happened outside Boston before supporting a rising against the established order. They denied the Foot Guards access to gunpowder.

A standoff developed. Amid shouting and finger-pointing, Arnold declared: "None but Almighty God shall prevent my marching!" He threatened to break into the powder magazine and remove the ammunition by force. Town officials gave way to what came to be known as the *rage militaire*, the popular passion that swept the colonies during the early months of the Revolution. Arnold and his armed men marched to Cambridge.

It was a decisive moment in Benedict Arnold's life. Always ambitious, he had been shrewd enough to weather the long recession and political turmoil that had crimped commerce in the years after the French and Indian conflict. He had braved the hazards intrinsic to sea trading and had made his fortune by hard work, smart dealing, and not a little smuggling. By 1775, he owned ships, wharfs, warehouses, and a New Haven mansion.

Thirty-four years old, with three young sons and a wife he loved, he did not need to assume the risk of rebellion. When he had opened his original apothecary shop he adopted the motto *Sibi totique,* "For himself and for all." In his early life, he had acted very much for himself. When the rebellion broke out, his passions ignited. He was caught up in the larger cause. Few could claim a greater impulse toward patriotism or a more fiery resolve to gamble all to break the colonies' bondage to Britain.

‿

Now, on June 24, 1776, a year into the conflict, a two-day journey brought him to Crown Point, a neck of land less than a mile across that jutted into the lake from the west shore. Two forts, one erected by the French, the other by British forces, both lay in ruins. The American soldiers gathered there lacked leadership, energy, and morale. They formed a picture of defeat.

Arnold continued fifteen miles to Fort Ticonderoga. The fort itself had lately been described as "in a ruinous condition," a post "more for show . . . than service." Indeed, Arnold could see little changed from when he had participated in its capture the previous May. He did not find General Schuyler, who, suffering a fever, had returned home to Albany. Arnold commandeered another boat on Lake George, which lay just over a rise of land, to continue on his journey.

As they traveled south, Arnold and Wilkinson saw increasing signs of civilization. At Fort Edward they took passage on the Hudson River and were greeted by well-built homes on both shores. In orderly fields, scarecrows flapped their arms over stands of young wheat and rye.

It was already night when they approached Albany, an over-grown village of some three thousand souls. The town had been founded as a Dutch trading post in the early 1600s, and even now English was only rarely heard in the streets. The business district was anchored on the river and stretched westward up a slope to a small stone fort. The collection of Dutch-pattern houses had spilled well beyond the original stockade walls.

The travelers landed at the waterfront a half mile south of town and climbed the hill to the mansion of Philip Schuyler. Unlike the busy, gabled cottages in town, the house was "attractive in its simple elegance," built in the style of grand English homes. It faced east across the river and was surrounded by immaculate French-style gardens.

Although it was almost midnight, the commander, recuperating from his illness, was still up, still working. He had returned to Albany for the healthier environment and to be closer to the nerve center of his area of responsibility, which extended from Canada down Lake Champlain, westward along the Mohawk River, and southward on the Hudson. His fever had broken only a few days earlier. He was glad to receive news from the north, however bad it might be.

Schuyler was a tall, slender man with the studious look of a Reformed parson. A portrait shows close-set skeptical eyes peering from either side of a billhook nose, his small head balanced on a patrician neck. His hauteur suggested his descent from Dutch aristocrats. Like them, he owned extensive lands around Albany. He had made a good marriage with the beautiful and wealthy Catherine Van Rensselaer, known as Kitty. A golden couple, they sat at the summit of Albany society and were the parents of three marriageable daughters, including Eliza, who in a few years would become the wife of Alexander Hamilton.

Wilkinson, who had a courtier's eye for detail, noted Schuyler's "strong, fertile and cultivated mind; with polished manners he united the most amiable disposition and insinuating address." The self-made Benedict Arnold admired Schuyler's easy dignity. The commanding general welcomed his visitors, his words spiced with the Dutch accent he had not quite purged from his speech—he and Kitty, like most Albany natives, spoke Dutch at home.

Schuyler had been educated by tutors and had lived his early life in New York City, socializing with the DeLanceys, the Livingstons, and other grandees of the colony, many of them his cousins. Arnold's education had been cut short—he had spent his adolescence and adulthood in the hard-edged world of trade. Like most sea captains, he had exerted his authority by means of a steely will, a profane tongue, and a hot temper. His manners could not match Schuyler's polish. One observer described Arnold's conversation as "indelicate . . . His language was ungrammatical and his pronunciation vulgar."

Although he had only distressing news to report, Arnold did not flirt with despair. He gave a calm assessment of the rebels' prospects for stopping the British advance. Schuyler listened. He had formed a positive impression of the man when Arnold visited him a year earlier after capturing Fort Ticonderoga and raiding St. Johns. He concurred with Charles Carroll, one of the congressional commissioners to Canada, who thought Arnold "will turn out a great man. He has great vivacity, perseverance, resources, intrepidity, and a cool judgment."

Arnold's theme was time. It would take time for the British to regroup and bring up the supplies needed to sustain the thousands of men of an invasion force. They would have to wait to draw on the summer harvest before plunging into hostile territory where farms were scarce. Because no roads penetrated the forested Champlain Valley, they would need time to construct vessels on the lake. Flat-bottomed bateaux, thirty feet long and tapered at both ends, which they could hammer together quickly, would not suffice. General Carleton would need warships to protect his troop carriers from armed American boats. They could not sail heavy Royal Navy vessels up the rapids of the Richelieu, so they would have to construct ships at St. Johns. More time.

Finally, having faced Carleton at Quebec during much of the

winter and spring, Arnold judged the colonial governor to be a cautious leader, likely to favor preparation over urgency. A veteran soldier and administrator, Carleton was certainly capable. But the eleven days he spent moving a hundred miles after the battle at Three Rivers had allowed the Americans to escape and had given Arnold the opportunity to enact his scorched-earth strategy.

Given these considerations, Arnold calculated that Carleton would not move south before late August. The patriots would have two months to rebuild their army, improve their defenses at Ticonderoga, and expand their fleet on Lake Champlain. Their chance of defeating the British military power was slim. Their hope was in delay. If Carleton lacked the time to prevail during the current fighting season, the Americans might create breathing room for their beleaguered cause.

ॐ

Schuyler, at forty-two, was seven years older than Arnold. As he listened to the account of events in the north, he calculated the responsibilities that the situation placed on his own shoulders. He saw war not just in terms of battles but as a vast web of connections that brought force to bear by concentrating troops and draft animals, arms and gunpowder, food and fodder, and equipment of all kinds in the right place at the right time. He knew that organizing these resources in a vast area that was still largely wilderness presented an enormous challenge, one exacerbated by a frugal and indecisive Congress.

A longtime member of the New York Provincial Assembly and an original delegate to the Second Continental Congress, Schuyler had joined the rebellion because of grievances about the nature of the British administration of the colonies. His argument with the king resembled the complaints of the feudal barons who had imposed the Magna Carta on an earlier monarch, not the impassioned tirades of Whig patriots.

While a friend called Schuyler "a gentleman of great independency of spirit," he remained dubious about the wisdom of declaring the colonies independent. Nevertheless, he had risked everything, declaring that he wanted to "sink or swim" with his country and to leave his posterity the certainty that he was "an honest American."

George Washington, knowing of Schuyler's extensive experience at acquiring and transporting supplies during the French and Indian War, had suggested him for leadership of the northern army. Congress had agreed. They wanted a man of "consequence," a man of substantial fortune who would display sound judgment during the struggle and "readily lay down his power" when the war was over. The delegates appointed Schuyler one of the four original major generals of the "army of the United Colonies." They hoped he could help Washington forge, from local militias and volunteers, a "continental" army.

Schuyler had ridden alongside the commander in chief when they left Philadelphia in June 1775 to take up their duties. Almost the same age, both men owned substantial country estates and speculated in frontier land. Both had fought in the French and Indian War. Both had served as members of the Continental Congress. Meticulous, proud, austere in habits, and ever attentive to detail, both were men of honor. Both were owners of enslaved people.

But they would operate in distinct theaters of war. Washington would lead a conventional army in the most populous regions of the country, first at Cambridge, then at New York City. Schuyler would employ both infantry and naval forces to defend the rugged sector north of Albany, from the Mohawk Valley to the far reaches of Lake Champlain. Washington could move troops and supplies by road as well as sea; Schuyler had to rely on water routes through a trackless wilderness. Washington would fight redcoats and a few loyalists; Schuyler always had to figure the role of Native American tribes into his calculations.

Recognizing Schuyler's familiarity with his own region, Washington had noted that his subordinate's "good Sense must govern in all Matters . . . I do not wish to circumscribe you within too narrow Limits."

As Arnold and his aide retired for some needed rest on that summer night in 1776, the commander of the Northern Department plunged into three urgent tasks. First, he had to rescue what remained of the crippled invasion army now stranded in Canada. He agreed with Arnold that General Sullivan should have pulled back to Crown Point and Ticonderoga on his own initiative. He immediately began writing orders to secure the withdrawal.

Second, his conference with Iroquois representatives, which was scheduled to take place in a few days, suddenly took on added importance. A raid by Indians and loyalists from the rear of Ticonderoga could unwind the entire American position. Keeping the Iroquois neutral while his army conducted operations farther north was crucial.

Third, Schuyler needed to augment the tiny fleet of ships on Lake Champlain, his principal means of blocking the expected British thrust into New York. The effort would have to be expanded as quickly as possible. He wrote to Governor Jonathan Trumbull of Connecticut for help. Understanding the difficulty of constructing a navy in the wilderness, Trumbull promised to send the militia general David Waterbury, an experienced seaman, along with two captains and several gangs of shipwrights, to help speed the boat-building effort.

The fate of the north would rely on the most mundane aspects of war—supply, logistics, organization, transport. "Our whole dependence is on you," Arnold had written to Schuyler a month earlier. A businessman above all, Schuyler was the only man in the country with the relevant connections, expertise, and local knowledge to take on the task. He would need to revamp a defeated army, build an effective navy, and forge a supply line into the far north.

It was not until five a.m., with a summer dawn washing the sky over the Hudson, that Schuyler finished writing the orders to get the process under way. As he listened to the songbirds already in full throat, he felt the tremor of his recent fever, the weight of a busy night without sleep, and the burden of responsibility for the precarious cause of liberty in America.

The situation in the north was grave. In a letter to Washington,

Schuyler did not mince words. His army, he admitted, was "broken and spiritless." He expressed "the grief I feel on the evacuation of Canada," but also the "hope I have that we shall maintain a superiority on the Lakes."

⌒

The day after Arnold's conference with his commanding general, another visitor arrived at Schuyler's mansion. Congressional delegates had named Horatio Gates, newly raised to the rank of major general, to take over from John Sullivan as commander of the Canadian invasion force. Gates was on his way north to assume his duties.

General Gates had served as a British officer in the French and Indian War of the 1750s. He had risen to the rank of major, but because he was of common birth—his mother was a housemaid—his prospects for promotion in the aristocratic British officer class were limited. In 1773, he sold his commission and moved to a modest plantation in Virginia. Having already spent years in America, he had become friendly with the Whig faction seeking more autonomy and relief from burdensome taxes. Gates became one of the voices for the rights of colonists. He volunteered to serve the cause once war broke out, leaving at home his wife, Elizabeth, and his teenage son, Robert.

At the time, colonial leaders viewed anyone with military experience as a valuable asset. In June 1775, Gates was made a brigadier general in the Continental Army. He was more experienced than Philip Schuyler, but his talents tended in the same direction—he excelled at administration. As the army's adjutant general, he helped George Washington organize the Continental Army outside Boston during the fall and winter of 1775–76. He advised the commander on the disposition of troops, the establishment of supply systems, and the organization of a medical department. He offered advice on the construction of fortifications to contain the besieged British Army.

Some American officers aped their British counterparts, treating enlisted men in a high-handed manner. Gates understood that men volunteering to fight for a cause were not of the same temper as conscripted soldiers. Firm discipline had to be tempered with fairness. A commander must not forget that he was leading free men. The approach won him high regard from the troops, especially the New Englanders he supervised at Cambridge.

The man who approached the entrance of Schuyler's mansion on June 26 was a month shy of his forty-ninth birthday. His face was long, his eyes pensive, his hair gray and thinning. His nose supported a pair of spectacles. While he may not have conveyed a martial demeanor, it would be wrong to picture him as a milquetoast. Contrary to myth, he was never referred to by his troops as "Granny" Gates. And with a long career in the army, he could easily assume the forceful, assertive presence essential to an officer.

Of the three men, Gates was the most easygoing and comfortable in his role, with a keen sense of humor and a genial manner. Well read and a fluent storyteller, he got on easily with men from all stations. But the affable Gates had another facet, rooted in his ultimately unsuccessful effort to advance in the British Army: he was a man of frustrated ambition. His reflex was to push himself forward and to denigrate rivals. Privately, he was growing critical of George Washington. He had curried favor with New England political leaders—John Adams in particular was a Gates cheerleader.

The general owed his current assignment to Adams. "I wish you was a major general," Adams had written him. "What say you to it?" Gates said yes wholeheartedly, and he soon found himself raised to the same rank as Philip Schuyler, although Schuyler held the superior position because of his seniority. Next, Adams announced to Gates: "We have ordered you to the post of honour, and made you dictator in Canada for six months." He added, only half jokingly, "We do not Choose to trust you Generals, with too much power, for too long Time."

On arriving at Schuyler's home on his way to take command, Gates let his host understand that Congress had, in essence, removed Schuyler as the northern commander and installed Gates in his place. Perhaps he thought he could bluff the reserved Dutchman into accepting the change. If so, he had misread his man.

Sensitive and self-conscious, Schuyler was quick to take offense.

A few years earlier, he had challenged a fellow colonial assembly member to a duel in broad daylight over a perceived slight. Although politically astute, he was at times impolitic in his dealings, asserting that "I cannot hesitate a moment between giving offence and doing my duty." In the current controversy, Schuyler kept his pique under control. He remained cordial but firm. Gates had been appointed to command the army in Canada. There was no longer an army in Canada. If he was to serve in the Northern Department, it would be as Schuyler's subordinate.

Schuyler wrote to George Washington that "if Congress intended that General Gates should command the Northern Army wherever it might be, as he assures me they did, it ought to have been signified to me." He added that both he and Gates "mean to be candid" and wanted the matter settled without "that Chicane, which would disgrace us as Officers & Men."

It was settled. Congressional delegates informed Gates that they had given him the command of the troops "while in Canada" and did not intend to "vest him with a superior command to General Schuyler." In spite of this initial contretemps, the two men were able to work together without rancor, at least for a while. In July, Schuyler reported to Washington that "the most perfect harmony subsists between us."

Not quite perfect. Gates would not forget. "I am no Dictator here," he wrote to Adams. "I have been Deceived, and Disappointed."

Circumstances and the fickle will of Congress had brought together a trio of leaders who would decide the fate of the northern campaign that season. In a situation demanding a miracle of logistics, Schuyler was the ideal man. Faced with rebuilding a shattered army, Gates had proven that he could bring order from chaos. And with the potential for a violent confrontation looming, Benedict Arnold was one of the most dynamic combat leaders available and an experienced seaman to boot.

The capabilities of all three were about to be put to the test.

3

The Great Warpath

IN JULY 1608, A YEAR AFTER BRITISH SETTLERS established their first permanent colony at Jamestown, Virginia, the French mariner Samuel de Champlain sailed up the wide mouth of the St. Lawrence River to a place the local people called Kebec, "the narrowing of waters." He and a few dozen of his countrymen established a small colony and began trading with forest people whom they called the Montagnais and who referred to themselves as the Innu, skilled native hunters who managed a vast trade network in the north.

Along with their allies, who included Algonquian-speakers to the north and east and Hurons to the west, the Montagnais had long been locked in conflict with the Haudenosaunee, who ruled an empire from their base south of Lake Ontario. Champlain referred to these latter tribes as Yroquois. The Iroquois Confederacy was made up of the Seneca, Cayuga, Onondaga, Tuscarora, Oneida, and Mohawk tribes, also known as the Six Nations.

Contact with Europeans had already brought change and disaster to the New World inhabitants. Disease, from measles and influenza to smallpox, had ravaged populations. The fur trade had given Indians access to European goods; the competition for pelts had fueled violence among tribes already hostile to each other.

The Montagnais wanted Champlain to join an expedition against the Kanien'kehá:ka, or "people of the flint." The fiercest of the Iroquois bands, they were known to their enemies as Mohawks, "man-eaters." They guarded the eastern door of the federation's territory. Champlain agreed to go along.

In June 1609, Champlain stood at the northern end of the long route of rivers and lakes that separated the Iroquois from their enemies to the east. It allowed almost continuous water transportation to a great south-flowing river that Champlain learned about from the Indians. Later that same year, Henry Hudson would explore the lower portion of the route for the Dutch. The Indians referred to the water route as "the Great Warpath."

Although most of the Europeans who had volunteered for the expedition turned back, the forty-two-year-old Champlain wanted to maintain his reputation with his Indian allies. The Indians were impressed by the spirit of this armored man and of his magical, thunderous stick, which could spew fire and smoke. With a small band of Indians and two French volunteers, Champlain paddled up the Richelieu River, passed the future site of St. Johns, and emerged into a narrow, brilliantly blue, island-clogged lake. He was the first European to see the body of water that would be named for him.

The party proceeded south, advancing more slowly now that they were skimming the edge of Mohawk territory. Champlain, an avid naturalist, noted the abundance of game that flourished in this contested no-man's-land where few hunters dared venture. Every night, the Indians accompanying him felled small trees and built a fort along the water's edge to guard against a sneak attack. As the lake narrowed they changed their tactics, traveling now only by night under the dome of stars. During the day they slept in their makeshift forts.

The Indians pressed Champlain to relate his dreams. He told them that he had envisioned enemy warriors floundering in the water. He had felt a desire to help them but heeded urgent warnings from his companions to let them drown. He described a mountain in the background. The Indians gave the account great weight. They knew that mountain.

The next night, as they paddled silently over the glass-smooth lake, the mountain Champlain had dreamed of suddenly loomed before them. They reached an arm of land that swept out from the western shore and choked the lake to barely a quarter of a mile in width. A river tumbled down just beyond it—the outlet from the yet-unnamed Lake George.

This was the magical place the Indians called Tekautaro:ken, "the meeting place of two waters." Europeans would later name the peninsula, one of the most strategic spots in North America, Ticonderoga.

From out of the darkness, ghostlike Mohawk warriors now appeared. Their heavy canoes, fashioned from the bark of elm trees, were less maneuverable than the nimble birchbark vessels of the northern Indians. The Mohawks decided to land on a sandy section of lakefront on the north portion of the peninsula and build a fort of their own. All night the two groups exchanged insults and dared each other to fight. Champlain and his two European companions remained hidden.

The confrontation began at dawn. Outnumbered by more than three to one, Champlain and his allies landed and approached the Mohawk fort. The Europeans were careful to keep out of sight— Champlain sent his French comrades into the woods on either side of the enemy. Each of them carried an arquebus, an early form of musket. The weapons, which could be loaded with multiple projectiles, were lethal at short range.

As the groups of fighters approached each other, the allied Indians suddenly opened their ranks to allow Champlain to step to the front. Sporting a shining breastplate, he walked straight toward the Mohawks and took aim at two chiefs marked by their feathered headdresses. His gun erupted in a flash of fire and a cloud of white smoke. The boom echoed from the nearby mountain and shivered across the water. His companions also fired. The chiefs fell. Surprise and panic threw the Mohawks into confusion. The fight was over in minutes, Champlain and his allies victorious.

✌

A silence had been broken. During the next two centuries, echoes of Champlain's first gunpowder explosions along the Great Warpath would never entirely die out. Conflict between the French and Iroquois flared in the 1650s with Indian raids on French settlements and punitive expeditions by Europeans into the Iroquois domain of the Mohawk Valley, ninety miles to the southwest.

Relations between indigenous peoples and the encroaching Europeans remained complex and nuanced as both sides maneuvered for advantage. By the end of the 1600s, the affairs of the region were being complicated by disputes between the French and the English settlers moving up the Hudson River. Queen Anne's War in the early 1700s saw fighting between the European powers along the Champlain Valley and ended with the boundary of New France being drawn at Split Rock, about halfway up the lake. King George's War of the 1740s brought more violence.

During the eighteenth century, the French built two forts at key points on Lake Champlain in an attempt to contain intrusion by Englishmen. They erected Fort St. Frederic in 1734 on the peninsula that formed the narrowest point in the lake. Some twenty years later, they built Fort Carillon fifteen miles farther south, near where Champlain's group had fought Mohawk warriors.

An uneasy peace collapsed with the outbreak of the French and Indian War in 1754, a conflict that became the Seven Years' War as it spread around the world. By defeating the French, the British wrested sovereignty over all of Canada. Fort St. Frederic became Crown Point; Fort Carillon was renamed Fort Ticonderoga. With Britain in control of the territory both north and south, the two forts no longer served much purpose. While still manned by a handful of British soldiers, they fell into disrepair.

✌

A dozen years passed after the 1763 Treaty of Paris brought peace to North America. In early May 1775, news of the outbreak of violence near Boston had not yet arrived in the Lake Champlain backcountry. The colonial rebellion was in its embryonic stage— patriot militia forces were besieging regulars in Boston, and the battle at Bunker Hill had yet to be fought. New England patriots looked around for targets.

At the request of Britain's military commander in America, General Thomas Gage, Canadian governor Guy Carleton had sent two of his regiments to Boston. That left him only eight hundred regular soldiers in the north, many assigned to forts in the Great Lakes. The remaining troops were strung out in small contingents at St. Johns, Crown Point, and Ticonderoga. Rebel leaders, without consulting Congress, decided to attack the latter two posts and establish control along the Great Warpath.

Connecticut officials gave the assignment to Ethan Allen, who lived in the Hampshire Grants east of the lake. Allen commanded 150 irregular vigilantes known as the Green Mountain Boys, who had opposed New York's claims in the region. He was eager to strike a blow not only against the British but against the Yorkers.

Benedict Arnold proposed the same operation to Massachusetts officials at Cambridge. Taking Ticonderoga would garner a large store of needed cannon, he explained, and help guard the colonies from a British invasion out of Canada. The Massachusetts authorities told Arnold to raise "a body of men not to exceed four hundred" in the western end of the colony and attack the fort. Learning that Allen was already on his way to seize the post, Arnold galloped ahead to catch up with him. After some wrangling, the two men agreed to share command.

On the night of May 10, 1775, Arnold and Allen surprised the sleeping Ticonderoga garrison. The attack had an element of melodrama—Allen claimed the fort "in the name of the great Jehovah and the Continental Congress"—but the action represented the first definitive victory of the war for the patriots, and one with important consequences.

The victorious militia took over the dilapidated facility and went north to capture the weakly defended post at Crown Point. Although Arnold judged Ticonderoga "not worth repairing," the fort provided a critical resource: the many cannon left behind by both the French and the British.

While the Green Mountain contingent celebrated by imbibing Ticonderoga's rum supply, Arnold kept the bigger picture in view. Allen's men had captured the estate of Philip Skene, a retired British major and ardent loyalist, who had founded Skenesborough (now Whitehall, New York) at the narrow southern tip of Lake Champlain, twenty-five miles from Ticonderoga. They also commandeered Skene's fifty-foot-long red-cedar lake schooner, the *Katherine*. Some of Arnold's men brought her to Ticonderoga, where Arnold rechristened her the *Liberty* and installed along her deck four cannon on wheeled carriages.

With a characteristic sense of urgency and the benefit of his considerable maritime experience, Arnold set sail north along the lake with forty men. Becalmed, they switched to rowboats, crossed into Canada, and proceeded quietly down the Richelieu River to St. Johns. They spent the night in a creek "invested with numberless swarms of gnats and musquitoes." At six o'clock on the morning of May 18, Arnold and his men surprised and captured a handful of British Army defenders at the fort in St. Johns without firing a shot. They took over the seventy-ton supply sloop *Betsey*, renaming it *Enterprise*.

The raiders also grabbed several bateaux, along with a supply of arms, including two 6-pounder brass cannon. By nine a.m. they were headed back up the river with their prizes and prisoners. They escaped just ahead of a contingent of British reinforcements hurrying to St. Johns from Montreal.

Canadian governor Guy Carleton had to admit to London authorities that Arnold, "said to be a Native of Connecticut and Known Horse Jockey . . . captured one sergeant and ten men, plus the sloop." The bloodless maneuvers on Lake Champlain pushed the Revolution further down the path to all-out war.

For Arnold, this short initial campaign ended badly. His insistence on operating according to what he considered proper military order rubbed the rustic Green Mountain Boys against their grain. They directed insults and even a few defiant potshots at Arnold. Ethan Allen followed Arnold's raid with a muddled, abortive attempt to establish a foothold near St. Johns.

Confusion about command responsibility ended in Arnold departing from Ticonderoga in June. He had used his own money to pay his men and was resentful of Congress for not supporting him.

On a trading voyage in 1774, Benedict Arnold had written to his wife, Peggy: "How uncertain is life, how certain is death." When he returned to New Haven after the raid on Lake Champlain, he found that Peggy had died a few weeks earlier, leaving him with three small sons, now in the care of his sister, Hannah.

Some members of Congress, shaken by the acceleration of events, considered handing Ticonderoga back to British authorities. The fort's guns would be returned after the "restoration of former harmony . . . so ardently desired." But they quickly realized that history had galloped ahead of any such timid recourse. The war was on.

4

Canada

ONLY WEEKS AFTER THE 1775 COUP AT TICONDEROGA,
members of the Continental Congress caught the surging revolutionary fever. Benedict Arnold, familiar with conditions in the
north, had already proposed an invasion of Canada, which he
thought advisable "for our own defense, as well as the advantage of
the inhabitants."

"Whether we should march into Canada . . . has been the great
Question," John Adams wrote on June 7. "It seems to be the general Conclusion that it is best to go, if we can be assured that the
Canadians will be pleased with it and join." Like many Americans,
Adams was deluded. Few Canadians shared his enthusiasm for
revolution, and many were mindful of the rabid anti-Catholic prejudices in most of the colonies below—their Church was referred
to as the "mother of Harlots."

In late June, congressional delegates declared that not only
would they refuse to return Ticonderoga or Crown Point to British authorities, they would embark on the first major offensive expedition of the Revolution—they would invade Canada. The plan
was to capture St. Johns, Montreal, and any part of Canada "which

may have a tendency to promote the peace and security of these Colonies."

By taking Montreal, the rebels would cut off the string of posts through the Great Lakes—Fort Detroit, Fort Pitt, Fort Miami, and others—that threatened to strangle them. They would also prevent Canada from being used as a base for the British military, from which the enemy could descend the Great Warpath to attack the colonies from the rear.

While most patriots still imagined the current conflict would end in reconciliation, the idea of liberty was in the air. Why not extend freedoms to the citizens in the north? Among those boosting the idea were Americans from the thirteen colonies who had relocated to Canada since the British takeover. Many were merchants looking to turn a quick profit—"licentious fanatics," the royal governor, Guy Carleton, called them.

Since the Treaty of Paris, authorities in London had wrestled with the question of how to administer this huge northern addition to their empire. Their decisions were influenced by Governor Carleton. Born in Ireland of Scottish ancestry, Carleton had received an ensign's commission in the British infantry at eighteen. He had served in Canada during the Seven Years' War, been wounded several times, and emerged as a general. He used his connections to gain an appointment as governor of the province in 1768.

In 1770, Carleton returned to England and spent four years pushing for legislation, known as the Quebec Act, that was intended to pacify the French inhabitants of the new territory through tolerant and humane treatment. Parliament agreed with the strategy, and the act, which went into effect on May 1, 1775, seemed a wise policy.

But although its provisions made sense to British ministers, the act did not achieve its objectives. By ratifying French civil laws and the Catholic religion, it irritated the citizens of the colonies to the south. By locking *habitants*, French-speaking peasants, into the semi-feudal seigneurial system that burdened them with fealty to a landlord and taxes to support the Church, it failed to elicit the affection of most Canadians.

Nor did the act allow for representative government in Canada, a measure that riled Americans bent on augmenting local rule. It rewrote the boundaries of Quebec and proclaimed that Canadian territory would extend down into the Ohio and Mississippi Valleys—a bear hug that infuriated American land speculators and potential western settlers. Its enactment would come to be included in the litany of reasons for rebellion listed in the Declaration of Independence.

On June 29, 1775, less than two months after the act became law, the delegates of the Continental Congress made their move. They instructed General Schuyler to put Fort Ticonderoga in order, to seize all enemy craft on Lake Champlain, and to march and sail an army north. They added the important proviso that Schuyler should act only if the invasion should "not be disagreeable to the Canadians."

Schuyler began his military preparations. He instructed his officers to assure the Canadians that "America . . . will not oppress." This was not a war of ambition. America was seeking only to correct the "misrule of tyrants." The objects of the armed invasion were "liberty, safety and peace."

✎

Schuyler, a newly minted major general in the Continental Army, faced a daunting task in July 1775. He had to form an army almost from scratch, train its soldiers, and find a way to transport and supply them during an expedition to the northern province. He knew from experience how hard it was to move a barrel of beef or a cannon in the rough American interior. He immediately set to work gathering armaments and building the fleet of transport vessels that would be needed to carry the army along Lake Champlain, and then to keep more men, arms, and rations flowing to Canada.

During the French and Indian War of the 1750s, Schuyler had served as a major in the provincial militia. Although he had a few brushes with combat, his main duties involved managing supplies for British forces. His mentor, British general John Bradstreet, was a savvy veteran who had developed expertise in moving troops and supplies through the forests and waterways of inland New York. While Schuyler was preparing the 1775 expedition, George Washington, now commanding outside Boston, listened to the ideas of the ever eager Benedict Arnold. He agreed with the young colonel that a second prong of attack would require General Carleton to divide his force, making Schuyler's conquest easier. Arnold suggested sending an army to Maine, where they could board bateaux and proceed up the Kennebec River. Once they got themselves and their equipment over the mountains they could travel downhill to the St. Lawrence River and emerge directly across from the citadel at Quebec City. Washington ratified the plan.

While Arnold prepared his force at Cambridge, Schuyler fretted over his own prospects. He commanded a mere thirteen hundred poorly trained men for an operation that would require at least four thousand. "If Job had been a general, in my situation," he complained, "his memory had not been so famous for patience."

As an aristocratic New Yorker, the general was unpopular among New Englanders, who considered him arrogant and lukewarm in his enthusiasm for the cause. Critics said he "lacked both energy and decisiveness" and was "deficient in assembling and training an offensive army." They could not understand the long delay as he gathered troops and supplies for the expedition. Some went as far as to suggest he was collaborating with the enemy.

A combination of urgent business in Albany and ill health kept Schuyler from leading the army when it finally moved northward in late August. His absence was another blow to his reputation. Field leadership passed to Brigadier General Richard Montgomery, a former British officer. His troops commenced a siege of St. Johns, which was defended by a few hundred redcoats and Canadian militiamen. Most of the inhabitants of the province showed little inclination to help either side.

The patriots methodically bombarded the fort and sank an armed schooner, the *Royal Savage*, that had been under construction at the St. Johns wharf. But it was not until November 3 that the British infantrymen inside the fort surrendered. The victory opened the way for Montgomery to easily take Montreal. His first objective was accomplished: Canada was half won. But his late start, combined with the weeks of delay at St. Johns, meant that he had little time to complete his mission before winter set in.

The Americans who stayed behind at St. Johns were able to raise the sunken schooner, patch her up, and sail her up the lake to Skenesborough. There she would be repaired and become an important part of the patriot fleet on Lake Champlain.

The second prong of the grand pincer movement also set out far too late in the fighting season. Colonel Arnold did not get his eleven hundred men to the mouth of the Kennebec until September 22. The troops, who included a battalion of exceptionally hardy Virginia riflemen, struggled northward through a malevolent wilderness. They battled temperatures that turned their damp clothes stiff with ice. They ran short of food. About a third of the men gave up and turned back without orders, the rest forged on.

Arnold hurried ahead to procure rations. His men were reduced to eating shaving soap, leather ammunition pouches, and a pet dog. One young soldier, who was accompanied by his wife, found himself unable to go on. He sat down on the trail and died. His spouse covered his body with leaves, picked up his musket, and continued down the trail. Arnold, who demonstrated a remarkable ability to keep up morale, managed to secure the needed food. He rallied his remaining troops on the bank of the St. Lawrence and found boats to transport them across to Quebec.

Too late. Governor Carleton had returned from Montreal and recruited enough armed men to defend the walled citadel. "Had I been ten days sooner," Arnold wrote to George Washington, "Quebec must inevitably have fallen into our hands, as there was not a man there to oppose us."

Even after Montgomery arrived with his troops to reinforce the siege, the Americans could make no progress. Delay, disease, and ill fortune determined the fate of the invasion. Montgomery, who had entered the war reluctantly, grew depressed. "Could I, with decency, leave the army in its present situation," he declared, "I would not serve an hour longer."

On the last day of the year, the Americans tried to storm the walls of the impregnable citadel. Montgomery died. Arnold was shot in the leg. At least fifty Americans were killed, four hundred imprisoned. "We have met with a severe check," Philip Schuyler reported to General Washington.

But the effort to win Canada did not end with the attack on Quebec. The delegates in Congress would not give up. In late March 1776, they sent General John Thomas, a physician and a hero of the fighting around Boston, to take command of the army in Canada. The delegates also committed eleven regiments, fifty-seven hundred men, to reinforce the effort. All for naught. By early May, this army was consuming six tons of meat and flour every day, all of it shipped at great effort and cost up the rivers and lakes.

When he reached Quebec City, Thomas found problems multiplying. As fast as the troops were arriving, they were falling ill with smallpox. On May 2, he heard that fifteen British ships had reached the mouth of the St. Lawrence. Five days later, they were in sight of Quebec. The siege was over.

During the retreat from Quebec City, one soldier remembered seeing sick men from the hospital "crawling after us" as the patriot soldiers sprinted toward boats on the St. Lawrence. In a pouring rain, the patriot troops rowed up the ice-clogged river. During the retreat to Sorel, Chambly, St. Johns, and finally Crown Point, the northern army came close to complete collapse. General Thomas, who had taken over command at Quebec on May 1, was dead of smallpox on June 2. By the middle of June, the Canadian expedition had reached its ignoble end.

5

---•———•---

Not an Army

FROM THE ENTRANCE OF HIS MANSION, PHILIP SCHUYLER could watch the white sails of working sloops glide up the Hudson River on the morning breeze. On that pristine midsummer day in 1776, the boats reminded him that the only thing that prevented the immediate descent of British troops against the disorganized, beaten American army at Crown Point was the meager fleet of armed vessels on Lake Champlain—two schooners and a sloop, each equipped with small cannon and manned by inexperienced crews.

Schuyler was familiar with boats and boatbuilding. He had sent his own sloops down the Hudson River and along the shipping routes to the islands of the Caribbean. Now he was engaged in an arms race with the British, who were certainly assembling a fleet in Canada.

Schuyler turned over the Americans' advantages and disadvantages in his mind. The colonists, like the English, were a seagoing race, their cities huddled along coasts and waterways. Much of their wealth depended on trade by sea. Seventy thousand Americans made their living at shipbuilding. They had helped develop the sleek, double-masted, fore-and-aft-rigged vessels known as schooners. They were also experienced at constructing the single-masted versions called sloops. Both types of boats could be handled by relatively small crews and were adapted to coastal sailing. (See pages 257–258.)

But colonists built their ships in coastal ports like Boston, New York, and Philadelphia. It would be a daunting task to transport naval supplies to a remote wilderness lake and to attract skilled craftsmen and sailors to the rugged interior.

Fortunately, Schuyler had a head start on the project. He had already supervised the construction of hundreds of flat-bottomed bateaux on Lake George to transport supplies and troops northward for the invasion of Canada. Responding to the determination of Congress to reinforce the northern army, he had continued the operation into the spring, overseeing the carpenters who hammered together another hundred boats.

The typical bateau was thirty feet long and six feet across the beam. Cheap and simple to build, a single boat could carry a dozen barrels or thirty men. Although not war vessels, these craft were even now doing service carrying the sick, defeated troops back from Canada.

The army's precipitous retreat threatened to open the lakes to a British attack. General Carleton had in fact received orders from Secretary Germain in March to "endeavor to pass the lakes as early as possible" in order to contribute to the success of General William Howe's planned attack on New York City.

During the spring, Schuyler set up another naval construction project at Skenesborough, where shipwrights could launch the boats directly into Lake Champlain. By June the first of the new warships was nearly finished. Benedict Arnold emphasized the importance of the effort in a letter to Washington. The British, he warned, "will doubtless become masters of the lake unless every nerve on our part is strained to exceed them in a naval armament."

༄

Schuyler spent the next few days conferring in Albany with Gates and Arnold. Because his important meeting with the Iroquois had been postponed, he was able to accompany the officers to the front lines. The three men headed north on the first day of July, traveling initially to Schuyler's country home in Saratoga, thirty-five miles north of Albany. Next they arrived at Fort Edward, the town at the head of navigation on the Hudson River. From there, the road split. The more well-traveled route headed northwest twenty miles to the southern tip of Lake George. The generals took the other fork, a recently improved but still raw passage along Wood Creek to Skenesborough. They inspected the dubious condition of the road and bridges along the way. Schuyler told of his hope to one day build a canal here to connect the Hudson to Lake Champlain.

By July 4 they were in Skenesborough. Philip Skene, the founder of the settlement, was a retired British officer who had seen action in America during the French and Indian War. The crown had granted Skene a patent on a choice tract of land in what was still wilderness. With the help of tenant farmers and enslaved workers, he built a community and a small industrial complex at the point where Wood Creek plunged into the lake.

The energetic Skene had constructed a dam, a sawmill, and a gristmill. He installed a foundry for extracting iron from ore and a forge where the raw metal could be hammered into tools. He had his men erect barns, a large warehouse, a coal house, a carpentry shop, and a barrel-making facility. All had been lost when Ethan Allen's vigilantes commandeered Skene's estate and his lake schooner. Patriots tracked down Skene and arrested the influential loyalist in Philadelphia.

Skene's settlement offered just what Schuyler needed for his shipbuilding operation: a source of wood and iron, a collection of buildings, and a convenient lakeside location that was as safe as possible from British intrusion. It was here that the rebels' energies would be focused through the next three months of 1776.

General Schuyler showed Gates and Arnold around the shipyard and introduced them to Harmanus Schuyler, assistant deputy commissary general for the northern army. Harmanus, a distant relative of Philip's, was overseeing the construction of new war vessels. Well connected in the local Dutch community, Harmanus was a former sheriff of Albany County, where he maintained the privileges of landowners, including the Schuylers.

All the men were acutely aware that more armed ships were needed to confront whatever fleet the British managed to put on the lake. Lacking the resources and expertise to build complex schooners, General Schuyler had so far put Harmanus to work on gunboats. Known as gondolas or gundaloes, these fifty-foot vessels were essentially armed barges. They were equipped with square sails on a single mast and long sweep oars for rowing. A wide "barn door" rudder facilitated steering. With a substantial cannon projecting from the bow and another jutting from either side, the gondolas would add to American firepower on the lake. Like the bateaux, they were flat-bottomed and easy to build. Their main virtue was that they could be constructed quickly. (See page 259.)

During the winter, Harmanus had supervised the felling of timbers and amassed a supply of lumber. General Schuyler pushed him to cut more. In May the general had sent thirty carpenters to the settlement, the first of what would be a growing workforce needed to complete the desperate task.

"Take Charge of the Carpenters, Ax-men, Teamsters & Blacksmiths," Schuyler had ordered on June 7, "do every Thing in your power to forward the Building of the Gundaloes." Harmanus wrote back to assure him that "one of the Gundalows is so far forward as having stem & stern rais'd tomorrow will begin to put in the knees."

Among Philip Schuyler's frustrations was the region's provincialism. Officials of Charlotte County, which included Skenesborough, had outlawed Sunday work in accordance with Puritan strictures. After the magistrates fined shipyard carpenters for violating the ban, the army commander had to plead with religious zealots to relent during the emergency.

One of Schuyler's strengths was his understanding of the value of intelligence. A web of informants was helpful for running a business and was even more crucial in war. He organized Native Americans, traders, travelers, and wilderness settlers to send him information. He had even recruited his eldest daughter, twenty-year-old Angelica, to forward information. She now sent him a letter from Albany with several bits of helpful news. She was able to pass on a rumor of a plot by the enemy to kill senior American officers in New York City, perhaps timed to coincide with the landing of British ships in the harbor.

By June 12, when General Sullivan was preparing to abandon his position at Sorel on the St. Lawrence, the construction of gondolas was already under way. Now, three weeks later, Harmanus had just sent the first two vessels to Ticonderoga, where workmen would add masts, sails, and rigging and hoist guns aboard. "We'll be able to launch One every week, if we have good weather," Harmanus declared with optimism.

By the last days of June, Philip Schuyler was also putting the best light on the situation in a letter to Connecticut governor Trumbull: "We have, happily, such a naval superiority on Lake Champlain that I have a confident hope the Enemy will not appear upon it this Campaign."

Schuyler's hope was balanced by fear. While directing the earlier work at Skenesborough by dispatch, he had applied a verbal whip to his subordinate. "Go on by Night as well as by Day," he wrote. "Early rising, a close attention to the orders I have given, will forward the Work with expedition & economy." In this peaceful backwater, it was easy to lose sight of the sudden violence that could erupt if the British brought warships up the lake.

The exhortations were not enough. To all three generals, the shortages of supplies and equipment at Skenesborough were obvious, the pace of the work troubling. Where were the carpenters and shipbuilders who could expedite the effort? The operations at the shipyard had to be accelerated.

༄

From Skenesborough, a boat carried the commanders up the long finger of Lake Champlain toward Fort Ticonderoga. They were unaware of momentous events unfolding elsewhere. The British king and his ministers had decided that the "undutiful children" in the American colonies needed to be slapped down decisively. Instead of a "sentimental manner of making war," the British authorities favored "one decisive blow." That blow was about to strike New York City.

The delegates to the Continental Congress and their generals had miscalculated. They had estimated that the British ministers would send a total of 22,500 troops to America. They had planned to raise 55,000 defenders. As it turned out, the proportions were reversed. In Quebec and New York, the enemy was able to land 48,000 redcoats, the largest expeditionary force in the kingdom's history. The Americans could muster no more than 22,000 fighters, many of them amateurs at war.

On July 2, ten thousand redcoats under General William Howe began to disembark at Staten Island. George Washington and his stunned headquarters staff looked out from the tip of Manhattan Island at a forest of masts in the harbor. The invasion gave weight to the British intention "to finish the rebellion in one campaign."

That same day, in a sweltering Philadelphia, delegates to the Continental Congress passed a resolution declaring "that these united colonies are, and of right ought to be free and independent States, that they are absolved from all allegiance to the British Crown." Two days later they would approve the final draft of the declaration, which included Thomas Jefferson's words: "We hold these truths to be self-evident ..."

By July 5, Schuyler, Gates, and Arnold had arrived at the landing slip below Fort Ticonderoga. The scene was not encouraging. The men originally stationed there had been joined by hundreds of the soldiers who had fled Canada. A quick inspection tour left the generals dismayed. The post had barely been improved during the previous year. Gates in particular recognized the unmilitary bearing of the fort and the slack discipline of its defenders. Something would have to be done, and quickly.

∽

The dismal scene the three commanders encountered at Ticonderoga could hardly prepare them for the spectacle at Crown Point. The post was situated eighty miles south of the Canadian border on the west side of the lake. What was left of the two old forts stood at the end of a two-mile-long peninsula that reached almost to Hospital Point (now Chimney Point) on the eastern shore. The channel at the bottleneck was only a few hundred yards wide.

After driving the French from the lake in 1759, British general Jeffrey Amherst had directed the construction at Crown Point of the largest fortification on the continent. During that winter, his men blasted ditches out of limestone and constructed a great five-sided bastion of dirt-filled timber casements. They raised stone barracks and other buildings inside and mounted cannon on the parapets. Much of the construction had been directed by Israel Putnam, an American officer in British service, later a Continental Army major general.

Once the British ended French rule in North America, Crown Point lost its strategic value. By 1767 it was already deteriorating, and the barracks remained unfinished. In 1773, a fire in a chimney set off a blaze that spread to the casements, which were covered with thick tar. The flames reached the fort's magazine, where the explosion of a hundred barrels of gunpowder demolished most of the fort.

Now, in July 1776, while the delegates in Philadelphia were proclaiming their willingness to risk their lives, fortunes, and sacred honor in the cause of liberty, the soldiers congregating at Crown Point were paying a higher and less abstract price.

∽

After Benedict Arnold had left Canada to report to Schuyler, General Sullivan had ordered sick soldiers ferried up Lake Champlain. With tired oarsmen heaving their bateaux southward against a headwind, the trip had taken four miserable days. One man said the oarsmen "rowed till I thought they would fall from their seats."

At the Crown Point landing "the sick were thrown on shore," and the boats headed back a hundred miles north to pick up more men. Those left at the waterfront found distressed soldiers by the "thousands, some dead, others dying. Great numbers could not stand." Many called out for help, but no help arrived.

The word used repeatedly to characterize the scene that the

three generals encountered when they arrived at the peninsula on the evening of July 5 was "indescribable." Even men familiar with the bloody, mangled bodies of warfare found Crown Point nearly beyond comprehension. Soldiers inured to shock declared it shocking. Colonel John Trumbull, the twenty-year-old son of the Connecticut governor, was the deputy adjutant general under Gates. He said it was "difficult to conceive a state of much deeper misery."

A military surgeon declared, "It broke my heart, and I wept till I had no more power to weep." Philip Schuyler wrote to George Washington, "The most descriptive pen cannot describe the condition of our Army: sickness, disorder, and discord, reign triumphant."

The peninsula was devoid of proper shelter. The soldiers were dispersed, John Trumbull wrote, "some few in tents, some in sheds, and more under the shelter of miserable brush huts."

Of the 11,000 soldiers who had been sent to Canada, more than half had simply vanished. Some had been killed by the enemy, some had died of disease, hundreds had deserted. Of the 5,200 who returned, almost 3,000 were incapacitated by illness.

Smallpox was the most grievous complaint. Soldiers were also afflicted with diarrhea, known as the "camp disorder." One man reported that he "had the dysentery, diarrhea, ague, and fever, etc. all in succession." The stench of filth pervaded the camp. The concentrated population was greater than that of all but the largest cities on the continent. Sanitation was primitive to nonexistent.

The few doctors available despaired at their lack of medicine for the men. Although the purgatives, emetics, and herbal compounds in use during the era may have had limited practical effect, they were important for boosting the men's morale. The doctors' obvious helplessness discouraged patients already in the grip of despair.

The area around Crown Point was a breeding ground for voracious insects, including battalions of aggressive blackflies whose bites raised painful welts. Attracted to the fetor of the camp in the heat of early July, they attacked the men in swarms, inflicting a buzzing torment on those who lacked the energy to swat them away.

General John Sullivan, whose command of the northern army officially ended with the arrival of Gates, gave the generals a tour of the installation. Their reaction was voiced by Trumbull, who wrote to his father, "I can scarcely imagine a more disastrous scene. I found not an army, but a mob, the shattered remains of twelve or fifteen very fine battalions, ruined by sickness, fatigue and desertion and void of every idea of discipline or subordination."

These beaten soldiers, who knew only defeat, who quivered on the edge of panic, were all that stood between the large, professional army to the north and the vulnerable colonies to the south.

~

On Sunday, July 7, General Schuyler convened a council of war at Crown Point. The general officers on the scene gathered inside the hot, ramshackle wardroom that was one of the few roofed buildings left at Crown Point.

Schuyler presided at the head of the table. Gates, the next most senior general, sat at his right hand. Then came a gloomy and resentful General Sullivan. He would soon express his intention to complain to Congress, even resign his commission, over his dismissal from command of the northern army. He requested leave to proceed to Philadelphia, and Schuyler was more than willing to see him go.

Also in attendance was Frederick William, Baron de Woedtke. The Prussian officer was an early arrival in what would become a parade of European adventurers, idealists, and self-proclaimed military experts attracted to the American war. Congress would learn to consider these volunteers with more skepticism, but in 1776 the delegates were still open to any help they could get. Woedtke's contributions to the cause were small, his taste for intoxicating drink large. He would die of illness a few weeks later.

Schuyler opened the meeting by emphasizing the gravity of the situation. The threat they faced was immediate. Bands of Indians and British light infantrymen were already making probes through the forest along the lake. British troops were rumored to be cutting a road along the eastern shore. It was certain they were building war vessels in St. Johns for service on the lake. The chaos at the American forts spoke for itself.

Benedict Arnold, only lately promoted to brigadier general, held the lowest seniority in the room. He sat at the end of the table and was given the chance to present his views first. Speaking with animation in the thick, hot air, he laid out a four-part plan.

First, he said, they should move the army out of the pestilential environment of Crown Point and regroup at Fort Ticonderoga. The current post was fatally contaminated with smallpox. Lacking fortifications, it was vulnerable to an attack by armed ships from the north. It did not make sense to risk stationing the army here.

Second, they should immediately transport sick soldiers far enough away to prevent the spread of illness. The sufferers must be put under strict quarantine and tended by doctors and men who had already been exposed to the pox. Both morale and fighting effectiveness depended on quick action to restore hygiene.

Third, they should hurry to repair the fortifications at Fort Ticonderoga and set up supply lines to sustain troops there. Arnold recommended adding another strong position by installing artillery on Rattlesnake Hill, across the lake from the current fort.

Fourth and most important, they should ensure that "the most effectual measures be taken to secure our superiority on Lake Champlain, by a naval armament of gondolas, row galleys, and armed bateaux." He felt they would also need a much larger warship, on the scale of an ocean-going frigate, to seal their mastery of the lake.

The goal of the plan was to give General Carleton pause, make him rethink his own strategy, and, with luck, delay the inevitable confrontation until the next fighting season. By then a more formidable defense could be mounted, and efforts to bring the French into the war on the side of the Americans might have paid off.

The officers were impressed by Arnold's grasp of the situation. Much of what he proposed had already been thought of by General Schuyler. Their discussion focused on whether to abandon Crown Point. None of the generals was eager to yield still more ground

to the enemy. If its fortifications had been intact and the area free
of illness, it would have been an ideal spot to stop the enemy. As
it was, the location was both vulnerable and infected. "Under our
present Circumstances, the post of Crown Point is not tenable,"
they concluded. "It is not capable of being made so, this summer."

The withdrawal from Crown Point proved unpopular among
junior officers and troops, especially those from New England.
More than twenty officers complained about the council's decision
to George Washington and to Congress. The men felt the commanders had ignored the legislature's order to "dispute every inch
of the ground in Canada." They pointed out that British soldiers
had earlier constructed a military road from Hospital Point on the
opposite shore of the lake through the backlands of the Hampshire Grants and into New Hampshire itself. If the enemy captured
Crown Point, they could set their infantry marching unopposed
into the heart of New England.

George Washington at first agreed with the New England officers' objection. He wrote to Gates: "Your relinquishing Crown
Point is in its consequences a relinquishment of the Lakes." Gates
was furious at being challenged, first by subordinates, then by a
superior who was 250 miles away. To order the troops to hold Crown
Point, he informed Washington, "would only be heaping one hospital on another," since "the clothes, the blankets, the air, and the
ground they walk upon" were infested with smallpox.

Philip Schuyler resented Washington's second-guessing even
more. He wrote that he felt "deeply chagrinned" at the interference
from afar. Although General Washington deferred to Schuyler,
Gates, and Arnold, the junior officers who had objected continued
to nurse their grievances. Since it was Benedict Arnold who had
first proposed the abandonment of Crown Point, much of their
resentment was directed at him.

By unanimous vote, the generals adopted Arnold's plan. They
made two alterations. Rather than abandon Crown Point altogether, they would station a regiment there under Arnold's command to serve as a forward outpost. And they would forgo building
a frigate. To construct, rig, and arm the flotilla of gondolas and row

galleys would strain the resources available. A larger ship was out of the question.

"I trust," General Gates wrote to Washington, "neither courage nor activity will be wanting in those to whom the business is committed." The events of the coming summer and autumn would determine whether that courage and that activity would be enough.

6

*Straining
Every Nerve*

HORATIO GATES'S MOST FORMATIVE EXPERIENCE OF WAR
had come on July 9, 1755. He had served in the British Army for
a decade, achieving the rank of captain. He was accompanying a
force commanded by General Edward Braddock deep into the
American interior to chastise the French, who were building a fort
at present-day Pittsburgh.

Without warning, French troops and their Native American
allies ambushed the column. Standard European musket volleys
proved ineffective in the densely forested, hilly terrain. Chaos ensued. The British ranks were cut to pieces, men scalped alive, General
Braddock killed. Gates himself was wounded early in the fight, his
life saved by a private who helped him off the field. Among those
who survived the catastrophe was a Virginia militia officer named
George Washington.

Gates saw how shock tactics could demolish a force's cohe-
sion. He learned the value of intelligence—a commander could
not advance heedlessly into a wilderness. The experience may have
formed Gates's lifelong preference in his military thinking for a defensive stance rather than an offensive one. Nor did he ever forget
that his life had been saved by a man in the ranks.

The general brought to Ticonderoga the same skills he had exercised at Cambridge. He had not been on the job long before an officer was writing, "Generalship is now dealt out . . . by our worthy and well-esteemed General Gates." The officer judged that "if our friends in Canada . . . will wait a few days, we will give them a very proper reception."

The enemy in the north was a continual concern, but far more pressing for Gates was the enemy that had already infiltrated his army—the variola virus. This mysterious vector of smallpox continued to rampage through camp and sicken men without mercy.

The early part of the Revolutionary War was fought during one of the continent's worst smallpox epidemics, and the disease shaped the course of the fighting. Smallpox had been a perennial scourge in Europe and had flared locally in America. Because it was spread not through tainted water or insect bites but by face-to-face human contact, it flourished in cities and in crowded military camps.

Smallpox had long been endemic in England, and British soldiers, like the rest of the population, would typically have survived the illness in their youth and gained immunity. Americans, particularly those from rural areas, were less likely to have been exposed. Rumors circulated that, as Thomas Jefferson said, infected persons had been sent "into our army designedly by the commanding officer in Quebec." Such a tactic was not considered beyond the realm of civilized warfare. An American soldier on the scene described the ploy as one of the "indecorous, yet fascinating arts of the enemy."

During the Canadian debacle, John Adams had observed that "the smallpox is ten times more terrible than the British, Canadians, Indians combined." When first infected, a smallpox patient had only a brief period of symptoms: a strong, bounding pulse and perhaps a night of bad dreams. During a twelve-day incubation period, he showed no sign of illness. But suddenly the victim was engulfed by chills, back pain, and high fever. Then came the eruption of red dots he had been dreading. The lesions swelled into bumps, the bumps became firm blisters, the blisters softened to fluid-filled pustules. The fever and other symptoms attacked with a vengeance.

Smallpox victims' torment was unrelenting—throat ulcers, sores around the eyes and lips, severe headache. Corrupted skin gave off a distinctive sweetish odor, described by one doctor as "a hen-house on a warm April morn." Another said it was "so loathsome and evil-smelling that none could stand the great stench."

After two weeks of intense suffering for the patient, the blisters broke and formed crusts. The fever abated, scabs hardened and fell off, and the person slowly regained his health. In many cases he was disfigured for life by pockmarks, but the ordeal left him with the consolation that he would never again get the disease.

Ten percent of previously healthy sufferers died. The disease could kill a far greater proportion of the feeble and malnourished or of those previously isolated from exposure. Pox took a terrible toll among the indigenous peoples of America. Shortly before the arrival of the Pilgrims in 1620 an epidemic killed nearly nine-tenths of the population of the Massachusetts Bay area.

～

Gates ordered that sick men be separated from the others and transported, with the help of soldiers already immune, to a new hospital set up beside the ruin of Fort George on the south end of Lake George, thirty-five miles from Ticonderoga.

The man most responsible for treating the epidemic there would be Dr. Jonathan Potts. The twenty-nine-year-old Pennsylvania physician had been practicing medicine in Reading when the war broke out. Like many families, his was divided between supporters and opponents of the uprising. Potts volunteered to serve with the army and was sent to Ticonderoga.

The doctor in charge of the medical department for the northern army at the time was Samuel Stringer, personal physician to Philip Schuyler. Stringer departed in late July in search of critically needed medicine as well as to try to finagle a promotion from Congress. He did not return north until October.

Dr. Potts was left to oversee the largest hospital in North America. Situated a three-day ride from Albany, the facility consisted of makeshift sheds with dirt floors, board cots, and leaky roofs of bark or brush. They gave at least partial protection from sun and rain, none from cold nights or swarms of biting insects. Some men were without clothing. Blankets were in short supply.

The Reverend Ammi Robbins, chaplain of a Connecticut militia regiment, visited the hospital and described "dreadful suffering." He noted that "the camp is in a most sickly state, ten or twelve in some instances, have been buried in one day."

One man who witnessed the primitive conditions at the hospital said, "I stood still & beheld with admiration & sympathetic anguish what neither tongue nor pen can describe."

Some patients came down with confluent smallpox, a more deadly variety in which lesions merged into an oozing mass. In the hemorrhagic version, the sufferer bled from his gums, nose, and eyes. Nor was smallpox the only ailment Dr. Potts treated. Dysentery and "bilious putrid fever" also stalked the wards.

The horror grew with the numbers of patients. Hundreds became more than a thousand. Then two, then three thousand. To care for them, Potts had four army surgeons and four surgeon's mates. There was no cure or effective treatment for the pox. Doctors still relied on medical theories based on the balance of "humors." The "jalap, ipecac, bark, salts, opium & sundry other capital articles" that Potts complained of lacking provided little relief even from symptoms.

Potts sent an appeal for the donation of old shirts, sheets, and aprons, which could be used for bandaging. He requested "good women to dry and cure" herbs, including sage, mallow, and wormwood, for use at the hospital. He would receive no real medications until September.

৵

Less obvious but deeply distressing were the ailments of the soul. The stress disorders created by combat, or simply by the disorientation of campaigning, had no name but afflicted many soldiers. Despair, shock, and the tears of unknown emotions drained men's strength and courage.

Robbins tended to a Massachusetts soldier suffering not only from sickness but from a profound loneliness. The youth pleaded with him, "I cannot die, do, sir, pray for me, will you not send for my mother, if she were here to nurse me I could get well.... She was opposed to my enlisting." Robbins gave him what spiritual comfort he could, prayed, and left him, concluding, "He cannot live long."

ご

Besides isolating those infected, the only protection against smallpox was to endure the disease (the efficacy of vaccination with the benign cowpox virus would not be discovered until 1796). It had long been known that deliberately infecting a person with smallpox, a process known as inoculation or variolation, usually resulted in a significantly milder case and a reduced chance of dying. The reason is still something of a mystery.

Inoculation usually involved inserting pus from a smallpox victim into a slit in a healthy person's arm. The process had two serious drawbacks. First, it incapacitated the person for several weeks while he endured the attenuated disease. Second, the sufferer could spread the full-blown version to others through contact.

As a result, inoculation became a controversial topic and frequently left military officers in a quandary. While still in Montreal, Benedict Arnold tried to stem the epidemic by ordering inoculations. Days later, General Thomas arrived and rescinded the order. Some soldiers underwent inoculation on their own, determined to head off the more serious form of the illness. Ultimately, George Washington would order inoculation for all soldiers who had yet to acquire immunity.

Unorganized inoculation stripped soldiers from the ranks and threatened to spread the epidemic. General Gates, although he understood the value of the procedure, did not have time for the prolonged quarantine that successful inoculation entailed. On July 16, he warned all officers and men to stay away from those who were sick and "by no manner inoculate or suffer them selves to be inoculated." He gave orders that any infected man should "be immediately sent to the General Hospital at Lake George."

Quickly removing infected soldiers, quarantining all the sick, and allowing only immune soldiers to come near the hospital gradually brought the epidemic under control. Gates could only thank heaven that the British did not choose to attack during the worst of his army's illness.

In the middle of August, the commander was "straining every nerve to annihilate the infection." By the end of the month he could inform General Washington that "the small pox is now perfectly removed from the Army." Many men remained sick at Fort George and smaller outbreaks would come, but for now the situation was under control. Conquering the disease had been General Gates's first battle, and he had prevailed.

❧

Morale was as important to the northern army as physical health. Like every military man, Gates well understood that the line between a mob and an army is fragile, easily erased by defeat, discouragement, fear, and lack of leadership. The loss of officers, as well as the sergeants and corporals who were the men's immediate supervisors, took a serious toll.

Gates made sure that these officers were quickly replaced. He sent down a steady flow of orders from headquarters to regulate every aspect of soldiers' lives. Discipline was tightened. Instant obedience was expected, respect toward officers taken for granted, and observance of military forms enforced.

Sergeants taught privates what to expect and quickly corrected them if they did not perform. Men were marched around the camp with halters on their necks for "abuse of the officers." Sleeping on sentry duty or stealing from local farms brought flogging before the whole army. Courts-martial became a daily routine.

In the past, members of different regiments had feuded and sometimes brawled over the regional rivalries that were endemic in the Continental Army. Yankee troops resented the supercilious Yorkers. A Pennsylvania officer wrote to his wife that all the New England troops were "low, dirty, griping, cowardly, lying rascals." He felt little in common with this "mixture of Negroes, Indians, and Whites," and declared, "The more I am acquainted with them the worse I like them." General Schuyler wrote to Connecticut governor Jonathan Trumbull about "the unhappy dissensions in the Northern Army, where some unfriendly or unthinking people have set up colonial distinctions."

Gates could not erase prejudices overnight, but he separated the men, assigning the New England regiments to the new position being fortified on the east side of the lake. Those from Pennsylvania manned the old French lines on the heights above Ticonderoga and formed the advance guard at Crown Point. Men from New Jersey were stationed at the fortifications on the sandy plain just north of the fort.

The troops were kept continually active. Up before sunrise, most of the men labored at digging and building fortifications until sunset. When they were not working they were performing the drills they had only roughly learned before. They assembled, marched, wheeled, formed firing lines, handled their muskets to order, then did it all again. And again. They trained in tactics. They stood guard duty. Fatigue became a constant—tired soldiers had little energy left over for misbehavior.

"General Gates," an American officer wrote at the end of July, "is putting the most disordered Army that ever bore the name into a state of regularity and defence."

∽

Neglect of hygiene can be fatal to an army, and the soldiers noticed an immediate change when Gates took over. He recruited barbers and ordered men to keep their hair "plaited and powdered." Officers issued eight pounds of soap for every hundred men as soon as it became available. Washing hands and faces and keeping their underclothes clean made men feel human and helped stem disease.

The general worked hard to make sure the troops had plenty of fresh food. Salt pork and flour could sustain the men, but fresh beef, potatoes, peas, and other vegetables were essential for rebuilding their strength.

Thirty-one-year-old Colonel Anthony Wayne, a tanner, surveyor, and politician from outside Philadelphia, had come north with his 4th Pennsylvania Regiment and performed admirably at Three Rivers during the retreat. He wrote home in August that "fresh provision is become more plentiful than salt & our people have recovered health and spirits." Commissary officers issued only kettles for the men to cook in. Soups and stews were healthier than roasted food, as boiling more reliably destroyed parasites. Orders were issued: "No broiling, frying." Diarrhea became less common.

Feeding an army was a challenge. Thousands of barrels of flour and salt pork had to be transported up rivers and bad roads. Cattle were continually marched northward to be slaughtered. Commissary officers had to locate, ship, and distribute to the troops mutton, potatoes, peas, beans, butter, bread, and cheese.

And beer. Gates made an effort to obtain barrels of molasses, and officers encouraged men to brew beer flavored with spruce twigs. One recipe called for seven pounds of spruce sprays to be boiled with three gallons of molasses. The mixture was then added to thirty gallons of water, along with a pint of yeast; the brew could be drunk after it fermented in the barrel for a few days. Although some reported that the result tasted like turpentine, the alcohol content made the beverage safer to drink than plain water, which often was contaminated. Besides propping up morale, the beer helped prevent scurvy.

Far too gradually for Gates's liking, the army resumed the character of a fighting force. Two new Continental regiments arrived from Massachusetts, sick men began to recover, and the troops' spirits slowly improved. By late August, the general would have fully eight thousand soldiers present and fit for duty at the two forts.

∾

Sunday was the soldiers' one day of rest, and Gates restored the tradition of worship that had slipped during the precipitous Canadian retreat. Although a minister who visited the camp said that Gates "does not pretend to a great deal of religion himself," the general understood the important function of chaplains and required all soldiers to attend weekly sermons.

More than form was involved. Many of the men, especially observant New Englanders, were devout. Brought up on the Bible, they saw in the unfolding of earthly reality evidence of God's will. Young men, far from home, uncertain of the future, shattered by defeat, needed spiritual succor. They needed to make sense of events rather than be overwhelmed by "the Destroying Angel," as one soldier put it.

Smallpox victims were being buried every day. Dr. Lewis Beebe, who attended men at Ticonderoga, felt that the epidemic "pointed out our own mortality, in the most lively colors." He could not understand how men who saw eternity so vividly reflected in their everyday experiences could continue to dare damnation by cursing and transgressing God's commandments.

Gates ordered "the drummers to beat the church call for prayers at sunrise" on Sunday and officers to "pay the strictest attention to prayer orders issued from superiors." He wanted the army to reject despair, to see meaning in their defeat, and to put their faith in a better future.

In July, a chaplain preached on a verse from Isaiah in which the prophet threatened the enemies of the Israelites. "All ye of far countries," he predicted, "ye shall be broken in pieces." The text went on to admonish the chosen people: "Sanctify the Lord of hosts himself; and let him be your fear, and let him be your dread." The patriot army had been cast down, but its enemies would not prevail. It was God, not the British, the men should fear.

7

Sometimes I Dream

WHILE HORATIO GATES STRUGGLED TO BRING ORDER TO the army at Ticonderoga, he also needed to discover the details of the British preparations in Canada. One alarming rumor from the north stated that the enemy was already at work on "three sloops and two schooners at St. John's, which they expected would soon be finished."

Gates relied in part on Lieutenant Colonel Thomas Hartley, who ran the day-to-day operations at Crown Point under Benedict Arnold. The twenty-eight-year-old lawyer had marched to Canada the previous year, and he understood that his troops now manned the front line of the patriots' northern defenses. As General Gates pointed out to him, he was to "constantly report all extraordinaries" and "procure intelligence of the motions of the enemy."

Hartley regularly dispatched patrols from Crown Point by both land and water. He also employed as scouts the band of Indians allied to the army. These were Stockbridge Mohicans, whose ancestors had been driven from their Hudson Valley homes by Mohawks and had settled near Stockbridge, Massachusetts, where they converted to Christianity. During the French and Indian War, they had taught the British the tactics of wilderness fighting. Now allied with the patriots, they bridled at camp discipline, but they were skilled at slipping through the woods undetected.

General Gates asked for a volunteer from among the troops to venture north, penetrate British lines, and bring back either information or prisoners who could reveal the enemy's plan. Lieutenant Benjamin Whitcomb stepped forward. He took with him two Americans and two French-speaking Canadians who had joined the patriot cause. At sunset on Sunday, July 14, they began paddling canoes from Crown Point against a fierce headwind. Straining north all the next day, they reached the Onion River (now the Winooski River north of Burlington, Vermont), where, "wind and rain being severe, we could go no further."

The storm continued for the next two days, and the men hunkered down onshore. They then enacted in reverse Samuel de Champlain's long-ago foray into enemy territory, moving by night, alert to the danger that could erupt from the shore at any moment.

Now thirty-nine, Whitcomb had frequented the Champlain region when he fought with the British Army during the French and Indian War. When peace came, he farmed a homestead in the Hampshire Grants. He married in 1769 and finally settled with his wife, Lydia, on a plot of land in Maidenhead, a small settlement on the Connecticut River forty miles from the Canadian border.

Whitcomb was a rough frontiersman. One contemporary described him as "a presumptuous fellow, entirely devoid of fear, of more than common strength," a man who drank to excess even during battle. On the trip north that July, he and his companions were soaked by rain, pommeled by wind. They slept on the ground under what shelter they could find. Most of the lakeshore was forbidding, the undergrowth thick. The men subsisted on a palm-sized slab of salt pork and a hard biscuit per day, washed down with lake water.

At some point, they left their canoe behind and made their way on foot. The "French Men being uneasy & not willing to go near St. John's," Whitcomb wrote in his journal, he instructed them to abduct one of their countrymen and extract what information they could before returning. He and his pair of companions continued toward St. Johns. Soon afterward, one of the two fell ill and turned back.

On Sunday, July 21, Whitcomb and his one remaining subordinate came within five miles of St. Johns. They could hear the drums that signaled a military encampment. They sat near the river all afternoon in another steady rain. They took note of boats passing by, each loaded with barrels of provisions. They observed thirty big bateaux in the water and more being hammered together on land. Workmen were engaged in sawing boards by hand, "appearing to Work with great Life & Activity."

They hoped to grab a lone soldier but judged from the number of guards posted that it would be difficult to take a prisoner near St. Johns. The next day, they ranged north along the east side of the river, moving twelve miles to Chambly. They found an unguarded canoe and paddled across to the west side. Making a rough count, they calculated that there were around three thousand regulars stationed in the area. They could see that the St. Johns–Chambly road was active, with wagons lumbering by loaded with barrels, tents, and military stores. Twice they were discovered by the enemy and had to dart off the road into the woods.

On July 23, Whitcomb's remaining fellow scout disappeared, perhaps deserting to the enemy. The lieutenant continued to lurk around the British camp. He reconnoitered up the road that led to Montreal and ducked in and out of the woods to observe the movements of armed Indians and a full regiment of redcoats.

Around noon on Wednesday, July 24, he spotted an officer, clearly of a high rank, passing on his horse with a small escort. The men were headed down the road from La Prairie, opposite Montreal, to St. Johns. What happened next would ignite one of the fiercest controversies of the campaign.

ߝ

On July 23, a copy of the Declaration of Independence arrived at Fort Ticonderoga. General Gates directed that, under a flag of truce, a copy be delivered to the British in Canada. Five days later, at the regular Sabbath worship service, General Arthur St. Clair, who led Pennsylvania troops at the fort, read the document to the gathered soldiers: "That all Men are created equal, that they are endowed by their Creator with certain unalienable Rights." The words were stunning to men raised in a monarchy. St. Clair remembered that they "threw their hats in the air and cheered."

&

For the construction of the urgently needed works at Ticonderoga, Gates turned to his chief engineer, Jeduthan Baldwin. Before the war, Baldwin had been a prosperous farmer near Brookfield in central Massachusetts. He had no formal engineering training, but during the French and Indian War, he aided the British artificers who erected Fort William Henry on Lake George.

When violence erupted in 1775, he traveled to Cambridge and helped construct the fortifications to keep the British Army captive in Boston. In June, his brother Isaac was shot through the breast at Bunker Hill and died of his wounds.

After George Washington forced the British out of Boston he sent Baldwin north to reinforce the troops in Canada. In May 1776, the engineer reached Chambly, where he found an army thoroughly shattered and in retreat. With smallpox rampant, he decided to undergo inoculation at once. His symptoms following the treatment were more severe than usual. "I broke out all over as thick as possible," he wrote.

On June 11, still "very weak and unfit for travel," he joined the precipitous retreat of Sullivan's army up the Richelieu River. Later, General Sullivan sent him ahead to find a defensible position somewhere along Lake Champlain and to prepare it for the army's arrival.

Once the commanders decided to make Ticonderoga the focus of their defense, General Schuyler directed Baldwin to take charge of putting the fort in order. He accompanied Schuyler and Gates to survey the east shore and made a quick trip up the lake to Skenesborough, where he directed carpenters in improving the sawmill and the shipbuilding facilities.

During the earlier war, the French had recognized that Fort

Carillon, as they called Ticonderoga, isolated near the end of the peninsula, was vulnerable to attack. In 1758, they chose to mount their defense on a ridge that cut across the neck of land west of the fort. General Louis-Joseph de Montcalm constructed a sturdy line of earth and logs fronted by a ditch along this ridge. British general James Abercrombie, a fifty-two-year-old incompetent whom provincial troops called "Nabbycrombie," ordered a head-on assault against the French line. In brutal fighting, the British were thrown back with sixteen hundred men killed and wounded; it would remain the bloodiest day on the continent for a hundred years.

Baldwin, who had commanded a company of Americans at that battle, understood the lesson. He instructed his men to repair the old French lines, which had fallen into disrepair. They erected new earthworks along the ridge, with menacing artillery batteries to cover any advance. A large camp and redoubt directly east of the line housed troops who could quickly man the barricades.

The engineer planned another line of defense along the wide plain that stretched north and slightly east from the fort, probably the place where Samuel de Champlain had fired his arquebus at the Mohawks 167 years earlier. The largest of the fortifications there, the Jersey Redoubt, overlooked the lake and was manned by Continental soldiers from New Jersey.

Baldwin put little effort into rebuilding the original fort, which was known to all as the Old French Fort. The crumbling citadel became the administrative headquarters of the army and held a number of barracks, a magazine for ammunition, and storage buildings.

While soldiers were busy hammering and digging on the peninsula around Ticonderoga, another corps was hard at work fortifying the thumb of land across the lake according to Baldwin's plans. The stubby peninsula had gone by the name East Point or Rattlesnake Hill. Soon, in honor of the newly declared nation, it became Mount Independence.

The wooded plateau there sat about a hundred feet above the lake. A slope gave access to a convenient landing spot. To the north and east it was protected by East Creek, an unfordable stream that flowed through a steep ravine. Artillery could easily dominate the quarter-mile gap between the two sides of the lake.

Soldiers set to work clearing brush and trees, digging, building. They killed "snakes of every description, though mostly black and rattlesnakes," a Massachusetts man wrote. "Had it been filled with devils, however, it would have made no difference to our soldiers, for they were proof against everything." Baldwin oversaw the construction of a star-shaped fort and a battery of cannon, along with wells, roads, cranes, barracks, and storage buildings.

Commanders recognized that the spot offered an alternative back door to the American position. By building a road to the south, they could bring up supplies via an inland route and establish an escape hatch for the army in an emergency.

A final element of the Americans' defenses was the fortification of the high ground that lay southwest of Ticonderoga's Old French Fort and overlooked La Chute River, which flowed down from Lake George into Champlain. Known as Mount Hope, this position was key to defending against an end run that would have given the enemy access to the American rear.

For the men of the rank and file, the work of constructing fortifications was daunting. They had to manhandle logs, drive oxen and horses, clear brush, erect palisades, hammer together frames of rough lumber, wrestle with stones, dig ditches, and move many tons of earth. Most of them, raised on farms, had spent their days at similar tasks from an early age. Working from sunup to after dark was nothing new. But in the damp heat of July and August, the nonstop effort was draining.

The mind of Jeduthan Baldwin spun with a kaleidoscope of urgent tasks. He was directing the construction of the fourth-largest human settlement on the continent after Philadelphia, New York, and Boston. The same morning the Declaration was read, Baldwin visited the various workers on the fortifications and, because no quartermaster general was with the army, paid for some carpentry tools that had been delivered. He noted that "I have the intire direction of house & ship carpenters, the smiths, armorers, rope makers, the wheel and carriage makers, miners turners, coal-yers, sawyers & shingle makers, which are all together 286, besides the direction of all the fatiguing parties, so that I have my hands & mind constantly employed night & day, except when I am asleep and then sometimes I dream."

8

Fired on an Officer

THE EASTERN HALF OF NORTH AMERICA WAS A DENSE expanse of forest. Residents speculated that a squirrel could travel from the East Coast to the Mississippi River without ever touching the ground. British and German soldiers who crossed the Atlantic had never seen anything like the towering trees of the New World. Such virgin forests had been gone from Europe for a thousand years.

This wilderness was seen by settlers as a forbidding menace. They referred to it as a "desert" and evoked the biblical description of "the waste howling wilderness." It was a place without sustenance and without comfort. The ground was covered with tangles of slippery deadfall and vines, the canopy so dense that it created a gloomy cavern of foliage. It was a place where one could easily become lost and perish.

Yet some found that, like Native Americans, they could become intimate with this gnarled landscape, could read the landmarks and find their way. During the French and Indian War, frontiersman Robert Rogers became famous for organizing a company of "rangers," experienced woodsmen who could range through the trackless expanses of the interior.

Rogers' Rangers were the model for a military unit that could live, scout, and fight in the wilderness. Discarding many of the practices of European armies, which proved useless in the forest, Rogers had developed new rules for warfare.

He told his men "to be ready on any emergency to march at a minute's warning." Carrying a musket, sixty rounds of ammunition, and a hatchet, they were to "march in a single file, keeping such a distance from each other as to prevent one shot from killing two men." Rangers should be able to campaign on snowshoes, venture far behind enemy lines, attack at night, and lay ambushes. Stealth and heightened awareness were essential. Units in the field should post sufficient guards and keep "one half of your whole party awake alternately through the night."

When the American rebellion broke out in 1775, these principles of moving and fighting in the wilderness were inherited by a number of frontiersmen who fought for the patriot cause, including Rogers' fellow New Hampshirite John Stark and a Virginian named Daniel Morgan, both of whom became Continental Army generals.

Benjamin Whitcomb came from a background similar to that of the men who had fought with the rangers. He had Rogers' uncanny ability to navigate a trackless forest. He relied on his own initiative, a necessity for scouts who often ventured alone through enemy territory and had to make quick decisions.

Finding himself in such a situation on a hot July day in 1776, Whitcomb squinted down the barrel of the heavy musket he had been carrying during the entire journey. He peered at the deep scarlet uniform, the gold braid of the officer's epaulets. He was close enough to be sure of his aim. Should he kill an unsuspecting man who was going about his business? He was an enemy, but this was not a field of battle. Thoughts stampeded through his mind in an instant and evaporated. He pulled the trigger.

Not waiting to see the effect of his shot through the smoke, the scout scampered down the raw road and cut into the deep woods. Now he had to avoid an aroused British guard. At one point he concealed himself under a pile of brush for hours until darkness fell. His account of the incident in his journal is matter-of-fact: "Fired on an officer & moved immediately into Chamblee Road being discovered, retreated back into the Woods, and Stayed till Night."

Setting out alone on July 27, Whitcomb carried his information back to his superiors. It took him ten days to make his way down the west shore of Lake Champlain as far as Crown Point.

Soon after his arrival, Whitcomb learned the consequences of the shot he had fired in the north. He had, like Samuel de Champlain, loaded his firelock with more than one ball. Both bullets had penetrated the shoulder of Brigadier General Patrick Gordon, who commanded the British 1st Brigade in Canada, a crack unit of three regiments.

With blood flowing freely from his wound, Gordon had been able to ride to the fort at St. Johns. He lived for a week in pain before dying of his injuries. The incident shocked and outraged the British high command. The fact that an enemy partisan could infiltrate so deeply into British territory was alarming enough. That any man claiming to be a soldier would fire on an officer from ambush suggested that the American rebels had thrown off all respect for the rules of war and for honor itself.

Even before Gordon expired, General Carleton issued a furious response. "The Rebel Runaways not having dared shew their Faces as Soldiers," he proclaimed, had now "taken the part of the vilest Assassins, and are lurking in small parties to Murder." He demanded that any of these "infamous Skulkers" who were taken prisoner should not be shot as spies but hung as common criminals.

After General Gordon died, Carleton put a fifty-guinea reward on Whitcomb's head—the ranger's reputation was well known to the enemy. The prize remained in effect for the rest of the war.

It was not only the British who were appalled by the act. When George Washington heard about the "assassination," he insisted it was an "indecent, illiberal and scurrilous performance so highly unbecoming the Character of a Soldier and a Gentleman."

James Wilkinson, now an aide to General Gates, pronounced Whitcomb's act an "abominable outrage on the customs of war and the laws of humanity," which produced "abhorrence" among his fellow officers. Colonel Matthias Ogden labeled the act "villainous," a word that still meant "lowborn" rather than "evil." Yet Ogden could not help admiring Whitcomb's courage and resourcefulness in penetrating enemy lines and avoiding capture. He praised "a peculiar kind of bravery that I believe Whitcomb alone is possessed of."

Wilkinson thought Whitcomb should be brought up on charges, but he admitted that "it was impossible, in the temper of the times, to bring him to punishment, without disaffecting the fighting men on that whole frontier."

It was an important point. American soldiers, particularly rangers like Whitcomb, although willing to submit to military discipline, continued to see themselves as free citizens, fundamentally equal to any officer. That was the cause for which they were fighting. The practice of drawing officers from the upper classes was not as entrenched in the American army as it was in the British. Many American soldiers saw no reason to kowtow to anyone.

Whitcomb's act took place in the shadowy moral frontier between everyday life and war. Although war inevitably unleashed actions that were primitive and barbaric, rules and customs circumscribed the violence. Who was to say where the boundary lay? What was to prevent the violence from spilling over? The questions would come up again in the Revolution and continue far into the future.

The shooting of Brigadier Gordon had practical consequences beyond the controversy. The British sent more light infantrymen and Indians south along the lake to scout and to assault unwary bands of Americans, including those sawing lumber near the shore. General Carleton for a time dropped his conciliatory stance and refused to receive messages from the Americans under flags of truce. The war was growing more bitter.

Whitcomb showed no concern about the reward the British had put on his head—a man taken as a spy was subject to execution anyway. The following month he returned to Canada with two other men on a second scouting expedition. General Gates warned that "you are positively forbid to fire upon, to kill, to wound ...

any one engaged in the service of the enemy except in your own defence."

The scout and his companions proceeded to the very spot where he had shot Gordon. At the time, Alexander Saunders, the quartermaster of Gordon's brigade, planned to ride to Montreal and was advised to avoid the remote road where Gordon had been ambushed. He scoffed that he would not go out of his way for Whitcomb or any skulking American. On the contrary, he said, he would "be very glad to meet him, as he was sure he should get the reward which had been offered."

Seeing Saunders coming, Whitcomb and his men burst from heavy brush, grabbed and disarmed the British officer, tied his arms, and blindfolded him. Four days later, the quartermaster was in Ticonderoga. When he would give no information, he was sent off as a prisoner of war.

In September, General Gates ignored the Gordon controversy when he asked Congress to promote Whitcomb to captain. He suggested giving him command of two companies of soldiers who would serve as unconventional fighters. Employing the principles of stealth and ambush developed by Robert Rogers and well suited to New World conditions, they would constitute the first in a long line of commandos and special forces in the American military.

9

Life and Spirit

"WE SHALL BE HAPPY, OR MISERABLE," GENERAL GATES wrote on July 13, "as we are, or are not, prepared for the enemy." His mood favored misery. The early effort to build and arm a fleet, the key element of that preparation, was lagging alarmingly.

George Washington, who was staring across New York Harbor at a massive British troop buildup, understood how critical it was to stop the enemy in the north. He dispatched troops from Boston to reinforce Gates, noting that it was "a matter of the greatest importance to have sufficient force to prevent the enemy passing the lake." Washington suggested that if the American flotilla there were "assigned to General Arnold, none will doubt of his exertions."

Gates agreed. He saw in Arnold his perfect complement. "How happy must every good officer be," he declared, "to find himself seconded by so capable and brave a spirit as that possess'd by Arnold."

Obstacles inevitably arose. Gates, who harbored a lingering resentment of Schuyler's authority, had written the commander to note that "I labor continually to get the Commodore to Crown Point with the vessels." The commodore was Jacobus Wynkoop, who was currently managing the Lake Champlain navy. Four days later, Gates complained to Benedict Arnold, "I think the Commodore seems slow." He was "baffled by the laziness of the artificers, or the neglect of those whose duty it is to see them diligently at their work."

Gates hoped that the pace of shipbuilding would pick up with the July 15 arrival of David Waterbury. The fifty-four-year-old Connecticut militia general was a friend of Arnold's. His farm in Stamford overlooked Long Island Sound, and Waterbury was considered "an able seaman." Gates assumed he would take command at Skenesborough, but Wynkoop continued to insist that he was in charge of all aspects of the ships on the lake.

Wynkoop was a holdover from General Schuyler's earlier efforts to prop up the patriot naval presence. That spring, with the army and its officers still committed to Canada, Schuyler had searched for someone to command the tiny fleet of warships already on the lake. Wynkoop was a mariner who had captained a merchant schooner sailing between Kingston, New York, on the Hudson River, and the West Indies. He had fought in the French and Indian War, and he held a respected position among the Dutch families of the Hudson Valley. He was also a captain in the 4th New York Regiment of the Continental Army.

In May 1776, Schuyler asked him to organize a maritime defense of Lake Champlain. Wynkoop recruited some soldiers to serve as marines and headed north. He referred to himself as commodore of the fleet on the lake, but Congress never precisely defined his role or rank.

Wynkoop's provincialism clashed with the insular anti-Yorker sentiments of the New England patriots. He found himself out of his depth as a commander, unable to expedite complex and urgent tasks or exercise forceful initiative.

General Gates complained that the sixty carpenters working at Skenesborough on July 15 "must be very ill-attended to, or very ignorant of their business, not to do more work." He wrote to tell John Hancock that the gondolas that had been built still awaited rigging. He concluded: "If the enemy gives us time to do all this, it will be well, if not, this wretched Army will probably be yet more unfortunate."

Gates wanted Benedict Arnold to take over shipbuilding at Skenesborough and push the project along. Following the July 7 council of war, Arnold had first counted and categorized all the men who had returned from Canada, compiling a listing of carpenters, blacksmiths, shipwrights, and sailors, whose skills would be critical.

Next, he sailed north with the two schooners and the sloop that constituted the initial fleet. His object was to pick up boards from the various sawmills scattered along the shore of Lake Champlain. Arnold had traded in lumber and could spot the type of seasoned planks best suited for marine construction. He ordered excess wood burned so that British raiding parties would not get their hands on it.

Scouting the many islands and inlets along the lake, Arnold took soundings and studied the shifting winds. He noted the dangerous shoals and rocks hidden below the surface. He went as far north as the inlet of the Onion River, about halfway between Crown Point and Canada on the east side of the lake. From there, he could peer across the lake with his spyglass and make out the distant shape of Valcour Island, near the western shore.

When Arnold returned to Ticonderoga on July 23, General Gates immediately sent him to Skenesborough to accelerate the progress of the shipbuilding. As a boy, Arnold had sailed with his father on trading expeditions to the West Indies. By the time he was twenty-five, he owned three ships of his own. He often went along on voyages—his decisiveness and sharp-edged personality were suited to a ship captain's duties. He filled his ships with livestock, lumber, and furs and traded them for mahogany, molasses, and enslaved people in the Caribbean basin.

Sailing into the Skenesborough shipyard on the sloop *Enterprise*, Arnold expected to see substantial progress. Instead, he came upon a post given to idleness and lethargy. Wynkoop had gone off on a pointless cruise along the lake. Some of the carpenters were finishing gondolas, but only one larger row galley had been started.

Although the naval yard was amply protected by the posts farther north on the lake, Wynkoop had decided to fortify his position at Skenesborough. He had ordered the men to build barracks and blockhouses instead of boats. Enervated by the summer heat, the civilian workmen went about their tasks without energy. Some had already fallen ill with the fevers that festered in the marshy settlement.

Arnold found two additional gondolas in the ways as well as a larger boat that was being built from frames he had confiscated at St. Johns before the army departed Canada. This small schooner, renamed the *Lee* after Richard Henry Lee, was sometimes called a cutter. Although it was shorter than a gondola, it had more firepower, carrying six cannon and ten swivel guns.

Furious at the lack of progress, Arnold issued orders to the carpenters to begin building additional row galleys, which were to be seventy feet long compared to the gondolas' fifty feet. Harmanus Schuyler, who had been following Wynkoop's orders, now reported, "General Arnold arrived here yesterday and thinks ten [gondolas] in number will be sufficient." In the meantime, the men were to "go immediately to work on building a Spanish galley."

The history of these Spanish galleys stretched back to antiquity. The word "galley" came to mean a vessel driven by both oars and sails. Galleys were the principal fighting ships of the Phoenicians, the Romans, and other peoples around the Mediterranean. They were also favored by Barbary pirates. (See the ship illustrations at the end of the book.)

During the Revolution, Americans adopted this style for warships on the Delaware Bay to protect Philadelphia. A galley was equipped with nine long sweep oars on each side for rowing. Two masts held its lateen sails, which were right triangles of canvas with the shortest side toward the stern and the hypotenuse attached to a long boom that crossed the mast. The boats had sleek lines and could tack easily as they progressed against the wind.

In contrast to the flat bottom of the gondola, the galley had a hull like that of a schooner or sloop, curved inward to join at its keel. This more complicated shape demanded a detailed knowledge of shipbuilding and made its construction more laborious compared to a gondola. But the result was a more maneuverable vessel. The galleys had a shallow draft, which made them ideal for coastal operations, and their dual methods of propulsion allowed them to accommodate changing winds or move in no wind at all.

Galleys featured a raised quarterdeck at the stern and a main gun deck stretching to the bow. Officers were housed in a small cabin under the quarterdeck, while the crew could take shelter in a space with a five-foot clearance under the main deck. On a gondola, only a canvas awning protected sailors from the elements.

Most important, galleys carried more firepower. The smaller gondolas were limited to three main guns firing over the bulwarks. The ten larger guns on the galleys fired through ports in their hulls. Their 18-pounders would give the American fleet its most potent punch.

Arnold's presence ushered in a new phase in the building of the patriot fleet. Luckily, the evening after he arrived, fifty-two more Pennsylvania ship's carpenters, who had built row galleys in Philadelphia, marched into town with their tools slung over their shoulders. They laid the keel of a second galley without delay. Another squad of carpenters showed up the following day and soon began work on a third galley.

The galleys would be useless without men to sail them. Bypassing General Gates, the eager Arnold wrote to Philip Schuyler to urge the commander to recruit "two or three hundred seamen" from Connecticut to man the craft that he could already envision. But attracting experienced seamen to the distant interior would vex the operation until its end.

On July 29, Horatio Gates wrote to Congress that General Arnold "is just returned from Skenesboro, where he has been to give life and spirit to our dockyard." He went on to sing his subordinate's praises: "Arnold (who is perfectly skilled in maritime affairs) has most nobly undertaken to command our fleet upon the lake. With infinite satisfaction, I have committed the whole of that department to his care, convinced he will thereby add to that brilliant reputation he has so deservedly acquired."

While Gates fortified Ticonderoga and Arnold ramped up activity at the shipyard, General Schuyler tackled the onerous duty of finding, buying, and transporting the diverse collection of equipment required by a functioning army and navy. For each item he had to find a vendor, negotiate a price, examine a prototype, approve the purchase, arrange transportation to remote Lake Champlain, and convey payment. He sometimes offered his own credit to complete the deal.

He was fortunate to enlist twenty-three-year-old Richard Varick, who had been a New York City lawyer when the war broke out. Varick became Schuyler's secretary and worked without stint to coordinate the vast supply system. Traveling around New York and New England, Varick hunted down needed equipment and hounded suppliers to expedite delivery. The items included everything from uniforms, spades, and cooking pots to bellows, lanterns, and grindstones.

Warships were complex machines requiring specialized equipment, most of it unavailable except in the shipbuilding centers near the coast. Arnold wrote Schuyler to emphasize that "many of the articles in my list, though trifles, are absolutely necessary, & cannot be procured here." He tried to be helpful by suggesting Connecticut merchants he knew who might supply them. He pressed Schuyler for more oakum, bar iron, frying pans, tar brushes, needles, and "about a ton of rum."

Congress had established a shipyard in Poughkeepsie, New York, on the Hudson River, to build frigates to thwart an enemy attack from the south. Varick tried to convince Jacobus Van Sandt, the yard's manager, to supply pistols, cutlasses, sheet lead, quick match, copper, and swivel guns, but these items were in short supply. He was able to scrounge slow match and six dozen large sails there. He purchased bolt rope, which sailmakers would stitch into the edges of the canvas. Building new ships always required a large amount of tar and pitch, used for waterproofing. Varick also acquired the masses of hemp fibers known as oakum, which were pounded into the joints between hull and deck planks and painted with pitch to seal the seams. Rope, which was manufactured in the rope-walks of coastal cities, was needed, as were anchors and the heavy cables by which they were let down and raised.

Varick purchased gear from Albany shipowners whose own vessels were bottled up in the river by the fighting and the British blockade at the mouth of the Hudson. He was able to buy, at "exorbitant rates," twenty-five anchors from river captains. "Neither the love of money, virtue to their country or persuasive eloquence of officers," he complained, "will induce some persons to part with a single article."

Varick's contribution was valued. Gates told him that "your love & Industry to serve the public cannot be too much prais'd or rewarded." Benedict Arnold wrote to Schuyler to let him know that "Captain Varick has been very industrious in procuring articles for the Navy." Arnold would later take on the young captain as his own aide.

∽

Once a vessel was seaworthy, the shipbuilders slid it down the greased stocks into the lake. Men rowed the unfinished hull north to the American post at Mount Independence, opposite Ticonderoga. There workmen used derricks on the high ground to install the boats' masts. Jeduthan Baldwin was in charge of organizing and pushing ahead this process.

Finishing the ships meant supplying the shrouds and stays that supported and stabilized the masts, and the intricate web of blocks, pulleys, and hempen lines that allowed the sailors to raise and adjust the sails. This work was as specialized as hull construction and could be just as time-consuming. It required the efforts of blacksmiths, splicers, knotters, and men well versed in the mechanics of sailing.

Also at Mount Independence, workmen hoisted and installed cannon. Plenty of gun barrels had been found at Ticonderoga when the fort was captured a year earlier, but the best of them had been hauled by sled to Boston during the previous winter and used to force the enemy out of the city. Not a few of those remaining were old and of dubious quality.

Gunpowder was the fuel of war at sea, where the essence of fighting was the artillery duel. But powder was in short supply in the northern theater for both the armed vessels and the forts. In early July, General Gates gave orders that soldiers should stop wasting powder by firing morning and evening guns and "unnecessary salutes." And in early September he demanded of Congress, "It is immediately necessary that fifteen tons of powder . . . should be sent to this post."

Lead for bullets and flints for firing muskets were also precious. To preserve the flints, Gates ordered that they were "not to be worn out by foolishly snapping the Firelocks." Fortunately, a vein of flint was discovered at Mount Independence, alleviating the shortage.

The handling of gunpowder was awkward and hazardous. On ships, it had to be stored and used in confined spaces close to smoldering lengths of match cord. It also needed to be kept dry, as any hint of dampness rendered it useless. The powder was most commonly measured into flannel cartridges and stored in the magazines or secure ammunition chests built into the vessels.

Accidents happened. On August 6, a crew had put the finishing touches on the gondola *Providence*. They sailed the boat a few miles down the lake and back on a practice run. As part of his crew's training, the captain ordered the men to fire a five-gun salute as they passed Ticonderoga.

A good number of the cannon supplied for the ships were British guns from the last war. Some were even older, dating back to the seventeenth century. Fashioned from cast iron and indifferently maintained, they were marred by cracks or scaling along the inside of the barrel. Both flaws made the guns dangerous to fire.

A soldier named Solomon Dyer was assigned to scour the barrel with a wet sponge after it was fired in order to quench any sparks. He did his job imperfectly. As he was ramming home a new cartridge, it exploded. With the blast, Jeduthan Baldwin commented, Dyer "was blown into many pieces and scattered on the water." What remained of his body floated to the surface three days later. His companions gave him a decent burial, no doubt mulling the volatile and unpredictable nature of warfare.

⤙⤚

Just as crucial as any of these supplies was manpower. Without shipwrights, riggers, and all the other specialized tradesmen, the fleet could not be finished. A galley would be officered by a captain, lieutenant, sailing master, and mate. Also needed were a gunner, a boatswain in charge of maintenance, a carpenter to make repairs, and twenty-eight seamen. Forty marines were assigned to fight off boarders and contribute musketry to the ship's firepower. A gondola carried a captain and two lieutenants, a gunner and his mate, and thirty-nine other men, half of them designated sailors, half marines.

The prospect of an encounter with the enemy on the lake did not excite nautical men any more than inland duty attracted shipbuilders. The coming of war had opened a thriving privateering trade off the Atlantic coast. Congress gave the captains of privately owned American vessels permission to hunt down and seize British cargo ships. Sailors who participated could look forward to substantial prize money. Those fighting on an isolated inland lake envisioned only hardship.

Benedict Arnold suggested a monthly eight-shilling bonus for seamen. Few rushed to take it. He again scoured the troops at Ticonderoga for anyone with maritime experience but found few sailors among the soldiers. Schuyler convinced Congress to offer more than thirty-two dollars a month to qualified shipwrights, a wage that was five times that of a private and more than most officers received. This inducement and the efforts of recruiting agents in coastal areas began, finally, to bring in a portion of the men needed.

Operating a sailing ship was a skill that generally took months and years to learn. Experienced officers could give orders, but the men had to know how to carry them out. Arnold pleaded for seasoned sailors: "We must have them. Our navigation without them will be useless—soldiers or landsmen will by no means answer without a number of seamen in each vessel."

Ultimately men had to be selected from the ranks, whatever their abilities. Regimental officers most often sent troublemakers and underperforming soldiers. Arnold wrote to Gates to complain that "the drafts from the Regiments at Ticonderoga are a miserable set," but he knew that his ship captains and officers would have to make do with whatever men were sent them.

Yet during August, commanders in the north dared to express optimism about their prospects. By August 6, Arnold announced that the galleys were "much forwarder than I expected, three will be launched in a Fortnight." He wrote to Schuyler that "the carpenters go on with great spirit."

Ships were being rigged at Ticonderoga, General Gates noted, and "our fleet grows daily more and more powerful." The real test of whether they had succeeded would come as soon as the new vessels "join those at Crown Point when General Arnold will sail with the whole down the lake."

10

Honor May Require

BEFORE GENERAL ARNOLD COULD SAIL OFF TO MEET THE enemy, a vexing administrative issue had to be settled. Just as Hamlet thought that to be great was "to find quarrel in a straw when honour's at the stake," gentlemen of the eighteenth century cultivated refined sensibilities that smelled a controversy in every slight, a challenge in every imputation. Often the way to settle the matter was to face each other with dueling pistols.

Excesses aside, the concept of honor contributed to the structure of the military and the wider society. Oaths were sacrosanct. Blatant self-interest stained a man's character. Adherence to the code marked his claim to be a gentleman rather than a plebeian. Officers in particular were held to strict covenants.

To restore order to the northern army, General Gates held a series of courts-martial at Ticonderoga. Panels of officers convened to hear charges against those accused of a misdemeanor or a breach of duty and to assign punishment. The process made the men aware that any lapse of discipline or offense against standing orders would not be tolerated. It assured them of a speedy trial and gave them the opportunity to defend their behavior. An officer would often demand a court-martial if he felt his reputation had been disparaged.

Most of these trials involved infractions in camp: sleeping on sentry duty, disrespecting officers, stealing from civilians or fellow soldiers. Others addressed the irregularities and disputes that had arisen in the chaos of the retreat from Canada. One of those to be judged was Moses Hazen. Then forty-three, Hazen had been born in Massachusetts and had fought with Rogers' Rangers during the French and Indian War. He performed well enough to be commissioned an officer in the British Army. With peace, he retired on half pay to Montreal, where he became a trader and land speculator. Hazen purchased several *seigneuries* near St. Johns, which gave him large tracts of land tended by serflike tenants. He was one of the Anglo-American opportunists whom James Murray, the first governor of the province, called "the most immoral collection of men I ever knew."

When violence broke out in the colonies to the south, Hazen proved an adept fence straddler. He dallied with the British, but by the time Philip Schuyler's northern army marched up the Richelieu in September 1775, Hazen was leaning toward the patriot cause. He soon enlisted in the war on the American side.

After the patriot army laid siege to Quebec City, Hazen returned to Montreal, where he assumed command on behalf of the invaders until replaced by Benedict Arnold in April. Arnold judged Hazen "a sensible, judicious officer, and well acquainted with this country." He put him in charge of Chambly and St. Johns while Sullivan's army retreated down the St. Lawrence.

Arnold and Hazen fell into a dispute in the middle of May during a botched effort to repel a British attack. While Guy Carleton's force proceeded up the river from the east, another enemy unit of 250 men, two-thirds of them Indians, moved toward Montreal from the west. They confronted American defenders on the north bank of the river at a place called The Cedars. The British besieged the 400 Americans; their commander lost his nerve and capitulated.

Benedict Arnold led a relief column to free the prisoners by means of a surprise attack. During the operation, Colonel Hazen, who accompanied Arnold, suggested they turn back for fear that the prisoners would be murdered. Other American officers backed the idea. A disagreement flared and the two men exchanged "reproachful language." The affair ended with a negotiated prisoner exchange and lingering bad blood between Hazen and Arnold.

By the end of May, the entire American effort in Canada was collapsing. The commissioners sent from Congress, including Benjamin Franklin, had given Arnold permission to confiscate supplies from Montreal merchants in exchange for promises of payment at a later date. On June 6, Arnold ordered a Major Scott to transport these supplies to Chambly and directed Hazen to take charge of them.

Hazen at first refused responsibility for the goods, which he felt had been unjustly confiscated from his merchant friends in Montreal. Finally he sent them on to St. Johns without proper documentation. They ended up on the wharf there. Someone— perhaps retreating American soldiers, perhaps local residents or merchants—broke open the crates and helped themselves. When Arnold arrived, most of the supplies were gone and the identifying labels were missing. No compensation was possible, leaving the Americans, and Arnold, open to the charge of thievery. Enraged, Arnold reprimanded Hazen in scathing language.

Hazen demanded a court of inquiry because of his superior's "undeserved reflection" on his character. In the chaos of the retreat, nothing could be done. But Hazen did not let go of this straw of insult.

Now in Ticonderoga the matter was to be sorted out. The court had to wait while Arnold pursued his urgent effort to get a fleet built at Skenesborough. But military justice was a priority, even if a critical officer had to be absent from his duties at a time when every minute was precious. Arnold was just as eager to see justice done as Hazen was to clear his name. The trial unfolded over the next two days. The result was very far from what Benedict Arnold expected.

ⓢ

Colonel Enoch Poor was the president of the court-martial, which included a dozen other field officers, several of them still disgruntled over the refusal of the high command to reinforce Crown Point. They had been meeting for more than a week, judging a variety of disciplinary matters. On July 31, they took up the case of Colonel Moses Hazen.

During his short military career, Arnold had won the admiration and affection of the soldiers serving under him. But his hair-trigger temper and displays of self-confidence bordering on arrogance had frequently rubbed fellow officers the wrong way. He was blunt, often tactless. He did not suffer fools. His meteoric rise ignited envy from many directions. He neglected to groom the egos of older men—Moses Hazen was eight years older than Arnold, Enoch Poor five years older. Nor did he afford these veterans of the French and Indian War the deference they expected for their experience.

Although the members of the court may have harbored resentment against Arnold, the evidence does not indicate that their proceeding was either biased or unfair. During the first day of the hearings, Hazen presented witnesses who swore that the goods Arnold sent ahead had never been in Hazen's possession—they had been looted when still under the auspices of Major Scott.

Hazen was a schemer, experienced in courtroom combat. He had used his time at Ticonderoga to make friends among the officers who were trying him. He had also conferred with John Brown, a Yale-educated lawyer from western Massachusetts. Brown's grievances against Arnold went back to the capture of Ticonderoga in May 1775. Arnold had impugned the courage of a Massachusetts officer named James Easton, in whose company Brown served. Both Easton and Brown became sworn enemies of the New Haven upstart. Like Hazen, they hoped to bring Arnold down.

The trial was complicated by the fact that "Major" Scott was in fact Captain John Budd Scott. Currently stationed at Ticonderoga, he served as the judge advocate or legal adviser for the court. Scott's position as both an officer of the court and a witness complicated matters. When Scott was called to testify on Arnold's behalf, Hazen objected. The court agreed that Scott was "so far interested . . . as to render his testimony inadmissible."

Arnold, who had seen the trial of an allegedly insubordinate officer turn into a judgment on his own behavior, flew into a rage. Scott "is not the least interested" in Hazen's trial, he asserted. He protested the court's decision "as unprecedented and I think unjust."

The point of a court-martial was to render military justice without prejudice. If a superior officer like Arnold questioned the court's impartiality, it struck at the foundation of the system. Colonel Poor noted that Arnold's demeanor throughout had been "marked with contempt and disrespect towards the Court." He demanded that Arnold apologize: "Nothing but an open acknowledgment of your error will be conceived as satisfactory."

The affair had moved into dangerous territory. The facts of what had happened on the wharf at Chambly faded into the background. Honor was at the stake.

On August 2, after a night spent seething over the perceived insult, Arnold responded in a manner that could only inflame the situation. He accused the court of "indecent reflections on a superior officer." Then he went further. He would, he said, as soon as military expediency allowed, "by no means withhold from any gentleman of the Court the satisfaction that his honour may require." He was in effect challenging the members of the court to meet him on the dueling ground.

That same day, the court found Hazen blameless in the affair of the looted supplies. A week later, some of the officers who had sat in judgment attended a celebratory dinner with the defendant. Having talked over the insult that Arnold had tossed in their faces, they ordered the general to be arrested for contempt of court and for "using profane oaths and execrations" and "menacing words" before them. For his part, Arnold claimed that at the end of the trial, Hazen had flung at him the "grossest abuse," probably an accusation of cheating Montreal merchants, and the court had "countenanced" the insult.

General Gates wrote to Congress that while "the warmth of general Arnold's temper might possibly lead him a little farther than is marked by the received line of decorum," he could not possibly accept the loss of his naval commander. "I was obliged to act dictatorially," he continued, "and dissolve the court martial the instant they demanded General Arnold to be put under arrest. The United States must not be deprived of that excellent officer's services at this important moment."

Gates wrote to General Schuyler that he was "astonished at the calumnies" of the junior officers against Arnold. He concluded, "To be a man of honor, and in an exalted station, will ever excite the envy in the mean and undeserving."

Later, as Arnold floated with his fleet in the cold water of the Canadian border region, awaiting an enemy force, a violent battle, and the prospect of death, he mused, "I cannot but think it extremely cruel when I have sacrificed my ease, health, and a great part of my private property, in the cause of my country, to be calumniated as a robber and thief—at a time, too, which I have it not in my power to be heard in my own defense."

Benedict Arnold would not forget.

II

Princes of the
Wilderness

IN 1745, WHEN PHILIP SCHUYLER WAS TWELVE YEARS OLD, French soldiers and allied Native American warriors descended the Great Warpath from Canada and attacked the village of Saratoga, north of Albany. They swept whooping into the Schuyler family estate on the Hudson River. The raiders killed thirty people and took a hundred prisoners. The bloody, scalped corpses included that of Schuyler's uncle, after whom he was named. In the wake of the raid, New York provincial authorities constructed a blockhouse and stationed militia in the settlement. The territory to the north emptied of pioneer families and remained a no-man's-land throughout King George's War, which lasted until 1748.

The violence was a keen reminder of Albany's proximity to the disputed frontier during Schuyler's childhood. Since the days his great-grandfather had immigrated from Holland in 1650, the family had lived near and drawn its fortune from the territory inhabited by Native Americans. Besides gaining ownership of large tracts of land, they carried on a lucrative fur trade with the Iroquois and other tribes.

Encouraged by his family, Philip learned to speak the Mohawk language. As a young man he traveled into the wilderness to live with Indians for a time and to become familiar with their customs. He understood the importance of trading fairly and catering to their rituals and sensibilities.

He inherited goodwill that traced back to his great-uncle Pieter Schuyler. Known to the Indians as Queder, Pieter had established cordial relations with the Mohawks and had acquired a reputation for honesty in his dealings. The Indians had long memories and honored Philip Schuyler for his ancestor's virtues. They respected him for his candor and intellect and called him Thoniyoudakayon, a transcription of a phrase meaning "his mind is old"—he had the wisdom of an elder.

✑

On Wednesday, August 7, 1776, while the men at Skenesborough and Fort Ticonderoga were hurrying their preparations for the British invasion they were certain was coming, General Schuyler was 120 miles away at German Flatts, a tiny settlement on the banks of the Mohawk River at the limit of white settlement. He looked out over a crowd of almost two thousand Native Americans, who stretched before him in an open field.

The afternoon was hot, the air laced with tobacco smoke. The heads of the warriors were shaved, each retaining a small tuft of hair interlaced with feathers representing defeated enemies. Their earlobes were split and weighted with ornaments, their noses pierced by rings. The faces of both men and women were tattooed.

Schuyler, arrayed in his best blue uniform and gold epaulets, began the proceedings by offering the tribal leaders a belt of wampum. "Brothers, Sachems and Warriors of the Six Nations," he declared, "with this string we open your ears, that you may plainly hear what the Independent States of America have to say." He told them he was about to "wipe away all mists that may interrupt your sight." Interpreters conveyed the meaning of his words to those who spoke no English.

It was the beginning of a long and carefully prepared oration. Reconciliation between the king and the colonists, he emphasized, was no longer a possibility. In measured words, he rebuked the tribes for actions that had broken the treaties so recently agreed to. He scolded them for paying heed to John Butler, a British agent at Fort Niagara, who had tried to get them to take up the hatchet for the crown.

The current conflict between the Americans and the British was a dispute that the Indians had agreed to stay out of. If any of the members of the Iroquois Confederacy wanted to side with the enemy, Schuyler said, they could leave now without being harassed. But they should know that the Americans would retaliate. Schuyler's tone was sometimes courteous, sometimes accusatory, but always firm and often "very warm" with anger.

೧

The Native Americans of New York and New England were vitally concerned about the course and outcome of the Revolutionary War. Early in the conflict, a patriot officer noted, "It is plain to me that the Indians understand their game, which is to play into both hands." For generations they had profited from making smart alliances when the white men fought each other—the Dutch against the English, the English against the French, and now the colonists against the authorities in London.

The power of Native Americans did not come from their numbers. At the time, the population of all the Haudenosaunee was twelve thousand and declining. The Mohawks had dwindled to barely more than four hundred souls. This compared with forty-two thousand colonists around Albany and up the Mohawk Valley. But the Indians had devised a method of fighting—slipping through the forests, attacking without warning, killing, and disappearing back into the wilderness—that made them an effective and feared force. In the current conflict they weighed their options. Many of them leaned toward the British because King George had restricted settlement in Indian territory. Others thought it more important to be allied with the winning side. Understanding this, Schuyler had arranged for Iroquois sachems to visit New York City and Philadelphia to view patriot military power.

The war created divisions in native societies, as it did among whites. The Oneida and Tuscarora nations favored the rebels; most of the other members of the Iroquois Confederacy were beginning to see their best chance in siding with the British.

The colonists, like the Indians, played a complex diplomatic game. Men like Philip Schuyler were outwardly respectful of Native Americans but privately disdainful. They sought to lure the warriors to their side—Congress authorized George Washington "to employ in the Continental Armies a number of Indians." At the same time, the Declaration of Independence referred to "merciless Indian Savages" and scolded King George for encouraging them.

৶

Many of Philip Schuyler's concerns in the Mohawk Valley flowed from the power and influence of the Johnson family. William Johnson had emigrated from Ireland to America in 1738 and settled along the river forty-five miles northwest of Albany. He acquired land and encouraged other Irishmen, Germans, and highland Scots to become tenants. With his close proximity to the Native American tribes, he gained an advantage over Dutch traders like the Schuylers, who pursued the fur trade from Albany. In both King George's War and the French and Indian conflict, he organized Iroquois warriors to fight for Britain, winning himself the title of baronet from the king. For twenty years he helped shape Indian policy and kept the Iroquois loyal to Britain.

Sir William died in 1774 just as colonists in America were choosing sides in the rapidly developing conflict. His son John inherited his father's land, title, and loyalty to the crown. When violence broke out the following spring, the situation in the Albany-Mohawk region grew perilous.

By May 1775, Sir John was publicly supporting the loyalist cause. His cousin Guy Johnson, who had taken over as superintendent of Indian affairs, led more than two hundred Scots and Mohawks to Canada by way of Lake Ontario to fight for the British. In August, General Schuyler delayed his invasion of Canada in order to meet with Indian representatives in Albany. He had warned Congress that if the Indians joined forces with the Highlanders and other

Tryon County loyalists, "they may with impunity not only march where they please ... but so effectively cut off all supplies from the Troops to the northward, that they must disperse or starve."

Heading the Indian delegation at that meeting was Tigoran-sera, a leading Mohawk sachem whom the British had dubbed Abraham. Abraham was a brilliant orator and a warrior who had fought for the British in the French and Indian War. Schuyler and the other commissioners informed the Mohawks that the king had "broken the covenant chain with his American children" at the behest of wicked advisers who tried to "slip their hand into our pocket without asking."

During that earlier meeting, Abraham and his people agreed to remain neutral in the current conflict, "not to take any part, but as it is a family affair, to sit still and see you fight it out." Before rushing back to his military duties, Schuyler assured the Indians: "We do not wish you to take up the hatchet against the King's troops."

The Mohawk Valley was quiet until January 1776, when Schuyler's intelligence network picked up a rumor that Sir John was stockpiling weapons at his estate, Johnson Hall. General Schuyler led a militia force of four thousand volunteers to disarm Johnson and his Highlander tenants. The incursion alarmed the Indians, and Mohawk sachems intervened on behalf of Johnson to engineer a compromise and avoid violence. Congress praised Schuyler for his "prudence, zeal, and temper" in the delicate affair.

But in May 1776, new suspicions arose about Johnson's loyalist activities. Schuyler sent a force to arrest him. Sir John, with almost two hundred followers and several bands of Iroquois, fled north through the woods to Montreal.

Schuyler diverted a regiment of New Jersey Continental troops under Colonel Elias Dayton on their way to reinforce the army retreating from Canada. They restored several small forts along the Mohawk and rebuilt Fort Stanwix, which dominated the route to Lake Ontario. The post, Schuyler said, would "impress on the Indians an idea that we are capable of acting with vigour, and that we do not mean to be trifled with."

〜

Schuyler had journeyed up the Mohawk River for the current conference immediately after the July 7 council of war at Ticonderoga. He arrived at German Flatts on the morning of July 16 along with two other Indian commissioners. The town straddled the Mohawk River, with a small fort on the south bank and the beginnings of a village (now Herkimer, New York) on the north.

The commissioners found 150 Iroquois waiting for them, far fewer than they had expected. It was the beginning of a series of delays that vexed Schuyler "beyond imagination." Tribesmen trickled into the camp day after day, bringing with them women, children, and dogs—each arriving party expecting to be greeted with a celebration, rounds of drinks, and pipe smoking.

An army officer noted that the Indians were "observant of those in Company, respectful to the old, of a temper cool deliberate." But, he wrote, "they are excessive fond of spiritous Liquors." Drinking corroded both their health and their judgment.

At German Flatts, the Haudenosaunee spent some of their time playing ball games, staging footraces, and performing ritual dances accompanied by drumming and singing. Warriors painted themselves with vermilion, black, blue, and yellow pigments mixed with bear grease. An observer noted that they "exert themselves to great fatigue." Schuyler knew the Indians would be insulted if he left German Flatts prematurely. He passed three weeks there, his impatience festering. Messengers arrived from the Senecas, the most westerly of the Iroquois, with excuses and apologies. One sachem had died, another had fallen ill. But Schuyler also received word that the Seneca leaders were using the delay to confer with British agents at Fort Niagara. They were hedging their bets.

Prickly to begin with, Schuyler was made more irritable that summer by nagging illness. He complained about his "ancient enemy," probably gout, which had attacked him "in the foot and Supported by an auxiliary . . . made a lodgement in my lungs." On July 24, Schuyler expressed his frustration in a letter to Samuel Chase, a Maryland delegate to Congress. Dealing with Indians, he wrote, was enough "to make one weary of Life . . . I would rather be the proprietor of a potato Garden & literally live by the Sweat of my Brow, than be an Indian Commissioner at a Time when you cannot prudently resent an Insult given by these haughty princes of the Wilderness."

Schuyler's comment spoke more to his own arrogance than that of the tribesmen. He had failed to grasp the moral landscape of Native Americans or to comprehend their long nightmare of usurpation. He carried in his heart a hard kernel of privilege and vanity that saw Indians, in common with his tenant farmers and his enslaved workers, solely as resources to be exploited.

~

Finally, on August 7, after the seemingly endless delays, the German Flatts conference convened. The Indians got off on the wrong foot by requesting that the commissioners express their sorrow for the death of a sachem killed while fighting with the British outside Montreal during the American retreat. Schuyler rejected the idea as an insult. He had no sorrow for those who broke their word and conspired with the enemy.

After some additional preliminaries, Schuyler stood to speak before the amassed representatives of the native tribes. Warriors of the Seneca, Oneida, Mohawk and other nations, along with a few Delaware and Mohicans, stared at him with impassive faces. The day was muggy, disturbed only by the buzz of flies and the low gurgling of the river. He addressed his remarks to the sachems directly in front of him. He reviewed previous meetings, citing verbatim Abraham's words of the previous year promising neutrality.

He chastised them for having "acted directly contrary to your solemn Engagement and broken that Faith which you plighted and which we depended upon." When American troops had marched on St. Johns, he said, Iroquois warriors had gone to Canada to help the British resist them. When he had come up the Mohawk Valley with the militia to disarm Johnson's loyalists, some of them had interfered. "You were very troublesome," Schuyler said, "and threatened us, altho we had sent you Word that no Harm was intended you."

He listed other transgressions. The Indians had assisted Sir John Johnson in escaping to the British, had consulted with Colonel Butler at Niagara, and had fired on boatmen taking supplies up the river to Fort Stanwix.

He continued in a similar vein, repeating himself, making sure he was understood and imprinting key points on listeners' minds. Talks progressed at a snail's pace as interpreters translated and the gist of the speech was passed through the crowd. Schuyler addressed his audience frankly, aware that Native Americans valued the well-spoken phrase and scorned empty verbiage.

He went on to praise the Oneida and Tuscarora for their restraint, but rebuked other tribes for specific offenses against neutrality. He scolded the Mohawks, insisting that they could not blame the drunkenness of individual braves for breaches of the peace. He told them it was the British who had disrupted trade in the valley, not Americans.

After reciting his complaints, Schuyler reassured the Iroquois of his friendship. He advised them to "attend to the voice of all the white people on this great Island. They say, that they have not injured you, that they wish to live in Friendship with all Indians and in particular with the Six Nations." At the conclusion of the address, he handed out additional belts of wampum to seal the understanding of his words.

Schuyler knew as well as any American officer that a diplomatic accord could have military consequences as important as a battlefield victory. He had insight into the subtle strategic thinking of the Native Americans. By minimizing the patriots' defeat in Canada and hiding their precarious situation on Lake Champlain, he was attempting to head off a threat that could undermine the American cause.

He did not try to persuade Iroquois warriors to join the patriots in their battles. He wrote to Congress after the meeting that the commissioners felt "that the attempt to induce the Indians to join us would have essentially injured us, as they might, and probably would, have concluded we were too weak for the enemy."

Now Abraham, the Mohawk sachem, rose to give the principal

reply to Schuyler's oration. He acknowledged the declared independence of the thirteen colonies. He had "no inclination or purpose of interfering in the dispute between Old England and Boston." He and the other sachems were prepared to renew their vow of neutrality.

Spokesmen who followed likewise favored peace, with the proviso that they could not necessarily control their impulsive young warriors eager to pick up the hatchet. Representatives of the Oneida and Tuscarora gave their assurance that they would never intervene in the ongoing quarrel and would remain friends to the colonists.

The talks had gone on for a week, with a pause on Sunday to allow the sachems to confer and interpreters to clarify specific points. By August 13, the sachems as a group were ready to acknowledge the ancient covenant sealed with Dutch traders at the end of the seventeenth century, "in the time of Queder." For the Americans, Philip Schuyler assured the tribal leaders that they would respect Indian territory as agreed to in the Fort Stanwix Treaty of 1768, which had settled the boundary line between Indian land and British settlements.

The conference concluded with more feasting, drinking, and smoking. The commissioners then handed out gifts: blankets, cloth, linen, knives, tobacco boxes, and cash. On August 15, at long last, the meeting ended and the commissioners headed back to Albany.

Philip Schuyler was relieved that he had neutralized the threat from the Mohawk Valley, at least for the time being. Now he turned all his attention to the situation on the lakes. He had received word from General Gates that although the American fleet was not yet finished, Benedict Arnold would, in a few days, be sailing northward on Lake Champlain. From there, he would keep a close eye on the enemy and, if needed, meet them in battle.

12

Setting Sail

HORATIO GATES'S NIGHTMARE WAS THE SUDDEN appearance of enemy warships at Crown Point. They could, after blasting his advance guard, bear down on Fort Ticonderoga with artillery powerful enough to smash redoubts and panic his fragile army.

To forestall the possibility, he had ordered Benedict Arnold to take over command of the fleet and to proceed down the lake with the vessels on hand—the three small schooners and one sloop from the previous year and whatever gondolas workmen could get ready to sail.

"Preventing the enemy's invasion of our country," Gates told his subordinate, "is the ultimate end of the important command, with which you are now intrusted."

Arnold proceeded to Crown Point to prepare for his move north. On August 17, a sudden emergency arose. A smoky fire lit by Colonel Hartley's oar makers, who were working seven miles down the lakeshore, signaled that they were in danger of attack. Arnold told Hartley to rush a hundred Pennsylvania infantrymen along the shore to protect the workers. He ordered two of the schooners, the *Liberty* and *Revenge*, to sail down the lake to blast the intruders with their cannon.

The crews of the two vessels weighed anchor and hoisted sails. "They were no sooner under way," Arnold later reported, "than Commodore Wynkoop, fired a shot and brought them to." After shooting across the schooners' bows from the *Royal Savage*, Wynkoop ordered their captains to heave to. They obeyed, dropping their sails.

The commodore was enraged. "I know of no Orders but what shall be given out by me," he insisted in a note to Arnold. "If an enemy is approaching I am to be acquainted with it."

The crotchety Dutchman had already wasted time, the northern army's most precious resource. Increasingly on edge, Arnold did not appreciate another show of defiance by a junior officer. He sent a reply to the commodore: "You surely must be out of your senses to say no orders shall be obeyed but yours." Arnold was in charge of the navy and commander at Crown Point. If Wynkoop did not comply, he wrote, "I shall be under the disagreeable necessity of convincing you of your error by immediately arresting you."

Unwilling to await an answer, Arnold rowed to the *Royal Savage*, climbed aboard, and talked to Wynkoop directly. Twenty years younger than the provincial businessman, Arnold unleashed a stream of invective. The two schooners were soon hurrying off to check on the emergency, which turned out to be a chance encounter. The enemy quickly retreated north.

When word of the dispute reached Horatio Gates, he boiled over. Because he viewed Wynkoop as one of General Schuyler's Dutch cronies, the incident touched on the buried tension between Gates and his commander. "It is my Orders," he replied to Arnold, "you instantly put Commodore Wynkoop in Arrest and send him prisoner to Head Quarters at Tyconderoga."

Gates wrote to Schuyler that he planned to send Wynkoop to him in Albany, "and I dare say you will without scruple, forthwith dismiss him the Service." Schuyler answered that "although I believe him brave, yet I do not think him equal to the command of such a fleet as we now have there."

For his part, Arnold asked Gates to afford the commodore leniency. "If it can be done with propriety, I wish he may be permitted to return home," rather than be punished or cashiered. Schuyler did send Wynkoop home. The erstwhile commodore appealed effectively to Congress and was restored to his position the following spring.

The dispute was overshadowed by a more pressing issue: the enemy was probing ever closer to the American base. Hope had been growing among American commanders that an attack this season was unlikely. Perhaps this was wishful thinking. It was time to move down the lake to gauge the enemy's intention.

ᴗᴖ

Benedict Arnold was ready to set sail, but as yet he had not been able to procure a medical man to go along as the squadron's surgeon. Arnold's involvement in the apothecary trade had taught him something of the healing arts, and he understood the limitations of medicine. He wryly asked Gates for a trained surgeon "or someone else who will answer to kill a man *secundum artem* [according to practice]."

But he knew that a doctor served a practical function in war. If he could ease a fever or sew up a wound, he allowed a man to fight again. In addition, the prospect of medical aid when wounded boosted the courage of those sorely tried by battle. "I don't think it prudent to go without a Surgeon," he wrote.

On Friday, August 23, General Gates named Dr. Stephen McCrea to be first surgeon to the fleet. McCrea reported to Arnold with his bag of instruments, a supply of medicine, and one assistant. Only twenty-one, McCrea was the son and grandson of New Jersey Presbyterian ministers. Although his medical education was not extensive, he had enlisted in a New York regiment as a surgeon and been sent north. Arnold was "very happy at his arrival as I was determined to have sailed the first fair wind, even without a surgeon."

McCrea came from a politically divided family. His sister Jane was engaged to a loyalist soldier. The following year, while she waited near Fort Edward to join him, she would be captured and killed by Indians allied with the British general John Burgoyne. Her lover would endure the unique horror of watching native warriors dance around the fire showing off her scalp. Thanks to a masterly propaganda campaign engineered by Horatio Gates, Jane McCrea's murder would become a cause célèbre of the Revolution and an enduring story in American folklore.

✍

A week earlier, Benedict Arnold's own sister, Hannah, had written to him, "I am sorry to hear you are going upon the lake.... Have been hoping you would quit the service but it seems you have no such intention."

He had no such intention. On August 24, the day after Dr. Mc-Crea came aboard, the wind swung around to the south under a cloudy sky. It was time for the ten-ship flotilla to sail toward an encounter with the enemy. That evening, after completing last-minute preparations—Arnold drafted some men from Hartley's regiment at Crown Point to complete the crews—the sailors hoisted the colors and the ships moved north in a stately procession.

Arnold made the *Royal Savage* his flagship. That fifty-foot schooner, which the patriots had sunk at St. Johns and then recovered, took the lead. The sloop *Enterprise*, about forty-five feet long and also captured in Canada, sailed beside her. Then came six gondolas, each about fifty feet in length. Most were named for the cities and states of their builders—*Boston, Providence, New Haven, Philadelphia*, and *Connecticut*. One was called *Spitfire*. The two smaller schooners, *Revenge* and *Liberty*, followed in the rear.

Pennsylvania carpenters had completed the hull of the *Philadelphia* at the Skenesborough shipyard on July 30. Other workmen had spent the previous month completing her rigging and installing guns at Ticonderoga.

Her captain, Benjamin Rue, another Pennsylvanian, was twenty-four. He had enlisted in a Continental Army regiment the year before and soon found himself reinforcing the invasion of Canada, where he had taken charge of a schooner on the St. Lawrence River. Skilled and enthusiastic, he had risen from private to ship's captain in less than a year.

Rue commanded a crew of forty-three officers, gunners, sailors, and marines. Many of the men had been drafted from New Hampshire regiments and some may have had experience at coastal or lake sailing. They crowded the fifty-four-foot-long, fifteen-foot-wide barge. Her main 12-pounder iron bow cannon had been cast in Sweden a century earlier. She joined a fleet that, while far from perfect, was the best defense the patriots had managed to construct in the seven weeks since they had begun the effort in earnest.

*

The crews welcomed the following wind, which allowed them to proceed under sail rather than by manning oars. Hundreds of soldiers watched from the shore at Crown Point and cheered as the boats passed. They would now be able to sleep more soundly, not having to worry about armed enemy vessels bursting out of the mist to launch a surprise attack.

The men on the boats, meanwhile, had endured two months of exhausting labor at Ticonderoga. They had suffered biting flies, thick heat, and nagging anxiety about an enemy attack. Sailing up the lake was a taste of heaven compared to camp life. The fresh smell of pine and hemp and pitch replaced the close, humid air that hovered around Ticonderoga. As they moved northward under a cloudy sky, the welcome breeze washed their faces.

The sailors covered only a short distance that day before Arnold decided to halt for the night. Thirty-two-year-old Bayze Wells, a militiaman from central Connecticut, had just been promoted to lieutenant the day before. Sailing aboard the gondola *Providence*, he was assigned to take soundings. He recorded in his diary that the fleet "Fell Down the Lake four miles then Came to in a Line of Battle had Good anchorage 4 fathoms [24 feet] water."

The sailors arose at dawn, ate a quick breakfast, and continued on. The south wind allowed them to skim past miles of forest broken here and there by isolated farms. Before the day was out, they had passed the wide reach of Buttonmould Bay and entered another narrow defile that led to Split Rock, where a mountain shouldered into the lake to create a choke point. They continued on through widening water almost to Willsborough, a peninsula thirty miles north of Crown Point. Here the lake stretched out to three miles wide, with a long open expanse to the north.

They anchored for the night near the eastern shore. Again, Wells wrote, they "Set a Watch and Prepared for the Enemy." Moving down the Great Warpath, the men had covered about a third of the distance to Canada. They did not know when or where they might encounter the British. Also concerning was the fact that the wind was veering northerly and the sky was becoming clogged with tumbling gray clouds.

That night they got a taste of the adversity that always threatened sailors. The clouds first masked, then devoured the nearly full moon. The air became restless. Drops of rain spattered on the canopies rigged over the gondolas' decks. The drumroll increased to a fierce tattoo. The wind veered around to the north. It whipped the rain under the awnings, giving the men on the decks a cold drenching. The pitching and heaving of the boats against their anchor cables had many of them vomiting over the gunwales. The night went on and on.

As a dim morning light finally sketched the landscape, the sky's angry face let them know they were not wanted there. Black clouds piled up and a northerly gale tore along the lake. General Arnold, who had a mariner's feel for the weather, sensed a rougher blow ahead. Instead of setting out into the teeth of the wind, he sent around orders that if the storm increased, the fleet should come to sail at two o'clock and seek shelter to the south.

Unlike the long swells that built on the ocean, lake storms set marching battalions of choppy whitecaps, a confusing tangle of stuttering waves that sent vessels dipping and plunging. Arnold had seen his share of heavy weather, but even he noted that "the hard gale made an amazing sea." He didn't wait until two—at one p.m. he fired a gun to alert the fleet to set sail and make for cover.

All the vessels managed to get under way except the gondola *Spitfire*. Her twenty-five-year-old captain, Philip Ulmer, tried to obey orders, but he found it impossible to handle his boat. The wind was driving the vessel perilously close to the rocks on the western shore. As waves leapt and fell, Arnold climbed from his flagship into a small boat and rowed over near the *Spitfire*. He shouted instructions to Ulmer through a speaking trumpet, telling him not to try to follow but to keep anchored and ride the storm out as best he could.

Arnold's risk-taking impressed the sailors on the other boats. The rest of the vessels struggled southward, leaving Ulmer's fate to God's mercy. Along the way, the mast of the gondola *Connecticut* snapped and sent sopping canvas down to blanket the men on deck. The sailors on the *Revenge* tossed a line across and took the disabled craft in tow.

The goal was to return to the more sheltered confines of Buttonmould Bay along the eastern shore. As they rounded the point and threaded into the shallower water, the schooner *Liberty* went aground. The rest of the vessels avoided the shallows and found a secure anchorage under the headlands. About five p.m. the *Liberty*'s crew worked her free and joined the others.

The storm raged for another day. When the *Spitfire* did not appear, Arnold gave her up for lost. He sent men onto land to find if local farmers had any news of British movements from the north. Keeping his eye on the bigger picture, he told them to ask if residents had heard anything about events around New York City. Northern officers knew only that the enemy had landed an army on Staten Island, threatening General Washington's forces on Manhattan.

Later that same day, the sailors cheered as the *Spitfire* rounded the point and sailed into the bay. Captain Ulmer described how he "rode out the Storm, tho exposed to the rake of Cumberland Bay . . . Fifty miles long." He had lost a bateau he had been towing and the storm had thoroughly battered his gondola, but the damage could be repaired.

The fleet remained pinned down by muscular northerly winds for another two days. Arnold invited the captains and lieutenants of all the boats to come onshore for what Bayze Wells described as a "most Genteel feast." They roasted a pig, held a marksmanship contest, and relaxed with "good wine, some punch, and a good old cider," toasting their general and Congress.

During the tense weeks to follow, such moments of leisure would be rare indeed.

13

Dare Cross the Lake

THE STORM COST GENERAL ARNOLD NEARLY A WEEK AT A moment of unknown danger. It was not until Sunday, September 1, that the wind again came around to the south. Arnold ordered the fleet to make sail. By that evening they had cleared Split Rock and anchored near where they had spent the night before the storm.

On Monday, the first word of an enemy advance reached the fleet. Arnold sent out a boat alerting captains to be ready for action. He dispatched a messenger to Ticonderoga to inform the fort of the threat. "We roused all hands up," Lieutenant Wells noted, "and prepared for battle on the shortest notice." The rumor proved false, but it reminded the crews they were venturing into enemy territory. That day they passed Willsborough and advanced as far as Schuyler's Island, a speck of land off the western shore. Some men went onshore there "to make Discovering."

The next morning, the fleet took advantage of a favorable wind to hurry another twenty-five miles down the lake. Passing Cumberland Head, a large peninsula that thrust out from the west, they spotted a group of twenty men with muskets on the shore, their first sighting of the enemy. Arnold ordered the ships to fire grapeshot from their swivel guns. He sent a detachment of riflemen to search the woods. They found nothing, but now they understood that Indians, Canadian militiamen, and British regulars were patrolling the lakeshore in the region.

That evening, September 3, the small fleet anchored off Isle La Motte at a spot that dominated the main channel of the lake. Ten miles to the north lay the entrance to the Richelieu River and the border of Canada. The next day, the fleet passed Windmill Point at the lake's northern end and entered the Richelieu. Arnold sent scout boats ahead and arranged his ships in a line of battle. It was a bold move. The Americans crept onward into enemy territory, accompanied by a chorus of frogs. Arnold and his men sailed six miles to Île aux Têtes, a low, marshy island that split the waters. It was said that in 1694, Abenaki Indians had defeated a band of Mohawks here. As a dark warning, they had decapitated their foes and mounted their heads on poles—hence the name Island of the Heads.

Here, twelve miles from St. Johns, Arnold and his men found several hundred enemy troops, mostly Canadians and Indians. The surprised soldiers, posted as sentinels, "made a precipitate retreat" down the Richelieu to Île aux Noix, the next obstacle in the river. This was where, two months earlier, the fleeing Americans under General Sullivan had made their last stand in Canada.

Having reconnoitered, Arnold dropped back south. For the next two days, he kept the fleet stationed near the head of the Richelieu. His ten-vessel armada appeared more formidable crowded into the river than it did on the broader lake.

General Gates had issued orders to Arnold before he sailed that left plenty of room for interpretation. He told Arnold that "it is my positive Order" not to sail past Îsle aux Têtes. "It is a defensive War we are carrying on," Gates continued, "therefore no wanton risque, or unnecessary Display of the Power of the Fleet, is at any Time, to influence your conduct."

At the same time, Gates wrote, "should the enemy come up the lake and attempt to force their way through the pass you are stationed to defend, in that case you will act with such cool, determined valor as will give them reason to repent their temerity."

After he arrived in the far north, Arnold began making his own decisions. He wanted the British to be aware of his presence. Stationing his fleet so close to them was a bluff. Although the fighting ability of his boats was limited, Arnold's brazen display might well make Guy Carleton hesitate, gaining the patriots time. General Gates had ordered him to use deception to influence the thinking of the enemy. He was to keep secret the fact that he would not pass Île aux Têtes. "I wish, on the Contrary," Gates had written, "that Words, occasionally dropped from you ... may, together with all your Motions, induce our own People to conclude it is our real Intention to invade the enemy."

Arnold did talk about making a new foray into Canada. He was sure British spies would get wind of the threat. The stratagem could start Carleton thinking about defense rather than offense. In fact, the Americans had no intention of moving aggressively. Their goal was to pin the British forces in Canada until winter made their further movement impossible. In a letter to Gates, Arnold predicted that "the enemy will not dare attempt crossing the lake," especially if the row galleys made it north in time.

༄

Arnold was always hungry for intelligence. He knew Carleton had at his disposal Burgoyne's mass of regular troops. He knew the enemy was building a fleet to protect this force as they advanced up the lake. Beyond that, details were sketchy. Now he informed Gates he hoped "soon have it in my power to send you a very full account of the strength of the enemy by sea and land." He dispatched small boats to scout the coves and inlets in the river and to explore the maze of islands in the northern part of the lake. Besides keeping an eye on British activity, the assignments made the sailors more familiar with the local waters.

He also sent scouts to probe northward. One group was led by the ranger Benjamin Whitcomb, who had raised the controversy by killing British general Patrick Gordon. He and three other woodsmen embarked from La Motte in a canoe, intending to slip past Île aux Têtes and observe enemy preparations further along the Richelieu.

A separate group of four spies was led by Ensign Thomas Mc-Coy, an Irish immigrant from Pennsylvania. The group included a tough New Hampshire ranger sergeant named Eli Stiles, who had made the trek over the Maine mountains with Arnold. These men moved north through the woods on the east side of the river. For good measure, Arnold hired a French Canadian named Antoine Girard for fifty dollars to go north and gain detailed information about British defenses at Île aux Noix.

◈

When on duty, sailors aboard large warships during the age of sail rolled their canvas hammocks and stacked them horizontally between supports that extended up from the ship's gunwales. In battle, the resulting barrier provided increased cover for the men working on the upper deck and made it more difficult for invading boarders to climb onto the ship.

Benedict Arnold realized that his gondolas, which sat low to the water, were vulnerable to boarding. The enemy would have plenty of marines available to swarm over the sides. Arnold ordered the captains to send men ashore to cut saplings in the woods. They would tie these inch-thick sticks into bundles known as fascines, a common element of field fortifications. Mounted along the tops of the ships' sides, they would serve the same function as the rolled hammocks.

On September 6, while patrolling near the entrance to the Richelieu, the captains were to send parties ashore to prepare these defenses "on the bows and sides of the gondolas, to prevent the enemy's boarding and to keep off small shot." Orders were to coordinate their landing and act together.

Job Sumner, the skipper of the *Boston*, proved overly eager. Eighteen of his men descended into a bateau and landed before the others were ready. Suddenly gunfire broke out onshore. The men were "attacked by a Party of Savages, who pursued them into the Water."

The ambushers were a group of Indians led by a British Army lieutenant. Their goal was to capture some prisoners who could provide intelligence on American plans. The enemy officer called for the Americans to surrender. Before he could take them prisoner, the rest of the American fleet came up and sprayed the shore with grapeshot. The British fled the hail of projectiles.

Additional patriot troops came onshore. They found that two of their companions had been shot dead. Another was grievously hurt and would soon die. Four more suffered wounds. A quick search of the area found an officer's hat with a button of the British 47th Regiment. So ended the first direct fighting between crews of the American fleet and the British. It was a taste of the murky, irregular warfare that gave the northern landscape a feeling of mortal danger.

&

That same day, back at Crown Point, Colonel Hartley heard "a very heavy cannonading down the Lake all this Morning it is undoubtedly between our fleet and the Enemy." Hartley sent a messenger hurrying to Ticonderoga to give General Gates the news and to ask for immediate reinforcements. Engineer Jeduthan Baldwin reported "all hands at work at Daylight preparing our batteries against the worst."

Gates sent word to Philip Schuyler, who immediately wrote to Congress that "it is probable that the enemy are attempting to cross the lake." He asked for the local militia to be called up. When the lake again fell silent, Hartley sent Lieutenant John Brooks north by boat to find out what was happening.

The shooting the men had heard was not the skirmish with the Indians. That day, two more vessels had joined the fleet. The *New Jersey* was the seventh gondola. It was accompanied by the cutter *Lee*, a hybrid between a gunboat and a schooner. When the boats were spotted, Arnold gave leave for every vessel in the fleet to fire its cannon.

The salute added to the show that Arnold was putting on for the enemy. Arnold's fleet had nowhere near the amount of ammunition he desired. The deeper secret, knowledge he could not share even with his own officers, was that Fort Ticonderoga was itself short of gunpowder. If attacked, Gates's troops would be forced to surrender or flee after firing only a handful of rounds. Arnold was sending a false signal to the British that the patriots could be extravagant with ammunition.

"We very distinctly heard 13 or 14 cannon shot," a British soldier noted. "All hands were ordered to throw up more works."

༄

The next day, the crews manning the scout boats out in front of the fleet heard the sound of axes and human voices from the points of land overlooking the American position at Windmill Point. It soon became clear that British soldiers were preparing emplacements for cannon. Once installed, the guns could be trained on any ship that dared enter the river.

The maneuver gave the Americans little option but to retreat. On Sunday, September 8, Arnold ordered the fleet to pull back seven miles south to the west side of Isle La Motte. That day, Lieutenant Brooks arrived from Crown Point to inquire about the earlier cannon fire. Arnold sent him back with a note to Gates informing him that they had fired a few shots at Indians. Now that the nights were taking on a chill, he asked the commander to send his men warmer clothes.

He reassured Gates about his current position. "I think we are very safe from gales of wind & this Anchorage good," he wrote. If storms came, they could scurry into nearby coves, where "the gundolas will ride safe any wind that blows." The position was "the best in the Lake to stop the enemy."

༄

The day after the fleet took post at La Motte, another gondola, the *New York*, arrived to add its guns to the effort. On board was Colonel Edward Wigglesworth. General Gates had informed Arnold earlier that he had appointed two officers to help command the fleet. Wigglesworth, a Massachusetts militia colonel, would be third in command. General David Waterbury, still supervising the boatbuilding at Skenesborough, would serve as second in command when he arrived in the north.

Wigglesworth was thirty-four, the son of a pastor from Ipswich. He had grown up on the Atlantic coast north of Boston. After graduating from Harvard he had worked as shipmaster for a firm of merchants in Newburyport, near his hometown. On his many trips as captain to the West Indies, he had probably met Benedict Arnold. In June, Wigglesworth had enlisted in the Massachusetts militia. Once his unit arrived in Ticonderoga, he was one of the officers taken from the ranks to supply the need for mariners on the lake.

In a letter from General Gates, Wigglesworth brought the news that Arnold had been anxiously awaiting. Two weeks earlier, on August 27, a battle had erupted on Long Island, across the East River from New York City. Gates quoted General Schuyler to report that British troops had "attacked our lines, but were repulsed with loss." Casualties had been heavy on both sides, with three thousand of the enemy and two thousand patriots fallen. "We wait with impatience for more particulars," General Gates related.

News of this "great and awful event," the first major battle fought by the newly independent nation, was sobering for those resisting the enemy in the north. It provided a grim reminder that the British forces were willing to use lethal force to put down the colonial rebellion. Men's eyes turned uneasily northward—the army that hovered only a few miles away was capable of unleashing similar violence on them.

Arnold, a born optimist, was heartened by the news. He wrote to Gates that the British losses at New York would "weaken and discourage them." He reiterated his core idea: "Time must gain us a victory." If he could delay the enemy, he said, he had "no doubt the Almighty will crown our virtuous struggles with success."

If the men huddled in open boats at the north end of Lake Champlain had known the truth about the situation at the other end of the Great Warpath, they would have been even more fearful for their safety. The initial reports of the battle were wrong.

British general William Howe had descended on the Americans with twenty thousand regulars, outnumbering the defenders two to one. Marching around the end of the patriots' position, the British had rolled up the entire line. They had killed or wounded more than a thousand men and taken another thousand prisoner. Casualties on their own side were light.

John Sullivan, who had departed Ticonderoga in a huff, had convinced Congress to appoint him major general. George Washington had put General Nathanael Greene in charge of the ten thousand American soldiers on Long Island. When Greene fell ill, command passed to Sullivan. The British struck. Sullivan allowed his men to be surrounded. He himself was captured. Poor planning, faulty intelligence, and uncertain leadership combined to bring the Continental Army dangerously close to annihilation.

Two days after the battle, the storm that had forced Arnold's fleet into Buttonmould Bay also swept New York City, blocking a Royal Navy thrust up the East River and allowing the bulk of the fighters on Long Island to cross to New York. Washington still held the city, but it had been a close call.

In his reply to Gates, Arnold repeated his demand for more—more clothes, more ammunition, especially more experienced seamen and gunners. His crews, exposed in the open gondolas, were taking sick at an alarming rate. The men drafted from the infantry had gained some experience in handling the boats, but seamanship was not a set of skills learned in a month. They could easily become confused in a sea battle.

What he wanted more than anything were the row galleys, which might give him a fighting chance against the enemy. He sent Robert Atkinson, a Champlain pilot recently released from the hospital, back to Crown Point "to guide the row galleys down the lake." He also sent back "another twenty-two men sick with ague."

A frustrated Arnold had complained, "When you ask for a frigate, they give you a raft. Ask for sailors, they give you tavern waiters. And if you want breeches, they give you a vest."

The same day that Wigglesworth arrived in the north, Congress in Philadelphia declared that the term "United Colonies" would no longer be used. "The stile be altered, for the future, to the 'United States.'"

Soon after Arnold stationed the fleet at Isle La Motte, the weather turned dirty. On Friday, September 13, Lieutenant Bayze Wells reported, "the wind south very strong, four of our Gondolas were obliged to move for a better harbour." The captains took advantage of nearby coves for shelter.

Conferring with Colonel Wigglesworth, Arnold decided that the wide, exposed channel at La Motte was not a favorable spot to confront the enemy. On September 21, after enduring what Lieutenant Wells called "a more windy night [than] I scarce ever knew," Arnold ordered the fleet south. They sailed nine miles to Bay St. Amand (now Treadwell Bay), an inlet on the New York side of the lake, just above Cumberland Head. Coves on both sides of the channel offered more defensive possibilities.

꙰

Keeping up his guard, Arnold sent the schooner *Liberty* out on patrol. He told the ship's captain, Mathias Primier, to sail back up to Isle La Motte and examine its ragged eastern side. While the *Liberty* was navigating the choppy water, a lookout spotted a man on the western shore. He was dressed like a Frenchman and was gesturing toward the ship. It became clear he "desired to be taken on board."

Captain Primier sent his ship's boat toward shore but advised caution. The crew backed in stern first, "swivel guns pointed and match lighted."

Primier hoped that the man was an informer. As the boat approached, the Frenchman continued his incomprehensible speech. The sailors ordered him to swim toward them. He waded into the cold lake up to his chest but made gestures indicating he could not swim.

He turned and made his way back to the shore. When he reached it, he gave "three Cahoops." Suddenly "three, or four, hundred Indians, Canadians & Regulars rose up and fired their muskets." The fusillade stunned the men on the boat. Three of them fell wounded.

The boat crew fired back with their swivel guns and muskets. Sailors on the *Liberty* let loose a broadside from its 2- and 4-pounder cannon, raking the shore with grapeshot.

The sailors in the boat heaved on oars, pulling back toward the ship. The firefight was short and violent. All three of the men who had been shot died of their wounds. As the ship continued its patrol, sailors spotted three hundred birchbark canoes pulled up onshore, indicating the presence of a large force of Indian warriors.

Gates had recently written to Arnold warning that "the Enemy are Subtile, and quick at Expedients; they may endeavor to Impose False Friends upon you." He reminded him to keep guard boats in the water and to be careful with the daily passwords that distinguished friend from foe.

By this time, Benedict Arnold could sense in his bones that the British were preparing to attack. He had located a place to make a stand. "I make no doubt of their soon paying us a visit," he wrote to Gates, "and intend first fair wind to come up as high as Isle Valcour, where tis a good harbour, and where we shall have the advantage over the enemy, and if they are too many for us, we can retire."

14

---◆---

A Considerable
Naval Force

AS BENEDICT ARNOLD WAITED IMPATIENTLY FOR WORD
from his scouts, the first bit of intelligence came from another
source. The American presence in the north had attracted a fugitive
from the British Army. Thomas Day, a New Yorker, had previously fought with the Americans in Canada. After he was taken
prisoner in Quebec, his captors had given him the choice of being
sent to England in chains or enlisting in the British Army. He
swore allegiance to the king and was assigned to a Loyalist unit,
McLean's Highland Emigrants. Late in the summer, this new regiment was stationed at St. Johns. Learning of the American fleet
lurking nearby, Day absconded and made his way up the river to
rejoin his former comrades.

Day lacked extensive knowledge of the disposition of British
forces on the Richelieu, but he did report "two schooners taken to
pieces and brought up" to the shipyard at St. Johns. He had also
seen a floating gun battery and had heard that the enemy possessed
the capability of crossing the lake to Crown Point in only two or
three days.

During that rainy week in late September, Antoine Girard, the
first of Arnold's spies to return, rejoined the fleet. He had scouted

the British forces at Île aux Noix and reported three thousand troops armed with forty cannon on the island. The position was impregnable against any American attack. He said he had seen an equal number of men at St. Johns, and more than 150 bateaux along the shore. He had heard rumors of several thousand more troops below the rapids at Chambly.

The Frenchman had seen two schooners at St. Johns. They were manned and ready to sail, each bristling with at least a dozen brass 12-pounder cannon. The enemy armada included three armed gondolas and several open boats carrying a single heavy gun each. He too had observed a floating battery loaded with artillery, along with a nearly completed two-masted ketch with twenty-four big 18-pounders on its deck. The entire fleet would be ready to sail in less than two weeks.

Alarmed, General Arnold sent a boat hurrying up the lake to take this information to headquarters. Then he learned that Girard had come in carrying a safe-conduct pass from a British officer at Noix. This made him suspicious that the enemy had turned his scout and sent him to the Americans "to give the foregoing account."

"I have every reason to think him placed as a spy on us," he now reported. He ordered Girard's arrest and sent him to Gates at Ticonderoga, "to be disposed of as you may think proper." It was all part of the slippery business of bluff and deception. Or was it?

Two days later, on September 18, the reliable Benjamin Whitcomb appeared with his squad of rangers and two prisoners, an ensign and a corporal from the British 29th Regiment of Foot. Both captives were "cautious of giving any information" under interrogation. They did tell Arnold that a ship was being built at St. Johns designed to mount twenty substantial cannon. Arnold reported to Gates: "The ship, the enemy says, will be completed in a fortnight."

The men of Thomas McCoy's unit had yet to be heard from. Arnold was concerned that Girard had betrayed the other American scouts. It was not until October 1 that Eli Stiles showed up. He reported that the others had indeed been captured. His information contradicted Girard's account and confirmed Arnold's suspicion of the Frenchman. Stiles said he had counted a hundred tents at Noix. Each accommodated ten men, for a total of one thousand, not the three thousand that Girard had reported. On the other hand, there were at least three hundred tents at St. Johns, indicating a large garrison there. Six hundred Indians provided with thirty-four large war canoes were also there, ready for battle.

The scout said he had lain concealed by the river when a boat passed containing General Burgoyne. He heard the general discussing the possibility of luring the American fleet within range of the batteries the British had built along the lakeshore.

Stiles reported seeing at the St. Johns wharf a vessel large enough to be an ocean-going frigate. She was not completed but was already "planked to her wales," which meant that her hull was finished and she would soon be ready to float. Two schooners were already prepared to sail. He saw nothing of the floating batteries reported by Girard and was suspicious of the Frenchman's report. Stiles said the British bateaux "appear twice as large as ours and carried fifty or sixty men."

A master of bluff, Arnold knew how the game was played. General Carleton was no doubt eager to make him think the enemy possessed an overwhelming advantage in ships, guns, and men, hoping to discourage any advance and perhaps frighten him into retreat. Yet, even allowing for disinformation, the combined reports gave Arnold reason to worry.

"I am inclined to think . . . that the Enemy will soon have a considerable naval Force," he wrote to Gates. He asked for an urgent shipment of six- and eight-inch howitzers, which could fire exploding shells at the enemy. He also wanted slow match, used to fire cannon, and more grapeshot and chain shot. He suggested that as many as fifteen hundred foot soldiers be sent down the lake and stationed on Isle La Motte, where they could support the fleet from the land.

∽

If the scouts and spies whom Arnold had sent north had enjoyed a bird's-eye view of the landscape, they would have seen a force that was indeed considerable being assembled in the triangle formed by Montreal, Chambly, and St. Johns. Thousands of troops filled tent camps up and down the Richelieu River. Two sleek schooners of war were moored at St. Johns, ready to sail. Hundreds of bateaux were available to transport British infantry up the lake. The soldiers practiced their rowing daily. Nearly two dozen gunboats with large cannon in their bows nodded by the wharfs.

A blasted ruin when Benedict Arnold left it at the end of June, St. Johns was now a vibrant settlement of soldiers, naval men, and civilians, all of them focused on building a formidable fleet of warships. The sounds of axes and saws, the ringing blows of blacksmiths' hammers on anvils, the smell of fresh pitch and new lumber, and the continual bustle of men and draft animals up and down the river testified to a focused and well-organized effort. All of it, from early morning to nightfall and beyond, was charged with a sense of urgency.

⁓

General Guy Carleton had seen a great deal of fighting before the Seven Years' War ended in 1763. The death of his friend James Wolfe at Quebec in 1759 haunted him. He had survived the hellish siege of Havana three years later. He had been wounded three times. He had fervently hoped he was done with war.

In 1768, the crown appointed Carleton governor and military commander of a peaceful Canada. He returned to England two years later to confer with officials about how the huge new colony should be governed. His stay, which he expected to be a brief consultation, extended for four years.

While he was there, Carleton paid a visit to Thomas Howard, Earl of Effingham. He had been friendly with the earl's father, a military man closer to his own age. According to family lore, Carleton's eye was taken by Lord Thomas's sister, Lady Elizabeth, whom the general had known when she was a child. Now nearly forty-eight and still a bachelor, the dashing military man and provincial governor was a prime match.

His portraits show a man with a pinched, tight-lipped face and weary eyes. He asked Lady Elizabeth's brother for her hand. She refused, having already fallen in love with Carleton's nephew. Her nineteen-year-old sister, Lady Maria, commented, "I only wish he had given me a chance." He soon did, and, reader, she married him.

A petite woman with bright blond hair and a dignified, ceremonious manner, Maria had been brought up and educated at Versailles. She proved an apt mate for the ruler of French-speaking subjects in Canada. The lenient policies Carleton recommended toward the Canadians may have carried his wife's fingerprints. Certainly members of the Canadian gentry were beguiled by her tales of the French court under Louis XV, an establishment dominated by his two mistresses, Mesdames de Pompadour and du Barry.

The couple already had two children when Maria accompanied Governor Carleton across the Atlantic in 1774. Soon after their arrival, the violent upheaval of the American rebellion and the subsequent invasion of Canada threw the province into turmoil. Carleton declared martial law and sent Lady Maria and the children back to England.

The man who had thought he was done with war found himself thrust into the middle of the desperate struggle between the forces of the crown and men who called themselves patriots. By holding out in Quebec through the winter of 1775–76, he had only barely saved the province for King George.

Now he seemed to hold all the high cards. He had at his disposal the powerful armada that had come from England, along with hundreds of experienced Royal Navy sailors. His problem had to do with geography. Lake Champlain lay a hundred feet above sea level. The Richelieu was navigable from its origin in the lake to St. Johns. From there it tumbled fifty feet over a dozen miles to Chambly. The shallow water made navigation impossible for large ships, especially in the fall, when the flow of water down the river was at its low point.

Carleton was also vexed to survey the results of the Americans' scorched-earth policy in Canada. The destruction of crops, carts, cattle, and all kinds of draft animals had left the Canadians in need of succor. Carleton had been forced to use some of the year's worth of rations brought across the Atlantic to sustain civilians. The lack of horses and fodder made moving around the country difficult.

❧

Carleton had foreseen the vulnerability that Canada faced once the southward colonies turned against the crown. Benedict Arnold and Ethan Allen had surprised Ticonderoga and Crown Point in June 1775 before Carleton had a chance to reinforce the positions. Their action opened for the Americans an invasion path to the north.

During the summer of 1775, Carleton wrote Admiral Samuel Graves, the chief British naval commander at Boston, requesting shipwrights and seamen to help regain control of Lake Champlain. Graves had not been able to provide immediate support, but word of Carleton's needs reached London. The floating relief column that arrived in Quebec in the spring of 1776 carried the nautical supplies and sailors from which the general could assemble a formidable lake fleet.

Captain Charles Douglas, who had commanded the first ship to reach Quebec, became chief of naval operations on the St. Lawrence River. General Burgoyne led the ground forces. Carleton continued to handle administrative duties in Quebec. Douglas was a forty-nine-year-old Royal Navy veteran with a quick mind, fluent in six languages. He considered the American rebellion "the most insolent, the most ungrateful, that ever reared an opprobrious head against an indulgent parent state."

Although the son of an earl, Douglas had earned his rank by solid seamanship. He considered various ways to counter the Americans' small fleet and their ongoing shipbuilding efforts. Constructing war vessels from scratch at St. Johns would take too long to allow the British an advantage that summer. He had to somehow get the ships in the St. Lawrence over the Richelieu rapids to the lake level.

Douglas had first organized Canadian militiamen and civilians to build a new road from Chambly to St. Johns and to strengthen the bridges over intervening streams. He then tackled the vexing task of bringing up the two schooners. He named Lieutenant John

Starke captain of the *Maria*, which had been named for Carleton's young wife. Starke was to winch that vessel onto a sled to stabilize her, then move the ship on log rollers up the gradual incline. But *Maria's* weight, even with masts and guns removed, proved insurmountable. She sank into the mud.

Starke was forced to undress the *Maria*, so to speak, removing the planks along her sides down to the corset of her ribs, baring her first to the waterline and then almost to her keel, and even stripping off some of her side timbers. Only when the vessel had been rendered a mere skeleton could men and oxen, sweating and blowing in the August heat, haul her foot by foot along the muddy road. Workmen used the same time-consuming method to get the second schooner, the *Carleton*, around the rapids.

During their invasion of Canada, the Americans had manned a gunboat named the *Convert* in the St. Lawrence. Captured by the British that spring, she was renamed *Loyal Convert*. The Americans had dragged the sixty-foot vessel down the rapids, and the British now dragged her back up, bumping and scraping their way to St. Johns. There the boat was fitted with a second mast and armed with additional cannon.

The supply ships sent from England that winter carried the frames for a dozen thirty-seven-foot-long gunboats. These were hauled up the river to St. Johns to be assembled. Carpenters built ten similar boats from scratch. They were slightly smaller versions of the gondolas that were the main armament of the American fleet. These open boats, equipped with a single powerful cannon in the bow, were propelled mainly by oars. Like the American gondolas, the gunboats had a mast and a simple square sail that could be used with a favorable wind.

For Carleton, defeating American resistance on the lake was only a first step. His goal was to move an army into enemy territory. He sent Lieutenant William Twiss of the Engineers Corps to St. Johns with orders to build flat-bottomed transport boats "calculated to carry from thirty to forty men with stores and provisions." About four hundred of these simple craft were constructed and readied to move the army southward.

The British also hauled up the rapids four longboats commandeered from their warships and fitted them out with small cannon. Rowed by ten men, the boats would serve as armed tenders and scouting vessels. Another two dozen longboats, without guns, would be used to transport provisions for the army or as scout or utility craft by the fleet.

∽

To oversee all this activity, Captain Douglas put Lieutenant John Schank in charge of the St. Johns shipyard. The thirty-six-year-old Schank, a future admiral, shared the mechanical ability for which his Scottish countrymen were noted. He had invented a device called a centerboard, which allowed a keel to be raised and lowered in a boat, giving the craft stability but allowing it to sail in very shallow water.

Unlike the Americans, who had to wait for carpenters and other craftsmen to arrive at Skenesborough and who often went begging for essential supplies, Schank soon had hundreds of shipwrights, riggers, caulkers, sailmakers, and blacksmiths at work constructing vessels. The builders could draw on the abundant stores of nautical gear brought over from England. The village of St. Johns pulsed day and night to the rhythm of pounding hammers and the hoarse breathing of saws.

Encouraged, British commanders decided to build another vessel from scratch at St. Johns. Carleton wanted a ship that could attack boats on the water and bombard land installations as well. This ship was referred to as a radeau, French for "raft." Large, almost square, and flat-bottomed, it would carry a frightening array of guns, including six 24-pounder cannon, the largest on the lake. Its capacious hold would serve as a floating ammunition magazine—the other boats could pull along the radeau's side for fresh shot and powder. The vessel carried several large mortars, from which it could heave large balls and exploding shells into American positions at Crown Point and Ticonderoga. Its shallow draft, which allowed it to sail close to shore, enhanced its ability to bombard land targets. And once the British arrived at the other end of the lake, soldiers could move the big guns to carriages for use in the field.

They named this ninety-foot-long floating artillery platform *Thunderer*. She was difficult to maneuver—her two masts carried sails that allowed headway only with the wind aft. Otherwise, straining sailors had to man long sweep oars to maneuver her. Her main advantage was the authority of her guns—a single broadside could send iron balls smashing through the sides of half a dozen opposing vessels.

∽

While workmen strained to assemble the floating weapons that would allow the British to sweep the rebels from the lake, General Burgoyne, commander of the regiments of soldiers, had a series of disagreements with Guy Carleton. Their conflict was magnified by the men's contrasting personalities. At fifty-four, Burgoyne was two years older than the Canadian governor. Carleton was flinty and formal—"he has a rigid strictness in his manner which is very unpleasing," a soldier complained. Burgoyne, on the other hand, had a "winning manner" and was "idolized by the army."

Early in the summer, more than two thousand Indians gathered around Montreal had offered their military services to the British. Most were affiliated with the groups of Indians who had converted to Catholicism and had previously been allied with the French. Many were Iroquois, but they included Algonquins, Hurons, Abenakis, and Nipissings. They were known as the Seven Nations, a reference to their seven villages along the St. Lawrence.

These Indians were attracted to the British cause in part by the prospect of war and the spoils and hostages that it might yield. Burgoyne, frustrated by Carleton's seemingly endless delay, wanted to be put in command of fifteen hundred Native Americans. He would take along loyalists from the thirteen colonies, led by Sir John Johnson, as well as Canadian militiamen and three battalions of redcoats. They would proceed up the St. Lawrence to Lake Ontario, sail to the British fort at Oswego, and descend the Mohawk

River toward Albany. It was the move that Philip Schuyler was trying to prevent by assuaging the Iroquois and reinforcing Fort Stanwix. Burgoyne felt the expedition would force the rebels to abandon Ticonderoga, Lake George, and all their posts north of Albany, opening the way for Carleton to secure the northern portion of the Great Warpath.

Carleton approved the plan, then hesitated. He was averse to using Indians on a large scale in a war against fellow Englishmen. He told Burgoyne he lacked the provisions to sustain such a campaign and canceled the operation.

Burgoyne next urged the Canadian governor to dispatch a substantial force of light infantrymen, troops who specialized in infiltration and woodland skirmishes. Reinforced by Canadians and Indians, they could move south through the woods and gain a position between Ticonderoga and Lake George. Relying on mobility rather than heavy artillery, another unit could then penetrate to Skenesborough, destroy the rebel shipyard there, and attack the American rear. The move might well panic the rebels into a retreat. The point of all his advice was to minimize the delay that was shrinking their chances of besting the enemy this season.

Carleton approved raids down the lake by light infantrymen and a few Indians, and ordered the formation of a small "Company of Marksmen" to serve as flankers for the advance corps. But neither tactic was likely to panic the Americans. Burgoyne and other British officers waited impatiently as the days ticked off the calendar.

✑

Most of the British naval vessels were ready by the end of August, just as Benedict Arnold was sailing north with his unfinished flotilla. Although Guy Carleton did not know it, this was the golden moment when his fleet, already powerful, had the best chance to sweep the Americans off the lake. With the defenses at Ticonderoga still under construction and the Americans' shortages of gunpowder and other supplies dire, Burgoyne's professional army might have unnerved the garrison and captured the fort. Carleton could have entered history as the general most responsible for a complete British victory in the war.

Others sensed the moment was right. On September 7, Carleton's artillery officer, Major General William Phillips, as frustrated with the delay as was Burgoyne, wrote to a fellow officer that "we must risk and depend on [this force] . . . it will be vain, nay madness, to wait for more." A British fleet manned with Royal Navy sailors, he thought, could easily handle the rebels. "I have great confidence that things will go well."

But Arnold's arrival at the entrance of the Richelieu, his loose talk about another invasion of Canada, and the sound of his cannon firing up the lake all had their effect on the cautious Carleton. He knew the Americans had begun the summer with four warships already on the water. He knew they had been hard at work augmenting their fleet. He had his schooners, his gunboats, the powerful *Thunderer*, but he wanted more. He wanted to be sure he would prevail.

Guy Carleton was hardly the first general to seek certainty in war. History is crowded with commanders who have requested more troops, more weapons, more advantage over the enemy before beginning an operation. But war is dynamic, conditions always in flux, and time, once lost, is lost forever. The savior of Canada now made a decision that would prove a momentous one for his country, for history, and for Carleton himself.

15

Prepared for
the Enemy

"WE ARE MOORED IN A SMALL BAY," BENEDICT ARNOLD explained in a September 28 letter to General Gates, "on the west side the island, as near together as possible & in such a form that few vessels can attack us at the same time & those will be exposed to the fire of the whole fleet." Five days earlier, Arnold had sailed with his warships into "an excellent harbor" beside Valcour Island, twenty-five miles south of the Canadian border and fifty miles north of Crown Point. "No doubt you will approve this measure," Arnold wrote. "If not, I will return to any of my former stations."

Gates did approve. He wrote that he was "pleased to find you and your armada ride in Valcour Bay in defiance of the power of our foes in Canada."

The uninhabited island stood near the north end of the long expanse of lake that gradually narrowed from Cumberland Head to the pinched-off strait at Split Rock, twenty-five miles south of Valcour. The American position at Crown Point lay twenty miles on from there.

Arnold understood that on Lake Champlain, he was fighting a hybrid conflict—a British officer used the term "terraqueous war." Wind direction and the relative position of the forces, the traditional factors of a sea battle, were an important part of it. But in the narrow lake, the terrain of the surrounding land also shaped the fighting. It cramped maneuvers, made winds less predictable, obscured vision, and offered opportunities for ambush. Valcour Island, two miles long, a mile wide, and covered with trees, rose 150 feet from the surface of the water, hiding ships gathered behind it from being seen by a force advancing along the main channel.

In the middle of the strait the water was sixty feet deep, but the northern entrance was shallower, with shoals that endangered large ships trying to thread southward. This was especially true in the autumn, when the level of the lake dropped by four feet or more. Low water also made the shallows close to land more treacherous. The rising land and trees on both sides gave partial shelter from winds as well as cover for infantry firing at the ships. All these elements were dancing in Arnold's mind as he tried to imagine how a meeting with the enemy might unfold.

༄

The climate in the Champlain Valley was colder than what many of the patriot sailors were used to in their homes farther south. September brought shrinking days and sharply cooler nights, with temperatures sometimes dipping into the thirties. As the month went on, morning frost sometimes glistened on the ships' gunwales and the men's breath steamed in the air.

Trees began to dress themselves in yellows. Three days after they moved to Valcour, the men awoke to see, under leaden skies, the mountains to the west whitened from an early snowfall. Autumn storms were a regular feature of northern weather. "We have continual gales of wind," Arnold would note on October 1, "and the duty very severe."

Like the majority of men in the eighteenth century, the crew members of the fleet lived their lives outdoors. They were accustomed to enduring cold and heat. Growing up on farms, they routinely worked through rain showers and sleet storms. Few were denizens of the drawing room. Their hands and feet were callused from childhood, their stomachs accustomed to periodic hunger.

They hunted and butchered animals. They tolerated dirt, sweat, minor injuries, and untreated illnesses. They knew the deep darkness of an overcast night without a fire.

When the fleet had come down the lake in late August, the humid summer weather left the men sweating as they rowed, hauled sails, and practiced handling the cannon. Flies and mosquitoes were still a problem. Now, a month later, the sun was slumping ever lower in the sky. Tense winds hissed down from Canada. The night air gnawed at exposed flesh. "A great part of my seamen and marines," Arnold wrote to Gates, "are almost naked." Wetness left men shivering even in balmy weather. Rain and lake spray made it difficult for anyone to stay dry on the boats. They lacked the tar-coated canvas coats and hats that men at sea traditionally wore to fend off the wet.

For the sailors on the gondolas, the duty was truly severe. The vessels were fifty feet long, but crews of at least forty men were needed to manage sails, fire the guns, and repel boarders. The men had barely enough room on their partial decking to lie down, and the boats lacked cots or hammocks.

Sleeping sitting up was common in the eighteenth century. Those sailors who were not on duty at night dropped down near their posts to lean against a section of bulwark. A canvas canopy gave some protection from the elements, but the sides were always open to wind and spray. In cold weather, the men spooned together to preserve body heat.

No provision was made on any of the boats for sanitation. Human waste went into the lake; water for drinking, procured from a reasonable distance, came out of the lake. Rations consisted of preserved meat and biscuits. Landing on shore to hunt for game risked encounters with British patrols and Indians. Each boat had a small brick fireplace where salt pork was boiled in several changes of water to reduce its salinity. Most food was served as a stew with peas and hard biscuits added to give it body.

Occasionally, boats coming up from Ticonderoga brought potatoes or vegetables purchased from lakeside farmers. Or they might bring a pig or scrawny bullock to be butchered on board, the fresh meat a welcome addition to the men's diet.

Tedious, physically demanding work consumed the men's daylight hours. They repeatedly raised, lowered, and trimmed the sails in order to move around the lake and to become practiced in seamanship. When the wind died, they rowed. Each man's hands had long since turned to horny claws from hauling ropes and handling oars.

"We are as well-prepared for the enemy as our circumstances will allow," Arnold noted. "They will never have it in their power to surprise us. The men are daily trained in the exercise of their guns."

To lift the mood of his officers, Arnold invited them to join him on Valcour Island the day after arriving at the anchorage. They savored a "most enjoyable entertainment," Lieutenant Bayze Wells said. The only dark note was an ominous sound from the distant north—the repeated boom of the British gunners practicing with their cannon.

⁓

From their earliest days, large guns were endowed with personalities. Their menacing mouths, deep voices, and fiery power suggested a presence. Some were christened with a woman's name, like Meg or Gunhilde.

A cannon was immensely heavy. A mass of metal was needed both to contain the forceful explosion of the gunpowder inside its breech and to dampen the violent recoil that would otherwise send it flying backward when the cannonball was blasted out the barrel. On land, the weight of a gun made it difficult to move—it sank in muddy roads and broke down bridges. On ships, the mass was easily counteracted by the buoyancy of the vessel.

Guns and ships had joined in a harmonious marriage during the sixteenth century. Armaments transformed naval vessels, which had been used to ram enemy ships and carry soldiers for boarding. Guns gave navies the ability to project power in a new way. Strategists on the island nation of Great Britain understood and took advantage of this fact more successfully than those of any other country. The American patriots shared the British perspective, even if they lacked the systematic training and experience at handling warships that the Royal Navy had perfected.

Guns were rated by the mass of the iron balls that they were designed to fire. The American cannon at Valcour ranged from 2-pounders to 18-pounders. The larger the gun, the more destructive the projectile. Bigger guns could also reach more distant targets. But any cannon was a formidable weapon, exploding with an earsplitting boom and throwing a lethal ball at high speed half a mile or more. The boats were equipped with multiple swivel guns, rated as 1-pounders. These were fixed to the gunwales to provide short-range fire. They were often loaded with musket balls to spray at the enemy.

Firing the big guns on water was an intricate and demanding task. The gunners had to load the cannon, then heave on a block and tackle until its muzzle jutted past the bulwark. Gondola crews wrestled with the 12-pounder bow gun, which weighed nearly two tons. When it went off it jerked back along a wooden skid to a position that gave access for reloading. The men then heaved on ropes to run it again into firing position. Each of the 9-pounder cannon that faced outward from the boat's side weighed more than a ton. They moved over the deck on carriages with small wooden wheels. Handling these guns was backbreaking, hernia-inducing work. Controlling them in the pitching chop of a lake storm required both strength and finesse.

The men went through the motions of swabbing the gun barrel with a damp sponge, loading a powder cartridge and iron ball, and heaving the piece into shooting position. The gunner inserted a quill filled with powder into the touch hole, aimed, and pretended to fire, over and over. They were only rarely allowed to burn powder in practice.

To facilitate aiming the guns, the officers taught crews how to use a spring cable. When a ship was fighting from a fixed position, the men would set anchors on opposite sides of the vessel. By tightening and loosening the attached ropes they could maneuver the boat, pointing it first one way, then another. Being able to turn the boat while it was motionless allowed them to bring each gun to bear in turn while the gun crews reloaded.

They performed these drills until the gestures were as automatic as the movements of a dancer. Then they practiced more. They needed precision—a fumble or misstep when handling gunpowder could result in a fatal explosion or a horrific burn. They also needed speed—in battle, firing had to be rapid and continuous.

It was not until the last days of September that the gunners were ordered to practice with live ammunition. They were allowed one round from each gun "fired about one mile at an empty cask" anchored up the strait. Arnold made a contest of it. Bayze Wells reported that his gondola, the *Providence*, "made the best Shots in the fleet."

Besides improving marksmanship, the practice gave the men a sense of their own power. Most of the crewmen had begun the voyage with no experience at their craft. They were learning, but how they would perform in the heat of battle was another question.

At night the men's muscles twitched as they worked the great guns in their sleep.

⁓

For now, the American cannon waited silently to assert their power. The slow drip of time in the northern lake eroded the men's nerves. The wilderness glowered, the men grew homesick, the continuous threat of violent attack made them hypervigilant. Stands of hemlock and ragged junipers curtained the shore, encouraging visions of danger.

Superstitious to begin with, the men inhabited a world of omens. The broad wings of a heron, the flash of a leaping fish, the brief whistle of wind through the rigging—all whispered of sinister events to come. The tension was a taut bow, its string notched into the arrow of the future.

The wait was difficult for a healthy man. But the exposure and damp left many of the crewmen suffering from fevers and agues, debilitating chills associated with various infections. The skipper of the gondola *Providence*, Captain Isaiah Simmons, came down with a severe fever. Lieutenant Bayze Wells complained of "the Itch." He gained little relief from a mixture of tallow, tar, and sulfur. While waiting at Valcour, Benedict Arnold sent sick men "who will be of no service for some time" back up the lake.

The men's anxiety was relentless. They were confined to a body of water where the enemy controlled the shore. From time to time they could visit Valcour Island itself, but elsewhere they were vulnerable to ambush. No one, including officers, knew what to expect. They only knew that sooner or later a British fleet would emerge from the north. Those ships would be manned by experienced sailors, crowded with professional soldiers, and armed with powerful guns. Most of the Americans were getting their first taste of extended time on the water. Many, new to war, had never fired a weapon at another human, never seen a man killed.

American scouts came in to report hearing "talk of crossing the lake soon" from British soldiers. Everyone was on edge. They were facing the king's troops. For generations, redcoats had been the embodiment of authority in the colonies. The inhabitants had obeyed royal dictates. To defy the king took effort and continual resolve.

Given their remote location and the lack of supplies that plagued the fleet, the men had to wonder whether they had been abandoned by their countrymen. No citizens cheered them on or provided support. Did anyone care about what they were doing here? News of the outside world was slow to arrive.

The sense of isolation grew by the day. Even the birds had disappeared. Now it was only a pair of crows carrying on a cawing conversation or a lone woodpecker far off in the forest who told himself a joke and could not stop laughing.

And if the days were hard, what of the nights? The moon, which had passed full a few days after they arrived at Valcour, had given relief from the profound darkness. But even bathed in that ghostly light, the nearby forests and hills suggested a darkness of the spirit. The men had to fight against gloom and discouragement. Now that the moon was coming toward new, the darkness deepened, feeding the men's worst imaginings.

Benedict Arnold understood the need for discipline on a ship. Yet American sailors, especially the inexperienced seamen who had been drafted into his service, were unaccustomed to the draconian rules that prevailed in the Royal Navy. Being flogged with a cat-o'-nine-tails or a rope end was a humiliating experience for a man who considered himself a free citizen. Arnold directed punishment to be administered with restraint. Just before sailing to Valcour, Bayze Wells reported that a man named "Ansel Fox was Cabbd twelve Strokes on his Naked Buttucks for sleeping on his watch." In the British Navy, Fox might have found himself swinging by his neck from a yardarm.

⌒

The fleet had sailed while still lacking many of its needed supplies. The men possessed little in the way of warm clothes. With continual dampness and hard usage, the uniforms they had brought with them wore out. They had come north in August. Now it was nearly October and the penetrating cold was wearing men down.

Just as crucial were spare sails and rigging. In the heat of battle, the equipment that propelled a ship became the target of gunfire. The enemy might blast chain or bar shot into their opponents' rigging. These whirling projectiles were intended to sever ropes and to tear through sails. If the lines, blocks, pulleys, and yards could not be replaced quickly, the vessel foundered.

Ammunition was also needed, but Arnold knew he could not expect a generous supply of powder and shot, given its scarcity at Ticonderoga. He would make do with what he had. He blamed Congress for the shortages. "I am surprised at their strange economy or infatuation below," he observed. "Saving and negligence, I am afraid, will ruin us at last."

More than anything, Arnold needed men. "We have but very indifferent Men, in general," he had written to General Gates earlier in the month. A "great part of those who shipped for Seamen know very little of the Matter. Three or four good gunners are wanted."

On September 18, he wrote, "I beg that at least one hundred good seamen may be sent me as soon as possible. We have a wretched motley crew in the fleet; the Marines the refuse of every Regiment, and the Seamen, few of them, ever wet with salt water." Three days later, he renewed his plea: "The men on board the fleet in general, are not equal to half their number of good men."

Gates blamed General Schuyler for the shortage of supplies. He sent a peremptory message to his superior, asking where were "the powder, lead and flints I wrote for so long ago? Pray hurry it up. The moments are precious, and not one of them should be lost . . . my hands are too full to write more."

To Arnold, Gates responded sardonically that he was sending north "every article that you Demanded in your last Letter on board the *Liberty* Schooner Except what is not to be had here— where it is not to be had, you, & the Princes of the Earth must go unfurnish'd."

❧

Arnold, aware of the larger strategic picture, waited impatiently to hear what was happening in New York City. The earlier report of heavy British casualties in the fight below had encouraged him. Would it affect enemy action in the north? He calculated that if Carleton were to "hear in time that Lord Howe is in possession of New York, they will doubtless attempt a junction with him."

General William Howe was very much in possession of New York. On September 15, a week before the northern fleet had repaired to Valcour, British troops had crossed the East River onto Manhattan Island well north of the city. If Howe had moved faster, he might have captured George Washington's entire army. As it was, the patriot troops had barely escaped, losing much of their artillery. The loss of a major port and one of the most important cities on the continent was a body blow to American hopes.

❧

Like the news, personal letters were slow making the tortuous trip north. While he waited at Valcour, Arnold received letters written some weeks earlier by his sister, Hannah. Two years his junior, Hannah was his closest confidante, the manager of his business in his absence, and, since his wife's death the year before, the guardian of his three sons.

Writing from New Haven, she passed on what she knew about the fighting around New York, painting a grimmer picture than the one he had received in official accounts. The children, she assured him, remained "blessed in ignorance."

Arnold had not seen his children in more than a year. Hannah assured him that they were well. Harry, just four years old, wanted Papa to buy him "a little horse and a pair of pistols" so that he could become a cavalryman. "As far as courage goes," Hannah wrote, he was like his father. She described the boy as "a little loving pup; he gives me twenty kisses a day for papa."

She had managed his business affairs as well as she could. She wrote that she had sold a brigantine he owned and invested the money in New York annuities. She suspected that the instruments would soon be worthless if the British captured the city. "If you ever live to return," she wrote, "you will find yourself a broken merchant, as I have sold everything on hand."

The grim news did not dishearten him. He had found a path to glory that did not involve great possessions. He would gain the esteem he had sought since childhood in the acclaim of his countrymen, hard won in the furnace of war.

Arnold had a worldly exuberance and carnal energy, which, rumor had it, induced him to indulge in amorous adventures in the Caribbean and to pursue French women during the siege of Quebec. Yet he remained under the influence of his mother's pious Puritan worldview. He saved many of her letters. Also named Hannah, she had continually reminded him to be ready for death. "Pray my dear," she had written him, "whatever you neglect do not neglect your precious soul." He should be always prepared to "step off the banks of time."

Her insights into mortality derived from hard experience. She had buried three of her children: Absalom at age three, Elizabeth at four, Mary at eight. Of the two surviving siblings, Benedict had been eighteen and Hannah sixteen when their mother died in 1759. Her death was the shattering event of their youth. Arnold's father, already given to drink, had descended into an alcoholism that bankrupted his children. He had wandered the streets of Norwich in an inebriated haze. Town officials cited him for being "disabled in the use of understanding and reason." His downfall was a deep humiliation for his son.

In closing her letter at this moment of great peril, Arnold's sister reminded him that he must not lose sight of the austere faith that their mother had tried to instill. "To the great Disposer of all events we must commit the issue," she wrote. "We all want to see you, but whether that happiness is again to be repeated to us, God only knows."

She sent him "four waistcoats and three pair stockings." She included a last message from Harry, who "sends a kiss to Pa and says, 'Auntie, tell my Papa he must come home, I want to kiss him.'"

16

No Landlubbers

DURING THE WAIT IN THE NORTH, ARNOLD HAD TIME TO brood. The resentment he felt over his treatment at the Hazen court-martial still festered. Word had reached him that some of those involved in that affair were planning to travel to Philadelphia to complain to Congress. Since the war started, Arnold had been too busy to make contacts among influential politicians at the nation's capital. General Gates, who viewed Arnold as indispensable, assured the younger man he would write to delegates and inform them that "every report to your prejudice is founded in calumny."

In fact, the War Board appointed by Congress had already decided they could not "approve the behavior of Brigadier General Arnold toward the court martial." His implication that the panel of officers should face him with loaded pistols would not do. But the board did not admonish him. Instead, the members referred the matter to George Washington, an Arnold admirer.

John Sullivan had become the commander of the army in Canada by default. When Congress replaced him with General Gates, he departed for Philadelphia, where he declared he would resign his commission. Instead, the delegates did him the honor of promoting him to major general, a position Arnold coveted. Sullivan assumed his new duties just in time to oversee the disastrous loss at Long Island.

Hearing of Sullivan's promotion, Arnold wrote to Gates with bitter irony: "When the enemy drives us back to Ticonderoga, I have some thoughts of going to Congress and begging leave to resign. Do you think they will make me a major general?"

༄

All of Arnold's frustrations and worries were minor compared to the fact that with a battle looming he had yet to receive the main armament of his fleet, the row galleys. It was on these vessels that his strategy of facing down the British depended. Without them he was on a glorified scouting mission. The summer's arms race had come down to this: could the patriots finish the galleys before the enemy attacked?

"I am greatly at a loss what could have retarded the gallies so long," Arnold wrote to Gates on September 23, the day he positioned the fleet near Valcour. Gates, in his turn, had written to Philip Schuyler that Arnold had "no doubt the enemy will soon pay him a visit; I hope not before we get the Row Gallies to his assistance—then succeed or fail, we have done our best. It is a lamentable case that our gallies must wait for cordage and for gun carriages to be completed."

Arnold knew that Schuyler had been dogged in his attempt to round up the canvas, ropes, guns, ammunition, and other supplies needed to complete these larger ships. "I wish the Workmen could all be employed, on One Gally & finish her first," he suggested to Gates. He noted of the British: "I expect them every minute."

༄

Finally, on Monday, September 30, a week after their arrival at Valcour, the men of the fleet cheered to see the broad lateen sail of the first galley appear over the horizon. It was the *Trumbull*, named for the Connecticut governor who had aided Schuyler in supplying and manning the ships. Captain Seth Warner, in command of the new vessel, directed her into the harbor beside Valcour.

Warner was a thirty-three-year-old Connecticut mariner. Benedict Arnold, who had known him before the war, had requested that he raise a company of seamen for the cause before he came north in July. Arnold asked Philip Schuyler to make Warner captain of one of the galleys. When the *Trumbull* arrived to join the fleet, Colonel Wigglesworth transferred to the galley, seeing it as a better vessel from which to exercise his authority as third in command of the fleet.

The rejoicing at the arrival of the vessel ended in a sour note. The *Trumbull*, Arnold noted, was "not half finished or rigged; her cannon are much too small." She carried only one 18-pounder in addition to her smaller cannon. She brought no supply of warm clothes for the men. None of the experienced sailors that Arnold had demanded were to be found aboard. Was this the best the country could do?

The ship did bring a letter. Gates informed Arnold again that he could not produce supplies out of thin air. Gunpowder and nautical stores were not easily come by. "Economy is the word," he wrote.

Arnold, facing a crisis on which the cause of liberty could stand or fall, was enraged. He scratched out a scathing reply: "I hope to be excused if with five hundred men, half naked, I should not be able to beat the enemy with seven thousand men, well clothed, and a naval force by the best accounts, near equal to ours." He informed Gates that "I don't expect to be able to keep my station above a fortnight longer."

October arrived the next day. Cold winds began to snatch leaves from trees. Nights turned frigid. On the boats, shivering sailors waited and waited. A flickering hope tickled their minds: the season was growing late, the threat had passed. They had instilled fear in the enemy. The British were not going to come out to fight. The patriots would soon sail back to warm fires and winter quarters wrapped in the cheers of their fellows.

But their optimism was tempered. It was also possible that the enemy attack was growing ever more likely as the days slipped past. Certainly the matter would be decided, one way or another, before October was half gone.

OCTOBER 1: Arnold drew up a "memorandum of articles which have been repeatedly written for, and which we are in the most extreme want of." He had little hope of receiving the equipment, but he wanted his request on the record. The items included "Tin Lanthorns . . . 1 Barrell Pitch . . . 30 Inch Pine Boards . . . Cloathing. for at least half the Men in the Fleet who are Naked . . . Rum as much as you please . . . One hundred Seamen, (no land Lubbers)."

OCTOBER 2: The day started fine, but by afternoon a gale had kicked up from the south. The sky filled with unkempt clouds, the wind blew and blew. Leaves fled the trees along the shore and danced in the swirling air. Waves drove the *Royal Savage* from her mooring—she collided with the gondola *Providence.*

OCTOBER 3: The wind kept up all day. Vessels adjusted their anchor cables to avoid more collisions. Still no sign of the additional row galleys. At night, cold rain poured from a black sky.

OCTOBER 4: Rain continued to fall like sorrow. The boats rocked with a ceaseless, maddening back-and-forth motion. Wind shifted north and blew wet under the canopies. Drops pocked the men's faces. Scout boats patrolled the main channel continuously. Men peered northward. No enemy came within sight.

OCTOBER 5: The weather cleared. The day was fresh, the sky a welcome blue.

OCTOBER 6: The Sabbath. The changeable wind veered and came from the south. The patriots cheered as two sails appeared from that direction. Yes, one of them was another galley coming to join them. The relief was palpable.

The *Washington* was nearly seventy-three feet from stem to stern and nineteen feet across. Her captain, John Thatcher, had been one of Arnold's comrades in the New Haven Foot Guards. The vessel carried General David Waterbury, who would serve as Arnold's second in command. Her appearance gave the northern sailors something to celebrate. Boats rowed around the fleet to distribute, at last, new warmer wool uniforms. The schooner *Liberty*, which had been escorting boats to and from Ticonderoga, rejoined the fleet that same day loaded with blankets and more warm clothes.

The two vessels brought a boon even more welcome: twenty barrels of rum, one for each of the boats. Rum, the distilled essence of sugar cane, was a balm and a tonic to all fighting men. It warmed the limbs, calmed the nerves, and charged the soul with something resembling courage.

Later that same Sunday, while the sailors were sipping their ration of grog, they were again visited with joy. The bright sails of a third galley appeared on the horizon.

The *Congress* carried two 18-pounder cannon, giving her the most formidable firepower of all the American vessels. The fact that, like the other galleys, she could be propelled in any direction by sweep oars and had a larger cabin set Arnold thinking that he would move his flag of command from the schooner *Royal Savage* to this new ship.

Arnold now had a force of seventeen vessels, a total of ninety-six substantial cannon, numerous swivel guns, and about nine hundred men under his command. Although another galley, named *Gates*, was afloat at Ticonderoga, she was not ready to sail. General Gates sent a letter down the lake. He knew that the officers' devotion to public service would not allow them to pull back from their present position "one moment sooner than in prudence and good conduct you ought to do." It was another ambiguous order that left the decision squarely on Arnold's shoulders.

Along with the welcome supplies, Waterbury brought bad news. More accurate accounts from New York told of the rough handling the British had doled out to George Washington's army. New York City was now in enemy hands. With the main Continental Army near collapse to the south, the entire length of the Great Warpath was vulnerable. The burden of the American cause rested more than ever on the men of the Champlain fleet.

October 7: Waiting. The wind came around yet again from the north and brought thick clouds. Crewmen drew and cooked two days' rations, taking advantage of the stores brought up by the arriving ships, which included fresh beef. That night a bitter, cold rain streamed down. "A very wet night," a crewman noted.

OCTOBER 8: More rain. Stores continued to be distributed to the ships and gondolas—barrels of pork and flour, bushels of potatoes, West India rum, cider.

OCTOBER 9: A wet wind from the south. Leaden clouds pressed down on the nearly bare trees.

OCTOBER 10: The wind continued very fresh from the south all day. The crews endured another night on the plunging, swaying boats. A glimmer of starlight broke through the clouds. The wind swung around to blow from the north. In the morning, the men sensed, but could not know for sure, that their long, anxious wait was over.

17

A Noble Sight

TO GENERAL GUY CARLETON, IT SEEMED ONLY PRUDENT. Build another ship, a frigate, square-rigged, heavily armed, able to sail quickly up the lake and crush any vessel the Americans could float. Benedict Arnold had proposed a frigate for his fleet in July, but time and a scarcity of resources had made that a pipe dream. For Carleton, obtaining such a ship would be easy. Shipwrights were already at work on such a vessel at Quebec City. They could dismantle the planks and frame, mark and catalogue each piece, haul all of the materials to St. Johns, reassemble and finish it.

But the effort would delay the attack up the lake, and, as Captain Charles Douglas said, "No considerable time is to be lost." Carleton decided to build the ship anyway. He wanted to be sure.

Royal Navy lieutenant John Schank oversaw the process. Carpenters pried the timbers apart and loaded them in longboats. They worked their way up the St. Lawrence, then the Richelieu. On September 7, while the first boats of the American fleet hovered around the north end of the lake, British builders laid the ship's keel at St. Johns. Work proceeded day and night. Schank and his engineer assistant, William Twiss, barely slept. Concerned that the vessel's draft would be too deep for some of the shallow spots in the lake, Schank added eight feet to her length to increase her buoyancy. This extended the ship to almost ninety feet long.

To build a vessel of that size in a makeshift shipyard in a remote colonial outpost was an epic feat. As they labored, the workmen's talk and laughter filled the village on the Richelieu. This would surely give the cheeky American rebels something to think about. This fine vessel would answer their posturing, their defiance of king and Parliament. These professionals, who served a God-appointed sovereign, could feel little but contempt for those whose ideas of freedom had driven them to rebellion.

Thick planks dropped one by one from the sawmill. Gangs carried them to the custom-built ways at the river's edge where the towering frame stood. Carpenters hammered them home, turning a skeleton into a hull. "It was no uncommon thing," wrote a British lieutenant, "for trees, growing at dawn of day, to form parts of the ship before night."

Captain Douglas ordered Lieutenant Schank to bring the large sloop-of-war *Canceaux* up to Chambly, strip the vessel of her stores, and haul her sails and anchors, barrels of biscuits and salt pork, spare yards and cables, extra blocks, timbers, cooking pots, lanterns, cutlasses, and carpenter tools up the river to be installed on the new ship. Most of the crew of the *Canceaux* would also switch to the frigate, the largest vessel ever seen on Lake Champlain, his majesty's ship *Inflexible*.

❧

The labor was prodigious: framing, decks, planking, hatches, grates, and ironwork all had to be fashioned by hand and installed. While they worked, the carpenters and sailors began to take in a sight that most had never seen. First isolated trees, then whole hillsides changed. Dogwoods, oak, and maples broke out in bronze and crimson hues. Hickories and birches turned yellow, sumac a dark purple. A vivid, silent kaleidoscope entranced the men as they worked. Less welcome were the cold nights and ever shorter days.

On September 29, at ten in the morning, carpenters swung sledgehammers to knock the wedges that held the sled on which the *Inflexible*'s keel rested. The vessel, twice the size of the schooners *Maria* and *Carleton*, slid down the greased ramp and splashed into the river. The sight was "beautiful to see," an observer remembered. Workmen, soldiers, and sailors along the wharf gave three loud cheers. Captain Douglas watched with "unspeakable joy."

It would take four more days for the shipwrights to install the frigate's three masts and to thread the complex web of lines, yards, and tackle that would allow her to ride the wind. Men worked feverishly, swinging provisions into the ship's hull, making the final preparations that would render her a fighting platform, a means of transportation, and a home for a hundred men. They filled her magazine with gunpowder but left off her cannon and ammunition for the time being.

Guy Carleton now had under his command five major war vessels and twenty-two gunboats. His fleet was armed with more than a hundred cannon, including powerful 18- and 24-pounders. He had seven hundred experienced sailors to work the ships. He had an army of three thousand soldiers immediately available to serve as marines and rowers. Other regiments of Burgoyne's relief force were stationed at posts from Montreal to Quebec in order to secure Carleton's base.

The commander had formed a plan, recommended by General Burgoyne, to have a portion of the army accompany the fleet. Now, although he had sufficient bateaux to move the troops, he abandoned the idea. He was worried about moving troops in unarmed transports, which would be vulnerable to hostile warships. Until he located and destroyed the American fleet, he could not risk offering the enemy such a target. He ordered General Burgoyne to hold his men in readiness around the northern end of Lake Champlain, where they could embark on short notice after Arnold and his vessels were dealt with. He directed the army commander to send several hundred light infantrymen and grenadiers southward to patrol along the shore of the lake.

On October 3, a stream of British ships and gunboats began to slip up the channel, round Île aux Noix, and sail to Windmill Point, the juncture of the river with the lake. The sailors were relieved to leave behind the confines of the Richelieu. As they emerged onto the inland lake, they were amazed to see flocks of passenger pigeons darkening the sky as they winged in their millions toward warmer climes.

The British troops now began a coordinated shift southward. The 1st Brigade of the army moved up the Richelieu to the edge of the lake, and the main force of Hessians at Montreal took their place at St. Johns. Army lieutenant William Digby noted, "We were all provided for the cold weather . . . with warm clothing such as under waistcoats, leggings, socks &c."

While British workers were putting the final touches on the *Inflexible* and preparing their other ships, they heard cannon fire from down the lake, a reminder of the enemy lurking somewhere among the islands to the south. On Saturday, October 5, a rumor reached British lines that a rebel force was advancing. In response, one soldier said, "We lay on our arms for four and twenty hours, but the enemy did not appear."

Two days later, as night descended, it began to rain. For two more days, a storm lashed the ships and cold sheets of droplets hissed against the water surface. The twenty men who occupied each of the gunboats, recruited from English and German artillery regiments, hunched under tarpaulins and endured the queasy pitch and roll of their open boats.

✧

British workmen and British ingenuity had accomplished a near miracle—the completion of the *Inflexible*, from the laying of her keel to sailing, had taken twenty-eight days. The feat astounded even her builders. The officers and men who guided her up the Richelieu had no time to get used to her sailing qualities or adjust her trim. As they approached a rain-drenched Lake Champlain on October 8, they stopped to mount her cannon. If the guns had been swung aboard at St. Johns, their weight would have risked sending her aground in the shallow river.

On October 10, the ship emerged onto the wider water, her

three tiers of square sails magnificent against dark clouds. "It certainly was a noble sight," a British lieutenant enthused, "to see such a vessel on a fresh water lake in the very heart of the Continent of America." Captain Douglas, who would stay behind to command the British fleet still in the St. Lawrence, was confident that the lake flotilla was destined to prevail. "As the *Inflexible* is of the party," he observed, "I am not uneasy about the event."

General Carleton watched with Lieutenant Thomas Pringle from the deck of the *Maria*. The commander had appointed Pringle to serve under his direction as commodore of the fleet, coordinating the movements of all the vessels. In doing so, he was following the traditions of the Royal Navy, in which rank and the order in which officers were promoted dictated assignments. Pringle, a member of a venerable Scottish family and son of a West Indies planter, had been a lieutenant for sixteen years, which gave him precedence.

The white ensign, which featured a simple red St. George's cross in its corner, flew from the major British vessels. The flags snapped against the austere lattice of bare lakeside trees. Fighting the choppy minuet of waves stirred by gales, British tenders brought more provisions to be loaded on the *Inflexible* as the fleet gathered at Point au Fer, two miles south of Windmill Point. Officers were encouraged when the rain diminished and the wind came around to blow from the north. Conditions boded well for an immediate advance up the lake. The *Inflexible* gave Carleton the confidence he had sought.

That evening, with a happy sunset glowing in the west, Commodore Pringle directed the fleet to take advantage of the breeze and sail seven miles up the lake to anchor for the night in sheltered coves at the south end of Isle La Motte.

Only one sour thought brewed in the back of General Carleton's mind. His fleet had been ready to sail at the beginning of September. The month of delay that constructing the *Inflexible* had cost brought him that much closer to winter. He was familiar with the northern cold. He knew that the weather could turn suddenly sharp and send fangs of ice out from the lake's edge. He knew that this entire body of water was destined to become a frozen plane over the next three months. Did he have time to fight the American fleet, rush down to Ticonderoga, and take the fort before winter set in? He was about to find out.

PART TWO

18

Make Ready

"ALL HANDS! ALL HANDS!"

Four-thirty of a frigid morning. The bosun's mates stormed through the sleeping ranks of men on the British ships spinning wooden clackers, sounding a grating wake-up call to startle the men out of their dreams. It was Friday, October 11. It was time to fight.

The sailors on the frigate and the schooners wrapped their hammocks. Those in the smaller boats stored blankets under tarpaulins. All scarfed down hot pork and beans and portions of bread. All talked of the exciting prospect of action. Generous rations of rum warmed stomachs. Men hurried to the bows of ships to relieve themselves through the openings of the heads, drawing up a rag on a rope to clean themselves with cold lake water. A pepper of stars defined the silhouettes of the distant mountains.

During the night, a teeth-clenching wind had rocked the British fleet at anchor. The crews, so long entangled in the details of preparation, would this day speed south and blast any vessels the rebels dared to bring out against them. In ten hours of favorable sailing, they could be at Crown Point, where the garrison would doubtless succumb to panic. Ticonderoga would fall next. Then, unopposed, Carleton's force would begin the march toward Albany, undefended.

Carleton had begun the year holding on to British sovereignty in Canada by a thread, his scope of authority reduced to the speck of land inside the walls of Quebec City. Now he would cap his brilliant campaign with a brilliant victory, and the rebellion in the colonies would be over.

⟳

With dawn not yet seeping above the horizon, Carleton and his officers, including the captains of the other major vessels, assembled in his cabin on the *Maria* for a council of war over breakfast. Knowing little about naval operations, Carleton would depend on Captain Pringle to issue sailing orders. Pringle had a small jaw and tight mouth. His busy eyes reflected his ambitious nature. He had come to America the year before as the first lieutenant of a navy ship. During the autumn of 1775, he had sailed back to England on a merchant vessel with dispatches describing the invasion of Canada by the Americans.

Relations among the top officers were tense. They were not accustomed to being commanded by an army general. Why was Carleton coming along on this naval mission? Lieutenant Digby was later critical of him for "hazarding himself on an element so much out of his line" by accompanying the fleet. Unfamiliar with naval procedures and tactics, Carleton had no purpose on board "except proving his courage."

His presence is not hard to explain. He was in overall command and wanted to be on the spot to issue orders. Having wrestled with a year's worth of vexing problems, Carleton was tempted by the taste of glory. What soldier would not be? He was not about to allow the navy men to claim sole credit for defeating the American insurgents.

General Carleton was the opposite of popular. Some of the naval lieutenants bore him frank ill will and resented his interference in a sphere they knew well. The ingenious, thirty-six-year-old John Schank, who would command the *Inflexible*, had overseen the construction of most of the fleet. John Starke, captain of the *Maria*, could boast of fourteen years' service in the navy—he had trained marines and seamen in Quebec. Edward Longcroft of the *Loyal Convert* had long naval experience as well.

That morning, as the men sipped tea in the commander's cabin, Carleton and Pringle explained to the officers the battle plan, such as it was. They anticipated one of two scenarios. The most likely was that they would encounter the American fleet in or near Cumberland Bay, seven miles south of Isle La Motte. The other was that Arnold would run south in order to gain protection under the guns at Ticonderoga. He might already have begun his flight as they spoke, in which case it was important for the British fleet to run him down.

It was easy for Carleton's mind to be drawn to this latter possibility. He had faced the Americans at Quebec and watched them retreat in disorder as soon as a force of regulars marched out to meet them. Arnold had already pulled back from his bold position at the north end of the lake, then retreated again from Isle La Motte. Carleton was advancing with a fleet powerful enough to strike fear in the heart of any rational enemy.

After Pringle issued his orders on board the *Maria*, the lieutenants hurried back to their respective ships to get under way. As the eastern opalescence began to erase the stars, signal flags instructed all ships: "Put out cookfires. Make ready for battle."

Sailors at creaking capstans hauled anchors off the bottom. All hands turned out to pull the sails into position and to stand ready at the big guns. The wind billowed the topsails, canvas snapped, the stays supporting the masts trembled.

Captain Georg Pausch, an officer with the Hessian artillery regiment, reported that "at 5 o'clock in the morning, we received orders to get in readiness for an engagement. We raised anchor and, with a favorable wind, got very early under sail." He would be commanding one of the twenty-two gunboats of the fleet.

The British formed up to proceed south on the lake. On the *Thunderer*, a stove was kept burning to heat iron cannonballs to a red glow. The incandescent shot could, when striking an enemy hull, set the ship ablaze. Vessels made of wood, canvas, and pitch and loaded with stores of gunpowder were vulnerable to fire.

✑

Whether Carleton and Commodore Pringle knew that Arnold's fleet awaited them behind Valcour Island when they set sail on the morning of Friday, October 11, is one of several mysteries that surround the battle.

General Von Reidesel, commander of the Hessians, later wrote that "it was reported to General Carleton, that the American fleet had been seen near Grand Island." Grand Island stood directly opposite Cumberland Bay. But on October 9, a longboat skipper had reported sailing around Grand Island "without discovering any traces of the enemy."

Lieutenant John Enys, an army officer on board the *Thunderer*, wrote in his journal, "On the 10th in the evening we got intelligence where they were."

In a letter submitted after the engagement, three disgruntled Royal Navy lieutenants who took part in the battle—Schank, Starke, and Longcroft—claimed that the high command "had information . . . the night before" about the enemy's deployment at Valcour. Both Carleton's actions that day and his later report left the question open.

It's possible that both depictions contained elements of truth. Reports might have reached Carleton that the American fleet was waiting in the Valcour channel. But the commander knew that the Americans could easily have shifted their position during the night. The surrounding lake offered many other coves and inlets where war vessels could hide. The favorable north wind made it likely they were running toward the safety of the American forts.

Pringle, more accustomed to fighting at sea than on a lake, probably assumed that even if Arnold was waiting behind Valcour, he would bring his fleet north to fight in Cumberland Bay—the British had fought and won a battle against the French there in 1759. It seemed to him a logical place for the fleets to engage each other, since both sides would have had more room to maneuver than they would in a confined strait.

Dr. Robert Knox, Carleton's personal physician and inspector general of the hospitals, was on board the *Maria*. He later reported that Carleton had been told that "Mr. Arnold had a fleet of 16 ships in Cumberland Bay."

Carleton and Pringle had settled on their own plans two days before. Now, with the wind at their backs, the commanders saw no reason to make last-minute changes based on scouting reports that could already have gone stale.

⟋⟍

The flag signals were hoisted up the stays again: "Form line of battle."

By eight o'clock that morning, all the British vessels were arrayed in ranks. They sailed down the channel, came abreast of North Hero Island on their port side. Two miles farther on lay Cumberland Head, a low-lying peninsula extending from the west, its trees just catching the morning sun. Beyond it, Cumberland Bay widened the lake to five miles. As the British sailed south, the bright sunshine of their confidence made them eager for a first glimpse of the enemy.

The water before them offered an unfamiliar environment to these saltwater sailors. On the ocean, hazards to navigation were rare and weather the main natural force to consider. On Lake Champlain, uncharted shoals, rocks, and small islands were common. The proverbial enemy of every ship's captain is land lying opposite the wind. A lee shore always spelled peril, and on this narrow lake there was a lee shore in every direction.

Captain Schank and the crew of the *Inflexible* in particular would have benefited from the shakedown cruise afforded any new ship. A vessel as complex as a frigate of war had its own personality and idiosyncrasies. Officers and sailors needed to get used to the ship's rigging, her humors, her feel. They could have adjusted her ballast to improve her trim. They could have run out and fired her big cannon to give the crews a sense of her strength.

No time for any of this. No time for the flotilla to practice sailing in formation. Pringle had laid out the arrangement in which the fleet would proceed, but he neglected to issue battle orders. Perhaps such orders seemed pointless to him, since he did not know how or when the fleet would encounter the enemy. He failed to anticipate the chaos that could ensue once a fight began.

British maps of the area were incomplete. Confusion existed about the strait where the American fleet was posted. Some officers referred to it as a bay or a channel; some seemed to think it was the mouth of a river. Like the many other islands on the lake, Valcour could block or deflect wind and limit maneuverability. It also obscured sight lines, allowing the kind of surprise that was impossible on open water.

◆

From the quarterdeck of the sixty-six-foot-long schooner *Maria*, Guy Carleton surveyed his powerful fleet. The first rank consisted of five vessels stretched across the lake in a line. The two largest ships made an impressive sight. The broad *Thunderer* had thick, curved sides and large cannon with both the range and power to intimidate any vessel on the lake. Beside her sailed the magnificent *Inflexible*, her three masts crowded with billowing white canvas. Just the sight of these magnificent ships was sure to unnerve the crews of the Americans' small boats.

The *Loyal Convert* was also in the front line. About the same size as the schooners, she carried three 9-pounder cannon on each side and a 24-pounder in her bow, a powerful addition to the fleet's firepower. The first rank was completed by the schooner *Carleton*, responsive to the wind and armed with a dozen 6-pounders.

In rows behind these ships sailed the twenty-two gunboats. These vessels, smaller versions of the American gondolas, were neither swift nor elegant. With a heavy gun in the bow and a load of ballast rocks in the stern to balance the weight, they bobbed awkwardly over the waves, driven by a square sail. But they were designed to pack a wallop. A couple of them carried 24-pounders, which matched the largest guns of the fleet. Others were armed with howitzers, which could heave exploding shells. Ten strong oarsmen could drive them forward if the wind failed. A gun crew of seven trained artillerymen meant their cannon would be handled by experts.

Trailing the gunboats, a collection of longboats taken from the ships in the St. Lawrence, some of them armed, carried provisions and several hundred soldiers who could serve as marines if it came to boarding enemy vessels. Some eight hundred Indians brought up the rear in an array of long war canoes. They could easily land to chase down Americans who might flee their ships.

Pringle had assigned the vessels a strict order in the armada. But with the brisk wind and the vessels' uneven sailing qualities, the formation quickly began to blur. Missing from Carleton's original plan were the hundreds of bateaux that would have carried the army and their provisions. General Burgoyne's troops would remain ready on land until the American fleet was neutralized.

And so they came down the lake, each man with his own thoughts as he pressed to his duties, rowing, paddling, trimming sail, watching, waiting. Just ahead of them the peninsula of Cumberland Head narrowed the lake to barely more than a mile. Behind it, the enemy most likely awaited them.

∽

Pringle's most critical failure that morning was to neglect exploring the lake ahead of him. His longboats were available as scouts, and some of them did probe the coves among the islands to the east. But he might also have assigned Indians in their canoes to fan out and search for the enemy. Perhaps he was in too much of a hurry, perhaps too confident that his impressive fleet would make short work of the Americans in battle, wherever they lay.

Just over a mile due north of Valcour Island, the much smaller tree-covered Crab Island stood at the southern edge of Cumberland Bay. Between that obstacle and Valcour a protrusion of land, now called Bluff Point, pushed eastward from the shore. A blunt peninsula extended from the west side of Valcour itself. The two landforms blocked a direct line of sight down the Valcour strait.

Only by sailing into the channel could British scouts have gained a view of the waiting American warships.

Dr. Knox, who observed the action from the crowded quarterdeck of the *Maria*, noted that the British armada passed Cumberland Head about half past nine, racing to the south. Valcour Island lay ahead off the fleet's starboard bow. The vessels had already stretched out over several miles, the larger, faster ships surging ahead of the bobbing gunboats. As Cumberland Bay opened before them, the officers peered across the empty water. "To our great mortification, we could discover no ships," Dr. Knox recorded. Cumberland Bay was empty. The discovery may have confirmed Carleton's notion that the rebels were fleeing up the lake.

The British fleet was galloping southward. The swift longboats had reported no sign of the enemy. Pringle had not ordered the midshipmen commanding them to navigate into the channel behind Valcour Island itself—an inexplicable lapse given the information Carleton had received about Arnold's most recent position.

Although Carleton held overall command, he left the naval decisions to the fleet commander, who was about to fight his first battle. Zealous and puffed up with the authority of his position, Pringle was eager to appear confident and decisive. In fact, he was literally venturing into unknown waters, seeing the contours of the lake for the first time.

Like any naval commander, Pringle kept the wind always in mind. This bright morning, it continued to blow briskly from the north, sometimes swaying to the northeast or northwest, perfect for driving the ships southward. They struggled to maintain their formation. With canvas spread on three masts, the *Invincible* had more motive power than any of the other vessels. The flat-bottomed *Thunderer* moved along handily but could not keep up with the *Invincible*. Nor could the schooners *Maria* and *Carleton*. The laden gunboats fell farther behind.

The officers who complained of Pringle's leadership during the engagement later noted, "You formed no plan nor made any disposition of the fleet under your command to attack them, which you was advised to do. . . . This neglect, whether proceeding from want of capacity or want of inclination was the true reason of their not being brought to action."

This judgment by experienced naval men on the scene has to be given weight. Pringle did face a complex, unfamiliar geography that varied as he proceeded south. He had no experience with lake sailing. His charts were rudimentary—Valcour Island did not even appear on them. Yet he made several serious puzzling blunders in his handling of the fleet during the morning hours of October 11.

Decisions had to be made at once about the fleet's disposition and actions. Should they heave to and send out scouts to explore the area? Should they ease the speed of the lead ships and reestablish their formation to prepare for a battle? Should they assume Arnold's fleet was gone and proceed south with all possible speed?

The favorable wind continued to hum in the ships' sails and the fleet continued to race the scudding clouds toward Valcour Island, which lay just south of Cumberland Bay. Pringle, with Carleton looking over his shoulder and the other ship captains waiting for his signal, stood on the quarterdeck of the *Maria*. He made no decision, took no action. The British fleet sailed on.

19

Engage

WHEN BENEDICT ARNOLD WAS THIRTEEN HIS TEACHER, A Congregationalist minister, wrote to his mother, picturing her son as "full of pranks and plays." His most recent stunt had been to climb to the roof of a barn that had caught fire. He horrified on-lookers by walking the ridgepole from end to end. Danger nour-ished Arnold. Chaos and violence ignited adrenaline-charged sensations that transformed fear into a vital sense of urgency. In action, he became himself.

For all soldiers, battle was an occasion for personal glory, but to Arnold it was more. He knew his family's distinguished lineage—an ancestor had been an early governor of Rhode Island. His father's disgrace and loss of fortune had spilled the family's honor onto the streets of Norwich. Arnold was drawn to any chance, any feat, that might refill the cup. When he awoke on October 11, he sensed that the enemy was near, that the confrontation he had spent three months anticipating was about to unfold.

To a seaman in the age of sail, the wind was the world. Over-night the south wind with its cloudy foreboding had quieted. Now a brisk breeze was mounting from the north, scouring the sky and bringing a fresh coolness to sweep the lake. The Americans, like their British counterparts, were up early. They were always on alert, with sentries floating in bateaux to the north, watching for a sail. Half the crewmen in each of the gondolas and schooners stood ready for action at all times.

Before dawn that Friday, Arnold had sent a squad of soldiers, along with some of the Stockbridge Mohican Indians who accompanied his fleet, to climb trees on the north end of Valcour Island and look for ships approaching. A guard boat was cruising out on the lake where sailors could keep spyglasses trained up the main channel.

As the sun came up, the crewmen marveled at the overnight snowfall that coated the distant hills. The mountains gleamed rosy white against the hopeful blue of the sky. The chilly wind hissed down from the north, moistening eyes and prompting men to hunch their shoulders.

Sometime around eight in the morning everything changed.

∽

"The guard boat came in fired an alarm and brought news of the near approach of our enemy," American lieutenant Bayze Wells recorded. Word shot through the fleet. "We had alarm," crewman Jahiel Stewart remembered, "that the Regular fleet was Coming on us." Another wrote about "six sail of the Enemy Being coming Round Comberlin head." From Cumberland Head they could be at Valcour Island in less than an hour.

The guard boat skidded around the end of the island, firing a small gun to alert the officers. The lookouts in the trees were soon reporting the same news: sails to windward, coming fast.

The men were amazed when they made out the lead vessel, with its three tiers of bright square canvas towering over the lake. It was a full-rigged ship, a frigate. None of them had seen anything like it on the lake.

Rumors had reached the men in recent weeks that enemy carpenters were building a large, heavily gunned ship, but Arnold had held out the hope that the two fleets would be roughly equal in strength when they met. Now it was clear that the British had gained a decisive advantage. To anyone who knew the destructive power of large cannon, the prospect of being on the receiving end of a broadside from the approaching *Inflexible* was daunting.

In the time since the arrival of the *Congress*, Arnold had shifted his flag from the *Royal Savage* to the more maneuverable galley. Perhaps because the galley offered a smaller cabin, he had left clothing, papers, and other personal effects on the schooner. He now sent up a white pennant along the stays of the *Congress*, calling his officers to hurry over for a last-minute council of war.

Small boats and skiffs rowed quickly to the flagship. The tense officers ducked under the deck beams and into the crowded cabin beneath the quarterdeck. The men swayed in unison as the chop made the vessel tug against its anchor. They were dressed for battle in their best uniforms. Arnold wore his blue coat, a sash suspending a sword at his side, one epaulet sparkling on his shoulder and gold rimming his tricorn hat.

The debate came down to a simple choice: stay and fight or weigh anchor and run. The discussion was carried on largely by Arnold and David Waterbury. The fleet's second in command had arrived only five days earlier on the galley *Washington*. Arnold liked and trusted the older officer—Waterbury was fifty-three to his thirty-five. Both were Connecticut men, both mariners. Both knew that men's lives, including their own, would depend on their decision.

Arnold laid out a battle plan. The gondolas would hold their current tight formation in an arc across the strait. Supported by the schooners and galleys, they would fight the British in Valcour Bay from fixed positions.

Waterbury objected. He saw the restricted bay as a death trap. British officers could blockade the north end of the channel while they attacked from the other end, crushing the American fleet in between.

The north wind, Arnold pointed out, would impede enemy ships advancing from the south.

But who knew how long the breeze would last? The British could wait at the end of the strait. If the wind swung round to the south again, the largest enemy ships would descend on the American fleet and shred the boats with cannon fire.

Arnold said he would send the *Royal Savage* and the galleys into the lake to lure the enemy to battle. The British would not be able to resist the provocation.

Waterbury continued to insist that they should meet the enemy in the open water, not "lie where we should be surrounded." The north wind gave them a chance to flee.

To escape down the lake before the British arrived held even more risk, Arnold pointed out. Even with a head start, the slower ships would have trouble outrunning the enemy.

Perhaps so, but a retreat offered the chance that at least part of the fleet would reach the relative safety of Crown Point and Ticonderoga. It was a risk worth taking. "I gave it as my opinion," Waterbury later said, "that the fleet ought immediately to come to sail and fight them on a retreat in [the] main lake."

Arnold reminded the men that General Gates's orders instructed them to hold out in the north for as long as it was prudent to do so. The time to flee had not yet arrived. Fighting in retreat was difficult. Pitting inexperienced sailors and gunners against crack Royal Navy men on open water invited disaster. With only three galleys, he could not protect the sluggish gondolas. By running they would be drawing the enemy closer to Crown Point. Their function was to stop or delay the British.

He kept one critical consideration to himself. The severe shortage of gunpowder at Ticonderoga meant that a concerted British attack there could overrun the fort.

To his men, Arnold voiced bright thoughts. He praised the captains. Seth Warner, who skippered the galley *Trumbull*, was a crack seaman. David Hawley, the captain of the *Royal Savage*, had smuggled a load of gunpowder through a British blockade. Waterbury and Wigglesworth were both adroit mariners and fearless fighters.

They could prevail in this battle. If most of the boats remained at anchor in the channel, the crews would not have to worry about the complicated tasks of sailing. Each vessel would have plenty of men to service its guns. Fighting from a fixed position would simplify their tactics. Their tight formation would prevent the British from closing and sending marines to board them. Intersecting lines of fire would stymie the ability of the British to maneuver. The enemy was far from invincible. "Carleton the Haughty," as Arnold called him, had not even sent out scout boats. The arrogance of the enemy would be their downfall.

Arnold possessed an almost preternatural ability to inspire men in desperate situations. His unwavering eyes and resolute voice snuffed out fear, doubt, and hesitation. His subordinates took sustenance from his overflowing confidence until they were as excited and optimistic as he was.

The discussion was over, Arnold declared. They would stay and face the enemy. If they were to die, they would die. But that day, they would fight for a cause greater than any of them. And they would win.

〜

Having received their orders, the officers quickly returned to their vessels. They directed their men to soak blankets with water and spread them over powder supplies so as to minimize the danger of fire. Sailors wet the decks and scattered sand to provide footing for the crews. They distributed buckets of water to fight fires and made sure sails not in use were securely furled, minimizing their exposure to enemy projectiles.

While the Americans were preparing, the British, surprised that they had not encountered an enemy fleet in Cumberland Bay, continued to sail south along the main channel of the lake.

"At ½ past nine," Colonel Wigglesworth noted, "Genl. Arnold ordered me on the Yawl to go to wind'd to observe their motions. I return'd at 10. & inform'd him they were round the Island of Valcour."

It was time for Arnold to make his move. He ordered the *Royal Savage*, along with the three row galleys, to set sail and exit the south end of the channel. They would move onto the open lake in full view of the British.

Arnold stood on the quarterdeck of the *Congress*, surveying the unfolding scene. The sun dodged new-made clouds as it climbed the sky. The brilliant light illuminated the familiar landscape as if from within. The area just south of Valcour Island was the widest stretch on the entire lake. The eastern shore lay ten miles away across an expanse of glittering, choppy water.

Arnold eyed the British vessels: the ominous frigate, the armed schooners, the small but menacing gunboats. All the preparation of the past three months—the frantic shipbuilding, the bluffing, the waiting—had come to this, a moment of decision. He was about to grip the waterwheel of his youth, about to descend into the turbulent sluice of battle.

According to Dr. Knox, the physician aboard the British schooner *Maria*, the fleet, hurrying south, passed the "river Valcour" about ten o'clock. He himself "descried a vessel close in shore." It's unlikely that a man on deck rather than a lookout high on the mast would have been the first to sight the enemy. Another account suggests that a midshipman in one of the longboats raised the alarm. It did not matter—Arnold's goal was to be seen by the passing fleet.

Knox recorded that Commodore Pringle sent a small tender into the mouth of the Valcour strait to investigate and fire an alarm gun if any American vessels were discovered. Lieutenant John Schank, captain of the *Inflexible*, related a different version: "At 10 saw a strange sail get under sail. Captain Pringle ordered the *Carleton* to chase her, soon after my signal was made for the same purpose."

Since the British sources do not report seeing the galleys, it may be that they did not need to venture far into the main channel— the enemy took the bait as soon as they spotted the *Royal Savage*. By this time, the principal British ships had already proceeded south of the entrance to the Valcour strait.

Benedict Arnold had assumed correctly that the British would not proceed up the lake unless they had a favorable wind. With the brisk northerly breeze, they could reach Crown Point in a single day. But once they passed him, the wind would work in his favor.

All agreed that the wind that day was blowing vigorously. A fifteen-knot breeze across the lake would have lifted three-foot-high waves and set numerous whitecaps flashing in the sunlight. Gusts would have ripped foam off the heaving water. The conditions made navigating in the confined waters of Lake Champlain a challenge.

Carleton described the difficult position to General Burgoyne: "After we had got beyond the enemy and cut them off, the wind, which had been favorable to bring us there, however entirely prevented our being able to bring our whole force to engage them."

If the intention of Carleton and Pringle was to cut off the American fleet, why did it take Arnold's sally onto the lake to lure them behind Valcour Island? If they planned to blockade the bay, as both later said they did, they underestimated the difficulty of bringing their large vessels around and heading into the teeth of the wind to achieve the opening of the channel.

Within minutes, the whole British fleet was in disorder. Captains shouted for their crews to come about. The larger ships continued to skid south up the lake. Their junior officers screamed orders to direct the complicated task of swinging around and beating into the wind.

Pringle must have realized he had made a mistake. Now the crews of the principal British ships found themselves south of Valcour Island, with American war vessels in their rear. The commodore's decision, ratified by Carleton, to sail without specific battle plans guaranteed confusion in a crisis. The reaction of the British captains gave every indication that Arnold had pulled off a complete surprise. The driving force of arrogance, which he had counted on, had as much to do with the developing imbroglio as did the northerly wind.

The situation raised another worry for Carleton. Was it possible that the Americans would now head north and train their cannon on the army troops? Their camps were undefended from the water and would be vulnerable to artillery fire. Arnold might even continue up the Richelieu and attack St. Johns.

ᴄᴏ

In their pursuit of the *Royal Savage*, crews swung the *Inflexible* and the *Carleton* around and tried to claw into the wind. They had to head northwest. The wind, as if deliberately perverse, now veered to come from that very direction, making their task even more difficult.

The *Carleton*, with its fore-and-aft rigging, was more manageable than the square-rigged frigate. Her skipper, James Dacres, managed to zigzag his way forward as he chased after the *Royal Savage*. The *Inflexible*, under Captain Schank, had to take a more circuitous route. When he considered tacking near the south end of the island, the pilot, who was familiar with the local waters, "acquainted me that I could not get in, at the same passage, after the Chase, but must run to the Southwest of the island," that is, the southwest side of Petit Island.

Commodore Pringle's contribution to the initial maneuvering was to hoist the signal flag that told all the other vessels: "Engage."

British Army lieutenant Thomas Hadden, who was aboard one of the gunboats, later claimed that the British pursuit of the American vessels "was without order or regularity." With no plan, the duty of the captain of each vessel was to pursue and fire on the enemy. Arnold had counted on the fact that the British would not, in the heat of battle, call off the action or wait for more favorable wind conditions. They would be drawn into the type of fight Arnold wanted.

ᴄᴏ

Naval combat was, by its nature, more dynamic than fighting on land. Ships and their powerful guns could be repositioned quickly, while field guns had to be hauled by teams of horses, and troops could only shift position at a walking pace. The result was a more chaotic and violent encounter on water, one where advantage could shift back and forth in a matter of seconds. Schank now reported that "we saw the *Royal Savage* bearing down, with intention to Engage the *Carleton*."

David Hawley, the captain of the *Savage*, had swung her around with the intention of confronting the slightly larger British schooner. But when he saw the massive *Inflexible* coming up in the *Carleton*'s wake, he hauled his wind and tried to get away rather than shoot it out with the enemy. His goal was to regain the Valcour strait and join the fleet according to Arnold's plan. Having cleared the rocks and ledges around Petit Island, he tried to make the turn around the sharp southwest corner of the larger island and come north into the channel. At that point, he ran into trouble.

With every tack, a sailing vessel had to pass through a perilous point head-on into the wind. If it could not swing through this heading, it would go motionless, a condition known as being "in irons," handcuffed in its movements. Its sails flapping, the ship would lose steering and risk being blown backward.

Caught by the variable and adverse wind, Hawley had trouble making the turn around the bottom of the island. Maneuvering into a headwind in a confined space with a crew that lacked experience was a tricky assignment. Arnold, watching the drama unfold, would attribute the vessel's problem to "some bad management."

Her crew hauled on lines. The wind came veering off the island in eddies. The schooner's sail first dumped wind, then fluttered uselessly. The *Royal Savage* was dead in the water.

On the *Inflexible*, Captain Schank saw his chance. He ordered his first mate to fire on the *Savage* with his ship's 12-pounder bow chaser cannon. In quick succession, the first significant hostile fire of the engagement boomed across the bay.

The American sailors, many of them plunging into their first battle, were startled by the realization that the crewmen on the enemy vessels were determined to fire the dangerous, flame-spouting cannon directly at them. The message was driven home by the guns' resounding blast, which shattered the inner dome of the sky.

The initial shot crashed into the *Royal Savage* and "sheared Her bowsprit," Schank wrote. "A second from the same hand struck her foremast, and the third killed A Man in the Cabin."

This matter-of-fact description belied the intense violence cannon fire inflicted on a sailing ship. A ball striking any wooden part blasted a spray of splinters, each a lethal projectile. A ship's stern was her most vulnerable target. A man killed by a 12-pounder ball could be mutilated beyond recognition. After smashing through the cabin, the ball would rip along the deck, compounding the destruction.

The Battle of Valcour Island had begun.

20

— · · · —

The Battle
Was Very Hot

IN THREE DAYS, PASCAL DE ANGELIS WOULD TURN fourteen. His stepfather, Seth Warner, captain of the galley *Trumbull*, had brought him along to see what war was. The boy's eyes widened as he watched the adventure of a lifetime unfold in front of him. In a short journal he kept during his stint on the lake, he remembered seeing the *Royal Savage* struggling, noting that she "could not Git up to the Line."

The three row galleys that had ventured out to challenge the British to battle were easier to propel in contrary winds than the schooner. They could resort to sweep oars to drive them directly into the wind. *Royal Savage* captain David Hawley had more trouble contending with the changeable winds at the end of the island. Fire from the *Inflexible*'s 12-pounder tore apart the *Savage*'s rigging, compounding the difficulty of handling her.

For the Americans aboard the schooner, the introduction to war was abrupt and terrifying. With the enemy astern and their vessel crippled, they could not defend themselves.

Captain Hawley saw there was no chance to bring the ship under control. His hope now was to sail her close enough to the island to allow the crew to escape being captured. He ordered the helmsman to steer the ship toward land. A minute later came the sound, awful to any seaman, of the schooner's hull scraping rock. The ship gave a sickening lurch and staggered like an animal with a broken leg. She ground to a halt, throwing men to the deck.

Fortunately for the schooner's crew, the wind was carrying *Inflexible* away, preventing her from getting into the channel to continue her bombardment. Now it was the British gunboats that began to menace the *Royal Savage*. Although their square sails were useless when advancing against the wind, their oars allowed crews to maneuver them adroitly. They could cut through the choppy water, driven by five strong soldiers on each side. Like a wolf pack, they approached the stranded ship from more than one direction.

"At this time the Gunboats came round the Island in the most masterly manner," Captain Schank recorded, "Each striving to be first, Never I am sure did boats behave so well in this world."

The guns kept up a staccato of fire at the *Royal Savage*. Their skippers shouted orders to oarsmen to bring them to bear—since the guns could not be swiveled from side to side, the entire boat had to be aimed. When the gunner touched a match to the cannon's vent an angry blast of orange flame flashed from its barrel, accompanied by a thunderous roar and an enormous eruption of dense white smoke. Cannonballs pounded the *Royal Savage*'s hull and tore through her sails. "One of her masts was wounded and rigging shot away," Arnold later reported.

Using his ship's boat and a crew of oarsmen, Hawley made a brief, futile attempt to tow the *Savage* free and haul her closer to the American line. Seeing that further efforts were pointless, he ordered his crew to abandon ship. Some of the men leapt into the rowboat or plunged into the icy lake water and struck out for shore. Others, unable to swim, hesitated.

The direction of the battle veered again. The gaggle of gunboats offered the American row galleys and gondolas an inviting target. "This firing at one object drew us all in a cluster," reported Lieutenant James Hayden, aboard one of the British gunboats, "and four of the Enemies vessels getting under way to support the *Royal Savage*, fired upon the boats with success." Chased by grapeshot and ball, the British gunboats first dispersed, then took up positions facing the American line to continue their barrage.

The *Loyal Convert*, the gondola the British had captured from the Americans, was also attempting to press the attack. Her square sail did not allow her captain, Edward Longcroft, to maneuver into the Valcour strait. Frustrated and eager for action, Longcroft took a crew aboard his ship's boat and rowed to the *Royal Savage*. The men scrambled aboard. They took several stranded Americans prisoner and heaved the stricken schooner's guns around to fire at the American vessels.

In the schooner's cabin, the British sailors found a surprising treasure: papers and clothing belonging to the American commander, Benedict Arnold, which had been left behind when Arnold had switched his flag from the *Royal Savage* to the *Congress*. The British sailors carried away part of this cache but were interrupted by American fire.

Jahiel Stewart, a crewman on the American hospital ship *Enterprise*, watched the events on the schooner as "the Regulars boarded her and fired from her to our fleet & the battle was very hot on both sides." Hot and loud. With twenty-two British gunboats, as well as the American gondolas and galleys firing simultaneously, the noise in the strait grew to a concussive roar that suffocated thought.

From the other side, Georg Pausch, the Hessian artillery commander, observed that American "gondolas, one after another, emerged from a small bay of the island firing rapidly and effectively. Every once in a while they would vanish to get breath and again suddenly reappear."

In this boiling free-for-all, American gunners bombarded the *Royal Savage*, now in the hands of the enemy. Captain Longcroft looked in vain for support from other British ships. To capture an enemy vessel of war was a key object of naval fighting. American cannon fire killed three of the boarders and forced the enterprising Longcroft to relinquish his prize. Arnold, watching from the *Congress*, noted that in the opening action of the battle, one of the most valuable pieces of the American fleet had been knocked out of action and nearly lost to the enemy. It was a bad beginning.

✌

The British faced their own problems. Much of the power of their fleet had been neutralized by the position of the American fleet and the contrary wind. The *Thunderer* had it the worst. Although she was capable of sailing a brisk nine knots downwind, her lack of a keel made movement against the wind impossible. Ensign Enys, who served on the radeau, observed that ships of the fleet "were obliged to tack in order to get into the Bay. This rendered the Vessel I was on board totally useless. . . . We fired some few Shot at the time we first Saw their fleet but I believe it might have been just as well let alone."

The *Thunderer*'s captain was forced to drop anchor before his vessel was blown down the shoreline. Although gunners fired her big cannon at the *Royal Savage*, they were warned off for fear of hitting the British gunboats.

General Carleton later wrote, "We had a narrow passage to work up, ship by ship, exposed to the fire of their whole line." His words echoed Arnold's description of his thinking to General Gates two weeks earlier: "Few vessels can attack us at the same time & those will be exposed to the fire of the whole fleet." His tactic was working. Pringle issued an order for the gunboats to form a line across the bay opposite the Americans. "This was soon effected," Lieutenant Hadden wrote. The fight was being carried by the heavily armed British gunboats, each crew keeping up a continual fire.

On the American side, Benedict Arnold and his men were surprised by the number and power of those same gunboats. He had been expecting seven or eight of these vessels, which were well suited to lake fighting. Now twenty-two boats, a few of them furnished with cannon larger than any he possessed, roared at his fleet.

The sun reached its zenith in the cobalt sky. Wild cumulus clouds, excited by the drama below, went flying by. The guns gushed tumbling white clouds themselves, the sulfurous smoke billowing in the wind. "At half past twelve, the engagement became General," Arnold observed, "and very warm."

∽

Around that time, Arnold squinted along the sight of one of the 18-pounder cannon projecting from the side of the *Congress*. He would later note that he had been "obliged . . . to point most of the guns on board the *Congress*, which I believe did good execution." It was a duty that a commander would normally have left to a competent gunner, but Arnold's men were unpracticed in the fine art of aiming a gun on the deck of a plunging boat.

He called out directions to the half-dozen men working the piece. They eased its carriage to one side using wooden crowbars known as handspikes. He tapped a wedge that supported the gun's breach. Although the barrel weighed more than two tons, its balance allowed it to tip easily on the pivots or trunnions that supported it. He adjusted the elevation upward.

He hesitated, coordinating the galley's rise and fall on the waves with the slight delay that occurred after the match was put to the gun's touch hole. He gave the order: "Fire!"

The big gun heaved backward and was brought up with a jerk by the thick rope looped around its breech and attached to the galley's gunwale. The jolt ricocheted through the ship. A blossom of smoke embraced the scene in front, then dissipated as the wind swept it south toward the enemy.

Arnold had been aiming at the British flagship *Maria*, which lay almost a mile away. He saw no sign that he had hit the schooner. In fact, he had missed, but just barely. The five-and-a-half-inch ball, a dense and lethal concentration of iron, flew straight at the distant ship. It passed over the main boom, from which the sail had been dropped.

Leaning over that boom watching the action were General Guy Carleton and his physician, Dr. Knox. In a later account of the battle, Knox noted that Carleton, while walking up and down the quarterdeck "with the most uncommon complacency of mind and intrepidity," had commented that the *Maria* was not close enough to the action. At that instant came the shocking near miss. No man could avoid flinching as a cannonball tore the air within a few feet of him. Carleton made no further mention of moving closer to the enemy guns. He asserted his dignity by remarking, "Well, Doctor, how do you like a sea fight?"

Such nonchalance was a pose learned by military officers. But the event had an effect on the battle. Commodore Pringle was all too aware of the peril that threatened the expedition commander. British Army lieutenant James Hadden suggested that because "the Com'r in Chief was on Board the Commodore," Pringle decided to move the *Maria* even farther away from the fight.

Pringle passed the order to John Starke, the schooner's captain, to ease the *Maria* southward until she was out of the danger zone and drop anchor. For Starke, acutely sensitive to the fine points of naval decorum, it was too much. He considered such an action cowardly. He changed his position but refused to lower the *Maria*'s anchor.

Starke may have been thinking about the case of Admiral John Byng, a British officer who not twenty years earlier had been court-martialed for failing to do his utmost in a battle against the French fleet off Minorca. Found guilty, Byng had been executed by firing squad on his own quarterdeck.

In any case, the *Maria* continued to hover on the fringe of the fighting. Pringle was criticized for the decision. The *Maria* was the best sailing ship in the fleet and carried fourteen 6-pounder cannon, two more than her sister ship, the *Carleton*. To take her out of the fight just as it was reaching a climax was a questionable move at best.

General Carleton presumably concurred with the maneuver, since he could easily have overridden the order, but his view was not recorded. He was a notoriously secretive man. Lieutenant Digby said that Guy Carleton was "one of the most distant, reserved men in the world." He admitted that the experienced commander possessed "a coolness and steadiness which few can attain." But his behavior that day, he said, was "very unpleasing."

Starke and the other lieutenants who lambasted Pringle noted that "yourself in the *Maria* lay to with the topsails, and was the only person in the fleet who showed no inclination to fight." The lieutenants' letter was no casual criticism. They asserted that Pringle might receive the proper "reward" for his handling of the battle under the twelfth and thirteenth articles of war. Those statutes stated that to "withdraw or keep back" in battle or to "forbear to pursue the chase of any enemy, pirate or rebel," was behavior deserving of a death sentence.

✺

Distant from the British flagship, the fight went on.

"During the affair," Captain Pausch observed, "it could have been a bit after one o'clock, the naval battle became very serious." It was a veteran soldier's sober way of saying that the Valcour channel had turned into a maelstrom of violence. On both sides, the men forgot themselves. In spite of their frantic labor, they felt light, manic.

"The wind was so unfavorable," Pringle reported, "that for a considerable time nothing could be brought into action with them, but the gun boats."

The American alignment, a rough arc stretching from the island to the mainland, presented further problems for the enemy. As a British boat came close to the middle of the line, it approached a focal point where all the American vessels could concentrate their fire.

The fight became a punching match between the American vessels and the enemy gunboats from "musket shot" range, about two hundred yards. Angry blasts erupted from each line every few seconds. Hits crashed into hulls and tore through rigging. Misses plowed the water and threw up geysers around the targets. Balls striking the stacked fascines blasted them to kindling. The American gunners tried to remember their hastily learned lessons—make every shot count, wait for the roll of your vessel.

The noise of the guns reared up on its hind legs. Men breathed smoke down sulfur-scraped throats. Their inflamed eyes swelled in their sockets.

All now understood an iron rule of naval warfare: in a battle, a ship offered nowhere to hide. On land, running away was at least a possibility. No man could run on water. Amid the deadly barrage, they could only envy the fish, safe in the subaqueous stillness beneath the waves.

After the battle, Captain Pausch wrote that "the rebels directed their cannon none too badly, because our frigates, as I later saw, were patched with boards and caulking." It was high praise for amateur gunners.

For his part, Carleton would later compliment his own gunboat crews for "the good service done, in the first action, by the spirited conduct of a number of officers and men of the Corps of Artillery." The crews of the gunboats kept up their assault "tho' under the Enemies whole fire and unsupported," Lieutenant Hadden observed, "all the King's Vessels having dropped too far to Leeward."

⌒

Not all.

For professional military men, a battle was more than a horrific and destructive ordeal. It was an opportunity. This was the great test for which they had long prepared. In a moment, a brilliant decision, a heroic act, or a stroke of luck could make an officer's career. Even in wartime, battles were rare. For ambitious men, they could quite literally be the chance of a lifetime. Action could bring a promotion, accompanied by power and wealth.

James Dacres was on an upward trajectory in the Royal Navy. Born in Gibraltar, a son of the secretary in the British garrison there, he had entered the navy at thirteen and made lieutenant by the age of twenty. With the outbreak of the American war, he was appointed second lieutenant aboard the *Blonde*, a fast, thirty-two-gun warship assigned to escort the troop carriers sent to reinforce Quebec. One of his passengers on the transatlantic voyage was General John Burgoyne, an ambitious officer in his own right.

After serving in the St. Lawrence River during the American retreat, Dacres was assigned to take twenty men from the *Blonde* and assume command of the *Carleton*, the fifty-nine-foot-long schooner armed with twelve 6-pounder cannon. The prospect of an easy victory over an inferior American fleet was a sparkling chance for glory and promotion.

In the middle of the afternoon, Commodore Pringle, perhaps hoping to sort out the confusion, sent up the flag signal for all his ships to drop anchor. *Inflexible* captain Schank reported rowing back to get Pringle's permission for his ship and Dacres's *Carleton* to attack the American line together. The idea was to obtain a position where they could break into the tight arc and disrupt the enemy formation. Pringle approved.

Still only twenty-seven, Dacres saw opportunity before him. From beneath his thick black eyebrows, he looked on the unfolding mayhem with a steady gaze. He had the advantage of a smart ship and a familiar crew. The men followed his crisp orders to trace a zigzag path northward.

Dacres was able, through a "lucky flaw" in the wind, to approach the center of the American arc. The *Inflexible* was unable to accompany him—the gust caught the frigate head-on and Captain Schank was forced to fall off again to the south.

From his quarterdeck, Dacres, a master mariner, peered across at an enemy that in no way resembled the ragtag collection of poorly managed ships he had anticipated meeting. Through his spyglass, Dacres could see that the row galleys were larger and more heavily armed than his own ship. Aboard the one in the center, he could make out the uniform of a senior officer, who must be the notorious Benedict Arnold.

The American gondolas were smaller but carried powerful 12-pounders in their bows. All were anchored under bare poles, only occasionally hoisting canvas to shift position. They did not have to worry about adjusting to the wind, only about keeping up a continual fire with their big guns.

Commodore Pringle noted that "the *Carleton* schooner, by much perseverance, at last got up to [the gunboats'] assistance." He regretted that "none of the other vessels of the fleet could then get up."

Dacres came up to the line where the British gunboats were keeping up a blistering fire at the enemy. He kept going. A momentary deflection of the wind by the trees of the island pushed the *Carleton* forward "nearly into the middle of the Rebel half-moon."

There he ordered his men to drop the *Carleton*'s anchor so that she would not be blown backward. Sailors rigged a spring cable, similar to the ones the Americans had deployed, and proceeded to haul the ship broadside and bring her main cannon to bear on the enemy. They began a "smart fire."

Benedict Arnold and his crews had a hard time scoring hits on the enemy gunboats. A British artilleryman noted that the vessels "being low in the Water made the Shot go over their heads." But the flat side of a schooner, much closer and with its sails and rigging towering above, presented a delicious target. Arnold sent out word to focus all guns on the *Carleton*. The schooner, Hadden noted, "immediately received the Enemies whole fire without intermission."

Soon "she was suffering most severely," a man on board remembered. Although practiced mariners, the British sailors had acquired little experience of battle during the years of peace since 1763. Now they watched as a cannonball knocked down their midshipman, Robert Brown, and shattered his arm. Before the stunned young officer could be led below, a chunk of flying tackle from the rigging struck Captain Dacres in the head. He fell unconscious to the deck.

Seeing no signs of life in their commander, the crew members lifted Dacres's bleeding body to heave it overboard. It was the standard way of dealing with fatalities in the heat of battle. The goal was to dispose of the dead man quickly, to minimize the pooling of blood on the deck, and to maintain the morale of the survivors.

The men looked around for direction. With two officers out of action, authority on the ship devolved to a petty officer, Edward Pellew, who held the rank of master's mate on the *Blonde*. Only nineteen, Pellew did not hesitate to assume full command of the *Carleton*.

In different circumstances, Benedict Arnold would have admired the young officer. Pellew had been born to a seafaring family in the remote Cornwall district of southwest England. His father died when Edward was eight, and the boy had to make his own way up from modest circumstances, starting as a ship's boy on a naval frigate when he was thirteen.

Lacking the fortune or patronage needed to advance, Pellew had relied on his native pluck. He grew to become a large, muscular youth with the agility and coordination needed to scamper up ratlines and furl sails among storm-tossed rigging. In February 1776, when Burgoyne had come aboard the *Blonde* in England to return to Canada, he was amused to notice Pellew performing a handstand from a yardarm that extended high above the water.

When they reached the other side of the Atlantic, the naval commander, Sir Charles Douglas, sent Pellew and the other *Blonde* crewmen to serve on the *Carleton* under Dacres. The assignment at first entailed a summer's worth of long hours and hard work preparing the ship. But for a teenager it promised high adventure once they set sail to seek out the enemy. Like Dacres, Pellew was eager to attract the attention of superiors. Now he had his chance.

His first commendable service was to recognize that while bloodied, Dacres still had life in him. He screamed at the sailors to keep them from tossing the lieutenant overboard. He ordered that the wounded man be taken below to join the injured midshipman, whose arm was even now being amputated.

Asserting his command of the ship, Pellew shouted out orders he had heard during the endless drill that had filled his six years in the navy. His shipmates automatically trusted him and began maneuvering the ship at anchor and firing the guns at the rebels as fast as they could load and aim.

For the longest hour of Pellew's young life, the *Carleton* was a pugilist fighting a mob. Iron fists slammed into her sides, making the thick planks crack and shudder. Lethal projectiles hissed overhead. Grapeshot clattered like hail. Splinters and tackle rained down from above, turning the air dangerous. The crew fired their 6-pounders again and again. The ship trembled with each blast.

Men fell. Some screamed; some lay deathly silent. Blood splashed and pooled in cracks and scuppers. Billows of swirling smoke seemed intent on drawing a choking veil over the awful scene.

Cheering on the American gunners, Jahiel Stewart noted, "We Cut her Rigging most all away & bored her through and through."

The pounding was beginning to tell. Water was pouring into the *Carleton*'s hull and already stood two feet deep in her well.

Still no British ship could come to the schooner's aid. All around, the British gunboats and American warships exchanged a torrent of unrelenting fire. Was it possible the patriots could actually win this battle?

21

◆━━━━◆━━━━◆

With Great Fury

AND HE GATHERED THEM TOGETHER INTO A PLACE
called in the Hebrew tongue Armageddon. To the patriots at Valcour
Island, raised on Bible verses, the imagery of Revelation was familiar. The words suddenly assumed a terrifying reality. *And there were
voices, and thunders, and lightnings; and there was a great earthquake,
such as was not since men were upon the earth, so mighty an earthquake,
and so great.*

The strait where the battle raged shook with the maddening,
unrelenting concussions of cannon. Young Pascal De Angelis, in
the heat of the battle aboard the *Trumbull,* noted that in early
afternoon "the Enemy Fleet attacked ours with Great fury, and
we Returned the fire with as Great Sperit and Vigar and the most
Desparate canannading."

Benedict Arnold's uniform stood out at a distance, and his
active leadership made him conspicuous to his own men as well
as to the enemy. The British directed fire at the *Congress,* which
dominated the center of the line, hoping to kill the charismatic
American officer. Their hits pounded the galley's hull, making the
ship tremble like a man suffering fits of ague. One cannonball, then

another and another, gouged the mainmast and cracked the vessel's long cantilevered yardarm.

Arnold, caught up in the exquisite excitement, could not get enough of the firing. The blasts of the cannon left his uniform spattered with powder, his face a dark mask pierced by the whites of eager eyes. He paid special attention to the vessel's 18-pounders, the most formidable cannon he possessed and the ones with the longest range. The echoes from every explosion were "tremendous," he remembered. The bay turned to a soundscape of uproar.

One of the men who served under Arnold declared that "he was our fighting general, and a bloody fellow he was. . . . It was 'Come on, boys'—'twasn't 'Go, boys.'" At times Arnold leapt into a bateau to have himself rowed to other vessels to relay instructions or to encourage and shout praise to the hardworking crews. He recognized that "we suffered much from want of seamen and gunners." Yet in spite of these shortcomings, the Americans were holding the enemy at bay.

The men knew about the *lake of fire burning with brimstone* and the *ever-burning Sulphur*. The taste of burnt gunpowder mixed with the metallic smell of human blood. They had been told of *horrid confusion heaped upon confusion*. Now an unrelenting pandemonium seemed to grip the world.

ᴈ

Arnold's gunners continued to direct their fire at the British schooner, the one vessel bold enough to approach their line. They were determined to destroy the *Carleton* as revenge for the loss of the *Royal Savage*. The repeated close-range blasts of the American cannon were so loud they left some men bleeding from the ears. All were consumed in an uproar that threatened to shake apart a man's soul.

A lucky American shot cut the *Carleton*'s spring cable. With the crew no longer able to maneuver her to broadside, her gunfire diminished. Edward Pellew, still in command of the harried vessel, finally spotted the "signal of recall" from Commodore Pringle's distant flagship. Now a new problem arose. Rebel fire had damaged the *Carleton* so badly that she was in no condition to obey the order. Sailors could not get her under way.

The schooner was pointing into the wind. To move, crewmen had to bring her bow across and then fall off to the south. But the jib sail, which would swing her around, was caught under a tangle of rope that had dropped from above.

Although he was for now the ship's captain, Pellew took on the duties of an able seaman. He crawled up the steep bowsprit and hacked with his knife at the mess of rope, trying desperately to free the crucial sail. While he worked, American crews fired at him with shot and grape. Marines took aim with muskets. The balls shrieked past him like demented insects. He found it impossible to set the sail or to catch enough wind to draw the ship around.

A crewman on the *Carleton* shouted that friendly boats were approaching. Captain Schank, seeing the schooner helpless, had sent two longboats from the *Inflexible* to tow her out of danger. Pellew ordered thick ropes passed down to them. The rescuers secured them to their own sterns. Ten strong-backed oarsmen in each boat leaned into their task. With much effort, still under a zinging barrage of American fire, they began to haul the schooner around and, with agonizing slowness, get her moving.

As the *Carleton* came broadside to the American line, another chance shot severed one of the tow ropes. A single boat could not move the waterlogged ship, which was now more exposed than ever. Pellew ordered men to fix a new rope in the ship's bow and pass it to the longboat. No one moved.

By that point, the teenage Pellew, drunk with the juice of battle, must have felt indestructible. Something had to be done. Someone had to do it. "Seeing all hesitate," one account related, "for indeed it appeared a death-service, he ran forward and did it himself."

Again defying a hail of fire, he managed to attach the line. The two longboats dragged the schooner away from the fight. As the press of fire eased, Pellew surveyed the damage. His vessel was crippled but salvageable. He ordered men to work the pumps and try to keep ahead of the water leaking in. He numbered his casualties—of the twenty men who had gotten the ship under way before dawn, eight were dead. Another six, including Lieutenant Dacres and Midshipman Brown, had been wounded.

Pellew's coolness under fire hinted at the course of the young seaman's career. He would rise to become an admiral and gain a reputation as one of the premier British frigate commanders of the Napoleonic Wars. The Cornish youth would one day be named a peer of the realm, the first Viscount Exmouth.

From the American line, the wind carried the faint cheering of the sailors. They had withstood the fire of the most intimidating ship sent against them so far and had mauled her badly.

The sun was taking on a golden hue as it slid toward the mountains in the southwest. Both combatants had taken painful punches; both were still standing. Arnold had put the British on notice that the Americans had the cause and will, the strength and means to stand up to a superior enemy. Guy Carleton looked on perplexed, frustrated, and impatient for his fleet to subdue these provincial upstarts.

The battle was not over.

❧

At the beginning of the eighteenth century, the French had begun stamping their cannon with the phrase *Ultima ratio regnum*, "the last argument of kings." Down the centuries, most guns had belonged to royalty and were indeed the foundation of their power. The cannon brought to bear against the American rebels at Valcour Island were King George III's ultimate—and, he thought, unanswerable—argument for remaining loyal to Britain.

Once the schooner *Carleton* withdrew, the battle was again carried on by the rugged British gunboats. They now formed their line some seven hundred yards back, out of range of grapeshot fired from American guns.

Stretched across the Valcour strait were nineteen boats manned by British seamen and soldiers of the artillery. Three more were assigned to expert Hessian gunners. The boats bore evocative names like *Invincible*, *Dreadful*, *Inferno*, and *Vesuvius*. Their crews worked unceasingly to fire their 24-pounders, howitzers, and other guns. Their array of extended oars, always moving to adjust and aim the boats, brought to mind the legs of giant water beetles.

Facing this array of boats were the American warships: the three galleys, each carrying eight to ten cannon; the eight gondolas, with three guns each; and the more lightly armed cutter *Lee* and schooner *Revenge*. The crews were firing all of the guns on all of the ships as quickly as they could load them.

With the heavier British vessels out of the contest, the two sides were almost evenly matched in firepower. But the British had several advantages: their heavy cannon had the power to break open a hull; their new bronze pieces fired balls more accurately and at a higher velocity than American cannon; and their gunners had greater skill at loading and aiming their guns. Yet as the afternoon wore on and the gun duel continued, the amateur American artillerymen continued to hold their own.

❧

Early in the battle, the cracks of musket fire, sounds that might startle a man from across the strait, could be heard in a steady rattle. Marksmen fired from the ships. Native American warriors and British commandos shot from the mainland and from Valcour Island itself, where they had landed and found cover. They kept up a steady fire, one patriot noted, "till we brought our brod side to bar on the Indians & gave them such dosers of grape shot which caused them to retreat in the woods."

To be under musket fire was unnerving. Bullets hissed past and thudded into masts and decks. The men were glad that their stacks of fascines blocked much of this fire. For all its noise, the racket of small arms amounted to little compared to the tremendous roar of the cannon. Each blast was an apocalypse. The big guns emitted concussive blows beyond sound, low-pitched explosions of air that hit men in their bowels and made them tense involuntarily. The water reflected each shot in a wash of ripples—the air trembled as if it would come apart.

These booms, roaring across the open water, came not as single notes but in monstrous chords, giant arpeggios of explosions. Again and again they merged into a single roar. And they continued, minute by minute, as the day lurched on toward dusk. The British gunboats fired more than a thousand rounds that afternoon. The Americans answered shot for shot.

Interwoven with the noise of the guns was a battle song of yelling. Officers roared orders for ears all but deaf from the clamor. They hailed nearby boats through speaking trumpets. Men flung hoarse curses—*Damn! The devil rot you! By the heavenly heart of God!* Men let loose warnings, cheers, snarls, prayers. Some screamed nonsense just to clear their brains of unnamable emotions.

∽

What made the watery battlefield most trying for the men was the prospect of random death. The deadly projectiles added terrible grace notes to the wild commotion. Men spotted a flash of fire and a mushroom of smoke from a distant boat. A taut second later came a shrieking metallic banshee rushing at a speed that took their breath away.

A cannonball was the fist of God. It might skip across the water. Might whiz past, ghostlike. Might crash into the hull, shaking the ship's skeleton to its deepest joint. Bar and chain shot had their own demonic squeals as they came spinning into the rigging, tearing ropes and shredding canvas.

Each fighter knew that he could blink his eyes and plunge into forever-darkness. Death grabbed men—shipmates, friends—and ripped the life out of them with sudden and hideous indifference. No one knew when he too might be a victim. Each realized that his future depended on a whim of fortune, that his dear life was a speck of thistledown.

The crews were working, sweating, and breathing in a cauldron of death. It was a fact that no man could endure and all had to endure. It was reality not for a brief, terrifying few seconds but for hour after endless hour.

To the men's haunted eyes, the scene took on an otherworldly quality. Time swelled and compressed, rushed ahead and stood still.

Sunlight pulsed. The liquid crimson of blood, shocking at first, became commonplace. A marine firing from the rigging of a gondola was shot. He fell only partway, held by his lifeline, and dripped blood onto the scene below. A man whose scalp had been grazed by a bullet went about his work with a veil of blood washing his face.

"Our decks were stain'd with blood," wrote Lieutenant Isaiah Canfield, a soldier drafted for lake duty on the galley *Trumbull*. Some of that blood was his own from a wound received in the battle. Elijah Towner, a seventeen-year-old Connecticut marine on the *Washington*, later remembered watching his lieutenant struck down by whirling bar shot, two balls joined by an iron rod. The same projectile killed another seaman. The young marine was standing so near his comrade that "his flesh and brains" splattered Towner's face.

༄

Jahiel Stewart remembered, "I was aboard of the hospital sloop [*Enterprise*] and they brought the wounded aboard of us." Men on all the ships saw sights they had never imagined: human bodies opened, white bone laid bare, the pulse of lacerated flesh. The eyes of injured men, pupils dilated, groped the scene with ghastly intensity. Ruddy skin turned a leprous white as blood spilled from torn arteries.

Supervising the firing of the great guns on the galley *Trumbull* was a twenty-one-year-old Rhode Island farm boy who, for the past four years, had been apprenticed to the shipbuilding trade. Benoni Simmons had taken an early stand against arbitrary British rule and joined in the burning of the crown revenue cutter *Gaspee* back in 1772. He had participated in the siege of Boston, marched to Canada, learned to handle artillery, helped build ships at Ticonderoga, and, as his widow wrote years later, "entered on board of the Galley *Trumbull*, Capt. Seth Warner, as master gunner at the rate of thirteen dollars per month." She related how, during the battle at Valcour, Benoni "had the misfortune to lose his arm by a shot from the Enemy."

"The Doctors cut off great many legs and arms," Stewart wrote, "and see seven men threw overboard that died with their wounds while I was aboard."

The bodies were heaved into the lake without ceremony. Dead men who had been intimate companions in laughter and misery slowly pirouetted beneath the water. Their battle over, they sank to the depths and were wrapped in the arms of eternity.

༄

Late in the afternoon, a cannonball fired by American gunners skimmed over the water and struck a gunboat manned by Hessian artillerymen and captained by a Lieutenant Dufais. The ball crashed into the hull just below the boat's 6-pounder bow gun, smashing through the planks above the waterline. It continued on, killing a man named Rossmer, one of nine cannoneers. It lopped off the leg of a rower behind him, then crashed into the boat's ammunition locker, setting off part of the gunpowder in a smoky explosion.

Captain Pausch, the Hessian commander, saw the catastrophe from his own gunboat and had to wait for the smoke to clear before he could recognize "by cords on their caps" that it was his men, not a British artillery crew, who had been hit. While he watched, another explosion heaved the stricken boat's ammunition chest into the air.

Pausch directed his men to row their boat over to assist. All was chaos in the foundering vessel. Some men had leapt into the cold water. The helmsman and a young drummer boy had burned to death in the eruption of flame. Pausch's men helped eighteen survivors into their own boat as the damaged gunboat listed alarmingly. That made forty-two men in Pausch's now dangerously overcrowded boat. The boat that had been hit was engulfed by lake water and sank out of sight.

"Here I had each moment to fear suddenly drowning both myself and all those with me," Pausch noted. One of the British gunboats, the *Infernal*, pulled alongside and took three men off. Sailors carefully rowed both boats to the rear.

The Americans took heart at having sunk an enemy vessel, but they had little to cheer about. The gunboats had pommeled the patriot ships again and again. The galley *Washington* was "hulled a Number of Times, her Main Mast shot through." Her captain, John Thatcher, had been wounded in the leg. Her sailing master had received an injury as well. A direct hit had killed her first lieutenant outright.

The *Trumbull* had also been badly damaged by enemy fire. A cannonball almost severed her mainmast; only the ropes of the rigging kept it from falling. When it did snap it plummeted to the deck and the blow "shivered it almost to pieces."

The gondola *Philadelphia* was struck again and again. As the sun disappeared over the trees on the western shore, a 24-pounder ball from one of the British gunboats crashed into that gondola's hull. Water poured in. Crewmen scrambled to patch the leak while others bailed.

The American lieutenant Bayze Wells summed up the day succinctly: "The battle lasted eight hours very hot." It was an ordeal that none of the men had endured before, and it would echo in memory for the rest of their lives. All day, the natural world seemed to pitch and tear; the wind, the waves, the swaying trees screamed and grappled in imitation of the fighting men.

Citizens of the new country had fought regulars from the old. Young, green volunteers had stood against veterans. Farmers had faced soldiers. All had endured the sickening exhilaration, the slow-motion horror of combat. All had looked death in the eye.

"There ensued a most terrible fire without the least intermission till half past five p.m. when the enemy drew off," was how Colonel Wigglesworth summed up the day.

Before the British pulled back, they took advantage of a diminishing wind to bring up their largest warships for one last go at the rebel fleet. First the radeau *Thunderer* struggled forward as well as her crew could manage and "tested its 24-pound cannons against the enemy" from long range. They had little effect.

Then the *Inflexible* finally made it back into the fight. In the twilight, her canvas towered majestically over the water. Handled by experienced Royal Navy men, armed with eight polished brass 12-pounder cannon on each side, she took up a position in the center of Valcour channel.

The autumn sky was exhaling its light like the sigh of an exhausted man. Dark seeped from the surrounding forests to cover the water. American gunners took aim at the inviting target, which Captain Schank kept well back from their line.

His crew swung the ship around. Schank gave the order. Her guns rang out in a single ripping explosion, a nerve-shattering climax to the day's desperate cannonading. The British naval commander, Charles Douglas, noted that "five broadsides silenced their whole line."

The firing from the *Inflexible* did inflict further damage on the beleaguered American ships, but it was darkness that finally brought the long ordeal to an end. The guns fell quiet. Stars began blinking to life in the firmament.

༜

It was not quite over. British commanders were concerned that under the cover of darkness, the Americans would make an attempt to recapture the *Royal Savage*. They sent a boatload of men, commanded by Captain Starke of the *Maria*, to set fire to the stranded schooner. Arnold's remaining papers and possessions were devoured with the ship. When the flames reached her magazine, kegs of gunpowder exploded, sending the flash of one final clap of destruction to light the clouds. She continued to burn, the wavering glow dancing for hours across the black water.

Fueled all day by continuous action, warriors on both sides now sank into a ponderous, deadening fatigue. Amazed at their own survival, they fought off sleep and turned their thoughts to the future.

The British officers understood their course. They would renew their ammunition, repair damage to their vessels, organize their forces, wait out the darkness, and attain a decisive victory as soon as daylight reappeared.

The American fighters were acutely aware of their predicament. They were trapped inside a narrow watery cul-de-sac. The steady northerly wind, which shielded them from a full-scale enemy advance, was dying down, but still it would complicate an escape if they tried to flee northward.

To the south, the enemy lay between them and the route to safety. Their ammunition was spent and could not be replenished. Their boats were mangled and leaking. The *Philadelphia* was in imminent danger of sinking into the black water—the galley *Washington* had already come alongside her to take off her crew. The land around them was swarming with British soldiers and their Indian allies.

They had paid a heavy price. Young Pascal De Angelis recorded: "A boat Came a Long side and took out our Wounded and carried them on board of the Hospetal sloop Interprise our Wounded were Lieut. [Isaiah] Canfield. Boatswain [Giles] Cone. Gunner [Benoni] Simmons. James Timberlake and Anderson are dead." Men who had greeted the dawn with bright faces had not seen the dusk. Those who had survived all asked the same question: What now?

22

Extreme Obscurity

AFTER THE ENORMOUS TUMULT, STILLNESS RETURNED TO the Great Warpath. It calmed the heavens and blanketed the water. It lay down in the hills. Like a great weight, it pressed on the exhausted men. Only the gulping murmur of wavelets and the faint wails and groans of the injured sounded across the dark water.

With a sigh of relief, the lake began to exhale mist—chilled air was rolling down from the hills and condensing the moisture over the water. The new moon had already dropped below the horizon on the heels of the sun. The night was lit only by the fire still burning on the *Royal Savage* and by constellations. Orion was beginning his climb over the eastern horizon to stare once more at the consequences of human folly.

Far up the lake, silence touched the ears of soldiers waiting at Crown Point and straining for sounds from the north. When no more reverberations rolled along the water, the officers there declared it over. The infantrymen would lie sleepless on their arms that night, not knowing what had happened to the fleet, imagining the imminent arrival of red-coated regulars.

Benedict Arnold congratulated his crew on the *Congress*. The men of the fleet had bearded the lion. They had bludgeoned one of the king's ships. They had sunk a gunboat. They had repulsed the enemy. He could not have hoped for more. The men he had labeled "indifferent," "a wretched motley crew," and the "refuse of every Regiment" had exceeded all his expectations.

And what of Arnold's own strategy? He understood that war was not a dumbshow of violence but a contest of spirit. Battles and campaigns turned on the courage of men and the perceptions of commanders, not just on the strength of the forces or the tally of casualties. Imagination, morale, will, and desire were what determined success or failure. And fear—especially fear.

By meeting the enemy in a forward position and keeping up a steady cannonade, Arnold had suggested to Guy Carleton that the Americans possessed abundant supplies of gunpowder. The fight that day had run counter to the British commander's notion that the American patriots were timid or insincere in their rebellion, or that they were unprepared for war. The provincials had fought with determination. They had inflicted damage. Carleton could not avoid the sinking feeling that a long and costly effort would be needed to subdue them. It was what Arnold wanted his opponent to think.

British Army lieutenant Thomas Hadden later gave his opinion that "upon the whole the British Fleet was fully a match for the Enemy." It was a telling admission. The Royal Navy of Great Britain had fought an impromptu collection of American vessels manned by untrained sailors and only matched them.

The Americans had put on a show for Carleton's benefit. They had paid grievously for the day's performance. Sixty or more men dead. Arms and legs shot off. Ships damaged. But they had not backed down. They had played the drama to the end.

Part of it was strategy, part the magic of Arnold's improvisations. As always, he had relied on a clairvoyant knack for reading a situation and reacting. Now he would have to come up with his greatest conjuring trick of all.

⁓

As soon as the guns ceased, Arnold sent messages to General Waterbury, Colonel Wigglesworth, and the boat captains to come aboard the *Congress*. The officers stood again in the cramped cabin where they had met that morning. They gathered around the same table, the boards now stained with the blood of the wounded men who had been treated there. Gore spattered their own uniforms. Their faces were dirtied with the soot of expended powder. Their ears rang. Their muscles ached. Fatigue buzzed in their brains.

They looked at each other with blinking, bloodshot eyes. It hardly seemed possible that as recently as eight o'clock that morning they had been young and eager. Now they felt ten years older, stunned by the passage of a day.

They recognized that the situation was a desperate one. All of their vessels had been damaged by the enemy cannonade. "The *Congress* and *Washington* have suffered greatly," Arnold would write to General Gates, "the latter lost her first lieutenant killed, captain and master wounded. The *New-York* lost all her officers, except her captain."

He went on to detail the damage to his main ships: a dozen cannonballs had pierced the *Congress*, seven of them "between wind and water," that is, in the space exposed when the ship heeled. The *Washington* had been hulled a number of times and her mainmast shot through. "Both vessels are very leaky and want repairing." The cutter *Lee* had lost all her officers dead or wounded.

Arnold reassigned men. David Hawley, captain of the *Royal Savage*, took over the *Washington* in place of the wounded Captain Thatcher. Junior officers and seamen in other vessels were ordered to step up to positions of command.

Nearby, a drama was unfolding aboard the gondola *Philadelphia*. The 24-pounder cannonball fired by a British gunboat was lodged in her hull at the waterline. The damage allowed lake water to pour in faster than her frantic crew could bail. Her bow was already canting. The *Washington* had pulled alongside to help. Men were trying to transfer supplies and ammunition to the larger ship. They stumbled in the dark, splashing in the cold water that crept over the *Philadelphia*'s decks. They began to scramble onto the galley. The last man leapt off. Her crew endured the dismal sight of their craft disappearing into darkness.

The reports of damaged vessels were alarming. So was the acute shortage of powder and shot. "Every vessels ammunition was nearly three fourths spent," Arnold would report. Some of the gondolas were down to fewer than half a dozen balls for their main guns. Their powder stores were dwindling. The enemy gunboats, on the other hand, were even now restoring their firepower from ample stores aboard the *Thunderer*. Arnold's commanders recognized that they faced an "enemy greatly superior to us in ships and men."

Danger was rushing toward the patriots with the dawn. The wind had slacked off. They could not know if it would continue from the north. They were in the very trap that David Waterbury had warned of that morning. Although some suggested escaping to the north, the shoals there were a danger to their boats, especially in the dark. Nor could they know if British warships had closed that route. They were sure only that the enemy awaited them at the mouth of the strait, and that hostile Indians and British infantry occupied both the western shore and Valcour Island itself.

Hoping to rally his officers, Arnold put the best possible light on the fleet's situation. He lavished praise on the performance of the crews. No men could have done better. He insisted that their situation was not as grave as it seemed. They would not surrender. He had a plan.

After a brief discussion, the officers all agreed on the course of action their commander laid out. It was their best, their only hope.

∾

"It was thought prudent to retire to Crown Point" was how the laconic Colonel Wigglesworth summed up the council of war. He continued, "I was ordered to get underway as soon as it was dark and show a light astern for the gondolas, in order to retreat up the lake as fast as possible."

Arnold's plan was as audacious as it was risky. Sailors on the American vessels would quietly raise their anchors and head south in the direction of the British fleet. They would escape not by retreating but by advancing.

By seven o'clock, two hours after the guns ceased, a pitch-black night had settled in. They were ready. Although battered, the *Trum-*

bull, from which Wigglesworth commanded, would lead the way, her experienced captain, Seth Warner, acting as pilot for the fleet. Using just her small spanker sail at the rear and the sweep oars as needed, he brought his ship as close as he dared to the western shore of the lake, then turned south.

Warner marked the stern of his vessel with a shielded lantern that gave a glimmer of light straight back to guide the gondolas. Sailors extinguished all other lights. The remaining vessels followed in a silent procession.

Officers enforced complete silence. Wounded men were moved to cabins, their involuntary groans muffled. Shirts were wrapped around the oars to quiet their movement in the locks. Sailors applied grease to the ropes and pulleys to prevent squeaking.

The damaged galleys *Washington* and *Congress*, bringing up the rear of the procession, were the most heavily armed of the vessels. If it came to a fight, they would do all they could to hold off the enemy. If they made good their escape, Benedict Arnold would be among the last to leave the bay.

They moved down the far side of the channel. The trees that lined the shore were etched in black silhouettes. They sailed inshore, daring the shallow water. During the eighteen days they had spent around Valcour Island, Arnold had insisted the officers take soundings so that they knew the profile of the strait by heart.

The night was alive with fear. The men imagined that the contest that had so recently gone quiet could spring to life in an instant. A British ship might come rearing out of the darkness, its guns erupting in flame.

To men stunned by a day of intense fighting, this ghostly procession could not have been more eerie. As they pulled on their sweeps, the sailors now and then felt the resistance of some obstacle floating in the water. A chunk of spar? A barrel? The floating body of one of the men heaved to a watery grave?

Flames still danced above the *Royal Savage* across the strait at the corner of Valcour Island. The light from the fire barely reached the far shore; it only illuminated the fog, further obscuring vision. The Americans heard the hammering of sailors making repairs on British vessels. They heard men talking, officers bawling orders. They crept quietly on. Many found themselves holding their breath.

As the vessels moved southward, the fog continued to build. Although it might serve as a protective blanket to shield them from the enemy, the captains, like all sailors, hated fog. There were no paths on the water. Fog blinded the helmsman and turned movement into a perilous groping. It raised the risk of the boats losing sight of one another and veering off, lost and alone, into the midst of the British fleet dispersed somewhere on their port side.

Seth Warner had so far provided unfailing guidance to the string of ships. Now, less than a mile south of Valcour Island, he began to veer eastward, away from the coast, to avoid the outlet of the Au Sable River. In French the name meant "sandy," referring to the deposits the stream spilled into the lake. The outlet known as Au Sable Point reached eastward, beyond the far shore of Valcour Island itself. Further deposits created shifting underwater dunes around the area. In the space between these shallows and Valcour Island lay the British fleet. If the captains were able to slip through, they could strike south in the wider lake.

It was a close call. Some boats scraped bottom, some came close to being hung up in the shallows. Jahiel Stewart, on the sloop *Enterprise*, recorded, "We run a ground but got off without much difficulty."

With silence and daring, the American flotilla threaded its way up the lake, slipping past the enemy, who were, Stewart noted, "betwick us and home." He continued, "We hoisted sails, put out our oars & made all the speed we could and they did not give us one gun nor we did not fire one at them." Colonel Wigglesworth confirmed that the fleet "row'd out clear of the enemy, without being discovered."

Captain Warner led them until they reached the open waters of the lake. They were still immersed in fog—only the compass and their knowledge of the surrounding waters gave them a sense of direction. They sailed and rowed on into the night. Providence had accomplished a miracle, but the drama was not yet over.

✒

The British officers and crews had endured a frustrating day. General Carleton had hoped that by now they would have forced Arnold to surrender his small fleet and begun their swift advance up the lake toward Crown Point. Instead, he had been forced to fight an inconclusive battle in an awkward location against a determined enemy. Although his casualties were minimal, the battering of the *Carleton* and sinking of a gunboat were embarrassments. The fight had subtracted another day from the dwindling campaign season.

During the night's intermission, repair crews had patched up the damage. Sailors resupplied ammunition cases. They made the ships ready for the decisive battle, which would open in the morning, unless the Americans were wise enough to surrender before it started.

The interlude went on longer than expected. As the sky brightened, the fog continued to obscure Valcour Bay from British eyes. Then the breeze increased, sweeping the mist away. The curtain went up. General Carleton assumed the final act was about to begin. Instead, he blinked his eyes—before him lay an empty stage.

The complacent British officers peered again through their spyglasses at the anchorage. It was not to be believed. An entire enemy fleet had vanished. All that remained were the scraps of flotsam bobbing in the shifting water.

Carleton was reported to be in "a rage" that the enemy "gave us the slip." He wrote to General Burgoyne that day, explaining that the night before, Commodore Pringle had ordered the British vessels to anchor in a line opposite the Americans, "expecting in the morning to be able to engage them with our whole fleet, but, to our great mortification we perceived at day break, that they had found means to escape us unobserved by any of our guard boats."

Great mortification. The decisions that had made the daring escape possible would be debated long afterward. To Ensign Enys on the *Thunderer* it was a mystery how the rebels had passed "between us and the shore unperceived by anyone." Commodore Pringle claimed that he had ordered his vessels to "anchor in a line as near as possible to the Rebels, that their retreat might be cut off." He blandly attributed their escape to "the extreme obscurity of the night."

For the British, the confusion that had begun the day before had continued to befuddle them during the night. Just to get into line, the *Thunderer* and the gondola *Loyal Convert*, the least handy of the British vessels, had to be warped northward. Rowboats carried the ships' anchors ahead and dropped them so that the ships could be winched forward by ropes.

Captain Schank, on the *Inflexible*, wanted to spread the British line farther toward the western shore of the lake. He ordered a supply boat to take a station in that direction as a lookout. "Just as she was going away," he wrote, "I received orders from Captain Pringle to send her to cruize, between the fleet And the East Shore." Pringle was concerned that the rebels might escape out the north end of the strait and come down the main channel of the lake. He used some of his craft to keep watch there.

But it was not this precaution, or the lack of vessels, that prevented the discovery of the fleeing Americans. The lieutenants who criticized Pringle in their letter to London claimed that as darkness fell, the *Maria* had shifted half a mile away from the bay's mouth, with the *Inflexible* anchored beside her and the *Carleton* nearby. They blamed the failure on Pringle's positioning of the fleet, "by which means the rear of the British line was at least one mile from the western shore." Because of this, rather than "the extreme obscurity of the night as you are pleased to say, the rebels escaped."

The gunboats, which might have been formed into an effective picket line, were never organized as such. Lieutenant Hadden, who served on a British gunboat, noted that the vessels, "having received a small supply of Ammunition, were unaccountably order'd to Anchor under cover of a small Island without the opening of the Bay." Petit Island lay well east of the entrance to the strait.

Other factors aided the Americans' disappearing act. The fog certainly contributed. The hours-long cannonade had left the sentries with numbed ears, making them less likely to detect the stealthy American boats. The flames of the burning *Royal Savage*, rather than illuminating the scene, drew the attention of the British sailors and diminished their night vision. Exhaustion and the cold of the frigid October night combined to sap the vigilance of the crews. Everyone had to be "wideawake and on the alert," Captain Pausch wrote. But maintaining a lookout after such an ordeal was not easy.

At least one British officer admitted "this retreat did great honor to Gen'l Arnold," referring to the American by his proper military rank, a sign of respect the British usually withheld from rebel officers. Even Guy Carleton spoke of "the great diligence used by the enemy in getting away from us."

The British officers' lack of familiarity with the terrain around Valcour hampered the night watch. Without an accurate chart, Pringle was ignorant of where the shoal waters began or where rocks might be hidden. Like any sailor, he was wary of approaching too close to land, fearful that a sudden gust could drive a ship aground. He thought it prudent to pull his vessels back from the western shore and form a line farther out in the lake.

None of these considerations barred the British from their crucial mission of containing an enemy who lay directly in front of them. What tripped them up in the end was a failure of imagination.

To Benedict Arnold, the night following the battle was full of possibilities. To Carleton and Pringle, it held only the certainty of their own fixed ideas. Just as they had been sure they would find the Americans waiting for them in Cumberland Bay that morning, they were convinced that the enemy would remain motionless in the channel opposite Valcour Island through the night. "To our utter astonishment," Dr. Knox reported, "under the cover of the night Mr. Arnold sailed thro' a part of our fleet."

⁓

On the morning of October 12, Carleton's rage translated into a rush of orders to get the fleet under way. The ships sailed onto the wide expanse of the lake. One persistent legend has it that during the move, lookouts thought they spotted an enemy ship two miles east of Valcour Island. The British opened fire from a distance. In time they realized that they were shooting at the rocky cliffs of a tiny island, whose few trees suggested the outline of sails. The speck of land is called Carleton's Prize to this day.

During the morning, British sailors saw a pitching sail of one of the American vessels far up the lake. "The signal was made to sail," Captain Schank wrote, "and we soon discovered the rest of the Rebel Fleet."

The chase was on, but with its characteristic restlessness, the weather on Lake Champlain intervened. "The wind then at south and freshing up," Schank went on, "the *Carleton* not being able to carry sail was under the land which soon proved to be my case with the *Inflexible*, for she was near sinking."

Attempting to sail into the headwind, both ships had taken on water. The mighty *Inflexible*, still on her maiden cruise, proved impossible to handle under the conditions. Lieutenant Butler, her first mate, noted that "under double reeft topsails, we (in a squall) lay along so much as to become water logged. Wherefore we wore & anchored in shore, as did the *Carleton* and *Maria*."

The heavily armed British radeau *Thunderer* also had a bad time of it. Her leeboards, which the crew swung down to resist the sideways force of the wind, were torn off by the gale. She heeled over so far that water poured into her gunports.

As another British officer noted, the "wind was so hard against us we were obliged [to] put back again." They had to "give over the chase for the present," General Carleton noted. The only consolation was that "the enemy has . . . been retarded as well as us."

⁓

During the night, the crews on the American vessels had rowed against an increasingly obstinate wind from the south. It was impossible for them to stick together in the dark. Seth Warner, still in the lead, knew that below Au Sable Point, a larger cape extended from the western shore. He veered the *Trumbull* eastward to stay clear of the land. At the same time he had to avoid several rocks known to lurk in this region only a few feet below the surface.

Without a chance to eat or rest, the American sailors had strained at oars all night against a contrary wind to avoid the certainty of destruction. Aching for sleep, each man's mind was edged with nightmare. The light just beginning to seep into the heavens brought the mixed possibility of escape or renewed battle.

As dawn broke on Saturday, October 12, Arnold found his fleet divided, his vessels damaged, and an angry squall coming straight at him from the south. The boats' captains had little choice except to find shelter. Most of the vessels gathered at Schuyler's Island, a flat, mile-long chunk of rock a few hundred yards off the western shore. In an entire night of rowing, they had progressed just seven miles—a frigate with favorable wind could cover the same distance in less than an hour.

But for now, the race was suspended. Most of the American fleet pulled in beside the low bluff on the west side of Schuyler's Island. The land gave them some protection from the ferocious wind. The boats were battered, damaged, and leaking. Arnold jotted down a letter to General Gates. "Most of the fleet is this minute come to an anchor," he reported. "The Enemy's fleet is underway . . . and beating up." In fact, the British were also dropping anchor.

He sorted out the vessels according to their condition. Three boats could not be salvaged in time. The gondola *Spitfire* had foundered during the night. Back in August, her captain, Philip Ulmer, had barely saved her from sinking as the fleet came down the lake. Now he made sure that she did not fall into British hands. Her crew sailed her into deep water and broke open her hull before scrambling onto other boats. She went down to join the *Philadelphia* at the bottom of the lake.

Another gondola, the *New Jersey*, had also taken on a large volume of water in spite of the sailors' efforts at bailing. She was too damaged to go on. Her crew set her afire and boarded other ships. The cutter *Lee*, smaller than the gondolas, was judged beyond repair. Sailors took her three miles across the lake and abandoned her near the mouth of the Onion River.

Five gondolas and three galleys remained, along with the hospital ship and the small schooner *Revenge*. "The Enemy came hard against us," Bayze Wells, aboard the gondola *Providence*, remembered, "So that we ware oblig'd to leave three Gondolas and make the best of our way."

After they devoured their first food in more than a day, the crews set to work with renewed energy to repair the ships. On board the sloop *Enterprise*, Dr. McCrea did what he could for the wounded. Some men were delirious with pain; some drifted in and out of consciousness. The sloop, which had received little damage, began tacking up the lake at once, escorted by the *Revenge*. Their goal was to cover the thirty-five miles to Crown Point that day if possible—they would have to wrestle a contrary wind all the way.

At two in the afternoon, Arnold felt the wind slacken a bit. He judged the *Congress* ready to sail. The *Washington* was still too badly damaged to confront the nasty weather. Although reluctant to further divide his force, Arnold gave instructions to General Waterbury to follow him as soon as practical. Arnold's crew fell to the oars. A steady wind plowed against them, pushing mounds of dark gray clouds.

Waterbury noted that his vessel was "so torn to pieces that it was almost impossible to keep her above water." In addition, the ship's canvas had been ripped in places during the fight at Valcour, and "my sails was so shot that carrying wind split them from foot to head." Remaining anchored at Schuyler's Island, he would need a few more hours of frantic work from his crew to get her in shape to sail again.

In the aftermath of the battle at Valcour, the *Washington* had taken on board most of the crew of the *Philadelphia*, including her captain, Benjamin Rue. They took over the duties of the men on the *Washington* who had been cut down in the fighting.

Arnold's idea was that the two galleys would serve as the rear guard for the remainder of the fleet. Waterbury and David Hawley, the *Washington*'s new captain, drove the crew to complete the repairs. Their work went on until evening, when the galley finally headed south into the gloom.

Before dark closed in, a lookout on the *Washington* spotted in the distance a flash of white, the sail of a British ship.

23

In Shattered Condition

THE GALLEY *TRUMBULL* HAD REACHED LIGONIER POINT, on the Willsborough peninsula, during the morning of Saturday, October 12. Finding himself six miles ahead of the other boats and facing a fierce wind roaring out of the south, Colonel Wigglesworth ordered Captain Warner to get as close as he could under the protection of land and anchor "to wait for the fleet & stop our leaks & secure our main mast which was shot in two."

The rest of the vessels also went to anchor much of the day rather than fight the weather. Later, as the wind moderated, Wigglesworth watched the hospital ship *Enterprise* and the schooner *Revenge*, both apt at sailing against the wind, reach his position. The captains reported they had left the rest of the fleet behind at Schuyler's Island.

Next, several of the gondola captains, who had steered their boats in close to the western shore, managed to claw southward. About midnight, *Boston* captain Job Sumner, who had dropped out of Harvard to join the rebellion, came abreast of the *Trumbull*. He found the galley's crew still working on repairs. An hour later, the *Providence* also reached Ligonier Point. Her captain, Isaiah Simmons, told Wigglesworth "that the Enemy had pursued us &

had taken 1 gondola, viz, Capt. Grimes." Moses Grimes had been the captain of the *New Jersey*, which her crew had been forced to scuttle. The fire they had set to destroy her had not taken, and she would indeed be lost to the enemy.

Finally, around one-thirty in the morning, Captain Warner hoisted what sail the *Trumbull* could carry and directed the men to heave on the sweeps to get the galley moving.

The American sailors were enduring their second night without sleep. Even as fatigue pulled on them like gravity, fear awakened spent muscles. Hope lay in driving their craft southward, one oar stroke at a time, into the headwind. Choppy waves lifted the vessel and let her drop with a rhythmic thud.

The darkness pressed against the men's eyes. Their minds, shrunken by lack of sleep, had room only for the repetitive action— thrust forward the oar, bite the water, heave backward. Icy spray came over the gunwales to slap at the rowers' faces. As the wind diminished, the weary men made better progress. Past midnight, a cold rain began to pelt them. They rowed on. Now pinpricks of sleet stung their faces.

"Weighed anchor with a fresh breeze to the southward," Arnold reported that afternoon. "Our gondolas made very little way a head. In the evening the wind moderated and we made such progress that at 6 o'clock the next morning we were about off Willsborough."

Before dawn, Arnold on the *Congress* passed the same spot where, seven weeks earlier, a storm had nearly scuttled the mission. The fleet, he noted, was twenty-eight miles from Crown Point. With luck, they would arrive there ahead of the enemy.

ᴄ♫

Some of the American captains, assuming the enemy could not continue to bear down on them under the conditions, gave their crews a respite by briefly dropping anchor during the night. Those who were not officers, not on watch, and not bailing from the well dropped to the deck, their minds already swarming with dreams. They slept fitfully for an hour, maybe two. Before the sky lightened, they were up and under way once more.

By morning, the well-handled *Trumbull* was again among the lead boats, having caught up with the rest of the fleet during the night. But the galley had managed to proceed less than five miles after leaving Ligonier Point. As dawn defined the shapes of glowering clouds, she stood opposite the outlet of Gilliland's Creek (now the Bouquet River). The *Revenge*, the *Enterprise*, and the remaining gondolas were working against the wind nearby. The *Congress* and the *Washington* brought up the rear. The fleet was entering the funnel that ended at the tight bottleneck of Split Rock.

The British fleet too was thrown into disarray by the contrary wind and darkness. Captain Schank admitted that as the earliest light brought the lake into focus, he saw two schooners in the distance across the lake and "taking one of them for the Enemy we Tacked and stood after her, but soon discovering our Mistake tacked and stood to the Southward." He had crossed to the other side of the lake to chase friendly ships.

"In the morning on Sunday, 13th," Colonel Wigglesworth summed up, "the Hospital Sloop and *Revenge* were ahead & the two galleys in the rear & the rest of the gondolas rowing up in Shore & the Enemy's fleet in chase of us, the wind dying away."

From the masts of the American ships, lookouts peering down the lake could now clearly see the sails of British vessels following them five miles to the rear. With twenty miles separating the Americans from Crown Point, Arnold thought the fleet had a good chance of reaching safety.

The odds were about to change. During the morning, as both fleets trudged up the lake, the south wind began to fall off. Through his spyglass, Arnold saw the topsails of the *Inflexible* balloon as she caught a following breeze. The lake's complicated winds were bedeviling the Americans. The southerly air still smacked their faces, as if in mockery, while an opposite wind aided the enemy.

The frigate was an ominous sight. With her enormous spread of canvas and a favorable wind, the warship could rapidly bear down on the smaller American vessels. During the time it took for the altered wind to reach Arnold's sails, the enemy had closed more than a mile of the distance that separated the two fleets.

"Enemy's Fleet were very little way above Schuyler's Island," Arnold wrote of that early morning. "The Wind breezed up to the Southward so that we gained very little by beating or rowing, at the same time the Enemy took a fresh Breeze from the Northeast and by the time we reached Split Rock were along side of us."

⁓

Two days before, the Americans had met the enemy while anchored in a favorable position and sustained by a well-considered battle plan. Now they were in the open water, in a stretch of the lake that gave the British room to maneuver. It was no longer the gunboats that would be attacking—those smaller vessels had been outpaced by the swifter British sailing ships. Now the patriots would face broadsides of 12-pounder cannon. Escape was essential. The men were literally rowing for their lives.

"I do not think the retreat was conducted altogether well," David Waterbury commented, "for to be scattered for seven miles in length it was too much."

Maintaining a tactical formation was one of the axioms of naval warfare. A lone vessel attacked by multiple enemy ships stood little chance of survival. Only by sticking together and supporting each other could the fleet have a chance. The desperate flight had, by Sunday morning, left the American vessels spaced out along the lake.

The British ships had also become disorganized. Lookouts on the *Maria*, Pringle's flagship, had spotted the rebel fleet at dawn. "After a chase of seven hours," he wrote, "I came up with [the rebels] in the *Maria*, having the *Carleton* and *Inflexible* a small distance astern; the rest of the fleet almost out of sight." The *Carleton*'s crew had accomplished a remarkable feat in getting the ship, so badly battered on Friday, back into the fight by Sunday. The gunboats, with their sails hoisted, lagged behind the larger ships but were coming on.

The Americans' goal was to race the enemy to Split Rock. The spot cut the lake in two, separating the wider water to the north from the narrow, river-like stretch to the south. The name referred to a mass of rock on the west shore rising nine hundred feet above the water. A narrow finger now known as Thompson's Point stretched toward the rock from the eastern shore. The gap was three-fourths of a mile wide. South of this opening lay a gut, none of it much more than a mile across, whose close shores would limit the enemy's room to maneuver.

The north wind finally reached the American sails. It blew both danger and hope. Their canvas filled and the fleet picked up speed. The foremost boats slipped through the gap at Split Rock. The hospital sloop and the schooner went first, then the galley *Trumbull* and the *New York*. The rest of the gondolas straggled through, followed by the *Congress*. But the *Washington*, still bringing up the rear, was lagging. As day broke, General Waterbury found himself almost as far behind the American fleet as he was ahead of the enemy.

"Began to grow calm," Waterbury later recorded, "and I knew the next wind would be North." Rowing the seventy-two-foot craft against a headwind had been a backbreaking task for the sailors. But the change of wind promised imminent danger.

"The enemy could spread so much sail," Waterbury went on, that they would inevitably bear down on him with their heavy cannon. To hurry the vessel along, Captain Hawley ordered the crew to attach square sections of canvas meant for the gondolas to the upper masts to serve as topsails. Catching more wind, the sails would drive the half-crippled ship forward. Waterbury saw little chance of escape.

"I thought it best to put my wounded men into the boats and send them to Ticonderoga," he wrote, "and row my galley ashore and blow her up."

As the British fleet gained on him, he sent his ship's boat ahead to the *Congress* and asked Arnold's permission to put this plan into action. His goal was to keep the enemy from taking his valuable ship as a prize. He also hoped to save his crew from becoming prisoners. He had already allowed Captain Rue and twenty-six of the men from the crew of the sunken *Philadelphia* to go ashore. They preferred to take their chances on land.

Then Waterbury heard back from Arnold: "I received for answer, by no means to run her ashore but to get forward as fast as possible and he would stop the fleet at Split Rock and there make a stand." This had been Arnold's idea as the last four gondolas, followed by the *Congress*, came abreast of Split Rock. He changed his mind when his spyglass picked out the British sailing ships coming on more quickly than he had hoped. As Waterbury relates, "When I came to Split Rock, the whole fleet was making their escape as fast as they could and left me in the rear to fall into the enemy's hands."

The Connecticut general resented the treatment. He felt that Arnold had made an error of judgment. Maybe the commander had not understood how damaged the *Washington* was. He had followed his own instincts and optimism rather than trust Waterbury's appraisal.

Arnold held to one last hope that he could form the fleet into a fighting unit. He ordered the *Trumbull*, as Colonel Wigglesworth related, to "lie by for the fleet, which I did, by stretching across the lake." He also sent a crew of men in a boat rowing southward to raise the alarm at Crown Point, and to ask that a supply of ammunition be ready there. To General Gates, he wrote, "On the whole, I think we have had a very fortunate escape."

୬

Not quite. For Waterbury, it was too late. Reaching Split Rock, Captain Hawley steered the ship down the channel between the necks of land and continued south along the narrow stretch of lake. He and his men could see the enemy ships looming larger and larger behind them. Waterbury said the enemy ships were "a Going three feet to our one."

At midmorning, the startled crew of the *Washington* was alarmed by the explosion of a 12-pounder cannon firing from the bow of the *Inflexible*. The horror of Friday's battle at Valcour was starting again. Men who had escaped death suddenly felt its icy breath on their necks. The roar ricocheted from the high rocks that lined the western shore. The ball splashed just short of the American vessel.

Waterbury understood that his ship was helpless. He could see the American fleet scurrying away to the south. "I found no Vessel to Make any Stop for Me," he later complained, "But all Made the Best of their Way for Crown Point."

The *Washington*, he noted, "was so Shattered She was Not able to Bear firing." The recoil of her cannon, he felt, would break the weakened timbers of the ship. Even had she been able to fire, the captain would have had to bring the ship around to confront the enemy with a broadside. To do so would have slowed her progress and allowed the more powerful British vessels the chance to pull alongside his ship.

The white canvas of the *Inflexible* loomed higher and higher as she approached. Every few minutes, her bow cannon shot out a 12-pounder ball, raising geysers around the *Washington*. The schooner *Maria*, coming up fast, was also firing at the rebel vessel.

David Waterbury faced an agonizing decision. If the *Inflexible* came alongside his helpless ship and fired at point-blank range, the powerful British guns would kill men wholesale. They could repeat the blows until the *Washington* was demolished. What would be accomplished? If he surrendered, he would save a hundred lives. But one of them would be his own, a fact that opened him to imputations of cowardice.

The *Washington* did not fire a single gun at the enemy. To save the crew, Waterbury told Captain David Hawley to have a man haul down the ship's flag as a sign of surrender. It was the Grand Union flag, with thirteen red and white stripes and the British cross of union in the corner—the Stars and Stripes had yet to be devised.

Waterbury himself presented the colors to the British boarding party, saving Captain Hawley, who had already lost the *Royal Savage*, the ignominy of having to personally surrender another vessel.

The enemy quickly took control of the *Washington* and declared the 110 men aboard to be prisoners of war. The British ships laid on all sail to catch and destroy the rest of the American fleet.

24

***

The End of the Fight

OPERATING ON LIMITED SLEEP AND UNDER INTENSE stress, Benedict Arnold continued to invent new options for his fleet. With the *Washington* lost, crews of the *Congress* and four nearby gondolas watched the British armada gaining on them from the north. Arnold now decided that no formation of American vessels could counter the enemy broadsides. He would not take a stand but would mount a fighting retreat in the narrow area of the lake that lay before him.

Anold ordered the hospital ship *Enterprise* to haul south to Crown Point as rapidly as possible. "We manned all our oars with three men to an oar," Jahiel Stewart remembered. "The Regulars began a fire on some of our fleet and the battle begun very hot."

Colonel Wigglesworth on the *Trumbull* had been "stretching" back and forth across the lake, slowing his progress as instructed. Now he too saw the British war vessels closing in on his galley. He exercised his own judgment. "I soon discovered," he wrote in his diary, "that the *Washington* galley, in which was General Waterbury, had struck, and that General Arnold was engaged with the ship and two schooners, and that he could not get clear. I thought it my duty to make sail and endeavor to save the *Trumbull* galley if possible."

Wigglesworth ordered Captain Warner to set the galley's sails to take advantage of the northeasterly wind. "We double manned our oars," he noted, "and made all the sail we could, and by throwing over our ballast got off clear."

Young Pascal De Angelis, aboard the *Trumbull*, confirmed that the crew, "closely pursued," used both sweeps and sails to speed southward. "We arrived at Crown Point about half after one o'clock," he wrote. "The end of the fight."

৶

For those on the other vessels, the fight was starting all over again. "At twelve o'clock we came up with his fleet," wrote the British physician Robert Knox, "when the battle became bloody and continued for two hours."

Captain Schank, on the *Inflexible*, reported that "at 10 Captain Pringle in the *Maria* made the signal to Engage." Schank fired his bow chaser whenever he saw an opportunity. "Our guns carrying a great way," Schank said, "overreached those of the *Maria*, not withstanding she was ahead of us."

They were proceeding south below Split Rock. *Inflexible* first mate Butler wrote that Arnold fired stern chasers at the British ships "but did no damage except to our Rigging and Sails."

Commodore Pringle, ever cautious, directed John Starke, captain of the *Maria*, to fire his 6-pounder broadsides without venturing too close to the guns of the *Congress*. Pringle was later criticized for staying "a greater distance when abreast of the Congress galley, than any officer inspired by true courage . . . would have done."

Benedict Arnold recounted that the enemy "kept up an incessant fire on us for about five glasses with round and grape shot, which we returned as briskly." After the enormous expenditure of ammunition on October 11, after the extraordinary escape from British clutches, after a day and a half of flight down the lake, the Americans still had teeth. They fought for two and a half hours, five turns of the sandglass.

The gunners on the remaining gondolas added some shots with their own cannon, but much of the fighting was conducted by the men aboard the *Congress*. Arnold was not trying to outdistance the enemy; rather, his intention was to keep them at bay and give the other vessels time to reach safety at Crown Point.

The enemy guns continued their drumbeat of explosive shots. The *Maria* and the *Carleton* swept in and out, firing as they went. The *Inflexible* maneuvered to pommel the *Congress* with shots from astern. As trying as the cannonade of October 11 was for the American crews, this slippery, ever-changing chaos was even more lethal.

"The sails, rigging, and hull of the *Congress* were shattered and torn in pieces," Arnold reported. His ship progressed south along the narrows toward Highlanders Bonnet, a low bluff on the eastern shore that someone thought looked like a tam-o'-shanter. It was there that the lake widened to four miles, expanding into Split Rock Bay on the west shore and Buttonmould Bay on the east. The latter was where Arnold and his fleet had taken shelter during the wicked storm of August 26, where the officers had gone on land to devour a feast and to shoot at targets.

The storm that slammed into them now was far worse than any they had imagined in that other lifetime. This was not a rainstorm but a cyclone of deadly projectiles. With more latitude, the enemy ships could more effectively surround the Americans. They cut off Arnold's last hope of escaping toward Crown Point.

"Still gaining ground on the Enemy," Captain Schank wrote, "I found myself near enough for grape. . . . In a little time more we began to fire the Swivels from the tops and at the same time giving them a broadside." It was a murderous combination.

Three of the British gunboats had caught up with the sailing ships and were battering the Americans with cannonballs. One of the shrieking projectiles tore apart the body of the first lieutenant on the *Congress*, Ephraim Goldsmith, killing him outright. The crewmen heaved his slack corpse overboard to join the skeletons of whales buried below.

Other men died. More were wounded. Men lay dazed and bleeding, their faces bleached, their comrades too busy to tend to their injuries. Some groaned, some cried out as if damned. All the sounds they made were dissolved in the repeated concussion of their own guns and the enemy's punishing response. Through it all, Benedict Arnold limped from one cannon to another aboard the *Congress*, blasting back at the enemy ships.

By the time it was over, twenty-three of the seventy-three-man crew of the *Congress* had been killed, their adventure on behalf of the new nation ended. Now, unless Arnold struck his colors, the seven British ships around him were preparing to move in and unleash a barrage that would destroy the American vessels and slaughter the crews. The men kept looking toward the general for a sign.

Finally Arnold gave the order—not to strike but once again to escape.

◦

After the British had secured the Lake Champlain region from France in 1763, a few settlers had begun to farm the fertile land between the lake and the Green Mountains to the east. One such pioneer was Benjamin Kellogg—his descendants would call him "the Daniel Boone of Addison County," referring to a stretch of land that fronted on the lake from Split Rock south to Ticonderoga. A Connecticut native, Kellogg had moved to the area during the 1760s, along with his wife, Comfort, and their children.

By the outbreak of the Revolution, Kellogg was a well-established resident of the disputed territory known as the Hampshire Grants—the town of Panton, in which he lived, had been granted a patent by New Hampshire authorities in 1761. He owned six hundred acres, which he worked with his son, Isaac, then nineteen. The rest of his five children were girls—the youngest, Sally, was ten years old. His house stood near the small indentation known as Ferris Bay at the southern corner of Buttonmould Bay.

Ferris Bay was named for another early settler. Peter Ferris, like his neighbor, owned a substantial tract of farmland. He grew wheat and raised sheep and hogs. An advocate of the patriot cause, he had opened his home to meetings of the local militia.

In April 1776, Congress had sent north a trio of commissioners to evaluate the campaign into Canada. The men had stopped at the

Ferris home during their month-long trek northward. The family members, who only rarely encountered strangers, watched in awe as a bald-headed figure wearing spectacles ducked inside and eased his portly frame into a chair. Benjamin Franklin, one of the most famous men in the world, had come to spend the evening by their fire.

Ferris was fifty-one in 1776. The youngest of his five children, named Squire, was fourteen. The Ferrises and Kelloggs were living an early version of the American dream—independent, prosperous, enjoying the fruits of their own hard labor, and situated beside a beautiful lake in a rough-hewn Eden that provided ample hunting and fishing.

On Sunday, October 13, the war arrived at their doorstep.

~๑

On the lake, within sight of the members of these two families, Benedict Arnold and his crew were at the center of a violent barrage of cannon fire from the British war vessels. Torn rigging dangled from the masts. Gunners continued to load and fire as Arnold shouted orders.

He had delayed as long as he could. The rest of the fleet had disappeared to the south. Arnold was determined not to surrender to his tormenters, not to allow them to capture his valuable warships and fighting men. He directed the helmsman to edge the beleaguered galley farther east. He knew Buttonmould Bay well. The broad shore offered no hiding place. But Arnold, as usual, had a plan.

With British ships circling on all sides, he gave the order to reverse course. Drop sails. Oarsmen heaved the *Congress* into the northeast wind. The galley surged forward as the crewmen pulled for their lives, three men to an oar. The crews of the four gondolas fell to their own oars.

The sudden reversal caught the British by surprise. They had been moving steadily southward to keep abreast of the rebels. They now had to come about and tack back against the wind.

Once he was clear of the enemy, Arnold changed direction

again. He ordered his crews to hoist canvas and make all speed up the length of Buttonmould Bay. He aimed his ragged flotilla toward the mouth of Ferris Bay. The cuplike opening was less than three hundred yards across. Arnold had made friends with Peter Ferris during his trips to and from Canada and his scouting expeditions on the lake. During the summer, he had dropped lines to sound the depths of the local waters. He knew the sheltered inlet was too shallow for larger ships to risk entering.

The British fleet swung around again and resumed their pursuit, firing from a distance. One after another, the American boats came into the confines of Ferris Bay under oars and canvas. The sailors drove them hard until they scraped against the stony bottom and lurched to a halt. The crewmen leapt into thigh-deep water and trudged to the shore.

Time was critical. The British sailing ships were already coming around to fire broadsides down the mouth of the tiny cove. Arnold ordered his men to tear open gunpowder cartridges, spread the powder on the boats' decks, and set them afire.

The men worked frantically to follow his grim orders. Marines hefted their muskets up the slope of the twenty-five-foot-high bluff that rimmed the cove and took positions, ready to greet any approaching enemy with fire.

Wide-eyed children watched the fight from the shore. Sally Kellogg would remember that "we saw the shipping a-coming in shattered condition." Another child reported of the American soldiers, "They were so black with the smoke of the powder that they could scarcely be told from Negroes and their clothes were all blackened with the burnt powder of the guns."

Pascal De Angelis—the next day he would be fourteen—took time on board the *Trumbull* to write in his diary: "The galley *Congress* Sustained the fire of the two scooners ship til about half after twelve When She and four of the Gundelows thrust into a small Crick on the east side of the lake and we Saw a Great Expution and supposed as General Arnal was aboard the Galley that he ordered them blown up."

Arnold told his men to leave the flags on the ships flying. He would not still the enemy guns by lowering them in surrender. It was yet another gesture of defiance. He would fight to the end, destroy his ships rather than allow them to be taken, and save as many crewmen as possible.

"The British fleet arrived at the mouth of the bay before the explosion of Arnold's vessels," Squire Ferris remembered, "and fired upon his men on the shore and on the house of Mr. Ferris, which stood near the shore." He was talking about his own house, his boyhood home. As the enemy ships moved closer, their gunners blasted the shore with grapeshot. The balls slammed into the log cabin as the members of the Ferris family huddled under shelter.

Below them in the bay, they watched the flames lick up the masts of the boats. The galley *Congress* and the gondolas *Providence*, *New Haven*, *Boston*, and *Connecticut* were engulfed by fire.

A British observer noted that Arnold "chiefly gloried in the dangerous attention which he paid to a nice point of honor in keeping his flag flying and not quitting his galley till she was in flames, lest the enemy should have boarded." The colorful swaths of cloth, the first national flag of the new nation, flapped in the rising heat and caught fire.

‹≈›

With her husband away, Comfort Kellogg had decided that the fastest way to reach safety was by boat. Joined by members of a neighboring farm family, she loaded her children into a bateau, along with whatever belongings they could grab.

The civilians struck out across Ferris Bay to flee south, away from the violence. Later in life, Sally recounted her vivid memory of those terrifying, exciting moments: "We shoved out into the Lake and fell in between Arnold's fleet and the British fleet. The Foremost of the British ships played away on the shattered vessels of Arnold's fleet, but happy for us the balls went over us. We heard them whis."

‹≈›

During their weeks of life afloat, the men had grown accustomed to the continually swaying decks. Now it was the solid ground that felt strangely unstable, that seemed to career and undulate. They found themselves lurching like drunken men until they got their land legs back.

Having come ashore, their instinct was to flee the British guns. Arnold would not allow it. They were to stand guard on the bluff, every weapon at the ready, to make sure that enemy sailors did not come into the bay in longboats and douse the fires before the American vessels were beyond salvaging. Only with those last powerful booms of the exploding ships' gunpowder was the commander satisfied that he had completed his mission. According to one account of the scene: "The enemy kept up a distant cannonade until our vessels were burnt to the water's edge."

For their part, the British were making yet another blunder. The *Congress* and the accompanying gondolas were spent. Pringle's decision to halt his drive down the lake in order to continue blasting them meant that the remaining American ships would get away. The pointless maneuver also delayed the arrival of the British at Crown Point, giving the defenders a chance to prepare.

Arnold feared that British troops and their Indian allies might set ambushes for them between Ferris Bay and Crown Point. It was now critical that he move his troops southward as quickly as possible. Peter Ferris and his family accompanied them, serving as guides.

Forty-six crewmen had survived from the *Congress*, along with some 150 sailors and marines from the four gondolas. The men fashioned litters from sail canvas. Taking turns carrying the wounded, they headed out, as one said, "by a bridle way through an unsettled wilderness." Except for some rolling hills, the land was flat. Ferris led them along an obscure path that wound ten miles to Hospital Point.

They had, Arnold wrote, "very luckily escaped the savages, who waylaid the road in two hours after we passed." Trudging through the woods and wading across streams, the group pushed south through the chilly afternoon. For the weary crewmen, every slight upgrade was a mountain. As day gave way to evening, anxiety flickered among the shadows.

❦

The violence at Valcour had erupted on Friday morning. Now it was Sunday evening. The men had barely had a chance to rest and had not taken a hot meal in almost three days. They had been hollowed out by gut-wrenching fear and withering fatigue. Finally they found themselves standing on the shore at Hospital Point, which reached out nearly to the Crown Point peninsula. They signaled the men on the opposite side of the lake, who had been alerted by Colonel Wigglesworth earlier in the day.

Colonel Hartley sent boats over. Arnold strode ashore, his mind reeling with exhaustion. He conferred with Hartley, then examined the rough barracks and gun emplacements that the Pennsylvania troops had built. It was clear that the fortifications were in no condition to resist a bombardment from the British fleet. If the enemy set off a panic there, the fear could spread to the militia troops waiting nervously at Ticonderoga.

Arnold gave the order—burn the entire place. Even the nearby houses of civilians would have to be destroyed. Their inhabitants had to depart, Jeduthan Baldwin observed, "in the greatest distress leaving all their household stuff, clothing &c. to the enemy, or to the flames. A melancholy sight."

Arnold was relieved to see that the British had not taken the opportunity to rush down on the forward defenses of the patriots that same day. His diversion had worked. General Carleton had continued his cautious tactics.

Arnold's actions had made an impression on the British general, had demonstrated a fanatical resolve both at Valcour Island and in the battle up the lake. He had shown Carleton the spirit of men fighting for a cause.

The work of destruction at Crown Point having begun, Arnold set out for Ticonderoga. He was rowed along the dark water and arrived at the fort at four o'clock on the chilly morning of October 14, "exceedingly fatigued and unwell, having been without sleep or refreshment for near three days."

It was, as Pascal De Angelis had put it, the end of the fight.

25

Want of Time

THAT SUNDAY, OCTOBER 13, THE REVEREND AMMI ROB-
bins was preaching a sermon at Fort Ticonderoga. The attention of
the soldiers, he noted, was taken up "by a smart cannonading from
the fleets which began in the morning. At noon express arrived
with accounts of the battle on Friday down the Lake.... All the
camp alarmed."

According to the engineer Jeduthan Baldwin, the troops received
"information that our fleet was in a shattered condition. About
three o'clock our Schooner came in sight. Soon after a Sloop &
then another Schooner & then the Row Galley & after a gondola."

Word shot through the ranks: the fleet had been crippled; the
British were master of the lake; the regulars were about to assault
the fort; the crisis had come. All the men were ordered to their
alarm posts. They stood gripping muskets as day gave way to a
long night.

Early the next morning, Colonel Hartley's troops from Crown
Point came into the fort by water and by land. They reported that
the enemy had occupied their post and were now only fifteen miles
away with nothing to stop their warships from sailing down on
Ticonderoga.

The two hundred men who had abandoned the *Congress* and four gondolas at Ferris Bay also began to trickle in, staggering with exhaustion. They walked around the fort in a daze. Some had left weeks before, some only a few days ago. They tried to regain their bearings. The aches and bruises they had ignored during the ordeal now lit up. Their regimental companions who had stayed behind questioned them about their experience of combat. Words failed them. A man's clothes spattered with blood, the look in his eyes, his stunned demeanor. Enough said.

Robbins was accustomed to comforting the sick, but the minister had little experience with battle injuries. "Visited the wounded," he reported, "and a horrible spectacle they were."

The men in camp asked about friends. Where was this private or that sergeant? Where was Lieutenant Rogers? A shake of the head, the blinking of weary eyes. Enough said. No words. Eighty men and more of those who had sailed north were dead or missing. Another hundred had been captured by the enemy. The fleet was blasted, only five of sixteen vessels left. They had anticipated the battle all summer; now it was hard to know what to make of the outcome.

Yet most of the nine hundred Americans of the fleet had lived through the violence. Benedict Arnold had lost the bulk of his ships but had saved most of his men. They would fight on.

⁓

General Gates put the best light on the result. He wrote to Philip Schuyler that although the enemy might "boast a victory, they must respect the vanquished." He was relieved that his principal combat officer had survived the maelstrom. "It has pleased Providence to preserve General Arnold. Few men ever met with so many hair-breadth escapes in so short a space of time."

He praised Arnold and his men for the gallant defense they had made against a superior enemy force. "Such magnanimous behavior," he asserted, "will establish the fame of American arms throughout the globe."

All summer the men at Crown Point and Ticonderoga had

imagined the king's troops only as a threat far to the north. On Monday, October 14, the anxious patriots manning the defenses saw the enemy in the flesh.

"A number of row boats approached our advanced post," Colonel John Trumbull recorded, "and there lay upon their oars with a flag of truce." The thousands of soldiers who had answered the alarm signal waited tensely on the ramparts.

"I found Capt. Craig," Trumbull went on, "with Gen. Waterbury and the other prisoners who had been taken in the recent action." He exchanged civilities with the British captain and they discussed the situation.

After the surrender of the *Washington* the day before, General Carleton had ordered that the prisoners be treated well. British marines brought them aboard the *Maria*, where the British commander told navy surgeons to look after the wounded "with the same care as they did his own men." He treated them to a drink of grog and praised their bravery. He only "regretted that it had not been displayed in the service of their lawful sovereign."

Carleton continued to imagine that the best interests of the rebels lay in returning to the fold as loyal subjects. He told the captives that they would be offered immediate parole if they agreed not to bear arms unless exchanged for British prisoners. He expressed regret rather than anger at the needless rebellion. "I never invaded your property," he pointed out to his captives, "nor sent a single soldier to distress you."

He invited Waterbury to his cabin and examined his commission. "I am happy to take you by the hand," Carleton said, "now that I see that you are not serving under a commission and orders of the rebel Congress, but of Governor Trumbull."

Jonathan Trumbull Sr., John Trumbull's father, had served as Connecticut's governor since 1769. He was the only royal governor in the thirteen colonies to join the rebellion. Although he was a patriot, he retained the authority vested in him by the king. In Carleton's view, his subordinates were not treasonous if they followed his orders. The blame fell on Governor Trumbull.

Carleton suspected that word of his lenient treatment would

make the troops at Ticonderoga more amenable to surrender. At least one of the captives succumbed to the inducement. Joseph Bettys, the mate of the *Philadelphia,* had remained on the *Washington* and had been taken prisoner. He decided to change sides and joined the King's Rangers, a British Army unit that performed scouting missions on the New York frontier. Patriots caught up with him six years later and hanged him for desertion.

Colonel Trumbull observed that Carleton's tactic "appeared to me to have made a very dangerous impression" on Waterbury and his companions. He prevented the prisoners from coming ashore. General Gates agreed that they should be taken to Skenesborough, then sent directly home. He did not want them to damage morale by painting for his nervous troops a picture of a merciful enemy.

David Waterbury went home carrying a heavy load of disappointment and rancor. He knew that his decisions on the lake had generated questions about his bravery. "I thought we were all friends while we were at Ticonderoga," he wrote to General Gates. He emphasized his long military record and his strict observance of orders and admitted, "I am very uneasy in my situation."

∾

Gates issued orders that the men of the regiments be "well acquainted with their alarm posts" and "alert in marching to support the works they are severally intended to defend." He knew that the British would now rush their army down from Canada and would, in a few days, be prepared to assault the inexperienced force he commanded. "This stillness," he told Schuyler, "will be succeeded immediately by a grand attack."

Arnold reported to Schuyler that the troops at Ticonderoga were busy reinforcing their lines, "which I am sorry to say are not so forward as I could wish." Gates commanded eleven thousand men, but with more than four thousand sick and others scattered to outposts, only about six thousand were ready for action. Overblown estimates put British strength at twelve thousand redcoats and German mercenaries. Gates told General Schuyler he needed nine thousand militiamen. The northern army commander asked

New York authorities to call up twelve thousand men. He alerted the governors of Massachusetts and Connecticut that even more troops might be needed.

On Tuesday, October 15, the British had not yet revealed their strategy. Gates welcomed the delay. The weather was fine for October. The southerly breeze would make it difficult for the British to sail their larger vessels up the lake. And Gates knew that every day that passed brought winter closer.

Yet it was inconceivable to all that the British would give up and return to Canada. The troops waited, their nerves raw. "Our situation is critical," William Tennent wrote to his wife, Susanna. "Should I never see you again, I wish you every blessing from the fountain of all goodness & beg you not to grieve for me."

That same day, Captain Benjamin Rue, skipper of the gondola *Philadelphia*, and sixteen of his men emerged from the woods to enter camp. Fleeing the *Washington* before her surrender, they had taken refuge onshore and found their way back overland without encountering any British patrols. Benedict Arnold was grateful to Rue for enduring the heat of battle at Valcour, getting the men off his sinking gondola, and saving them for the cause. He issued a declaration "to certify that the bearer, Benjamin Rue, late commander of a Gondola, in the service of the United States, Lake Champlain . . . deserves the esteem and applause of the Country for his good conduct and bravery in the late engagement against the Enemy's fleet."

That afternoon, gunfire alerted the garrison. The men working on fortifications dropped their shovels and ran with muskets to their alarm posts. They waited in tense anticipation. A noise in the brush had alerted a sentry, who barked out a challenge. When he received no reply, he fired. It turned out the intruder was an ox "which was taken for one of the enemy" and fired on "for not giving the Countersign when demanded." The garrison stood on alert all night; the fate of the ox was not recorded.

Colonel Anthony Wayne, destined to become one of the most flamboyantly courageous of the American officers, was among those anxious for battle. During this period of waiting, he wrote to his brother-in-law that "the whole body of the enemy are now within two hours march of us—and we expect to see them every moment." He was sure the coming contest would be a bloody one, imagining incorrectly that the British outnumbered them. "But if we are to die, we are enough," he said, paraphrasing Shakespeare's *Henry the Fifth*, "and if we Conquer the fewer the men the Greater the share of Honour."

On Thursday, October 17, a rumor reached the fort, Baldwin noted, that "Carleton said he would be in possession of Ticonderoga before Sunday & on his way to Albany where he was to have his Winter Quarter." The next day a hundred sick Pennsylvania men at the hospital on Lake George dragged themselves back to Ticonderoga, determined to conquer or die with their countrymen. "These poor emaciated worthy fellows," Anthony Wayne said, "were entitled to more merit than I have time or ability to describe."

The Sunday after the battle on the lake, General Gates ordered an elaborate religious service. The minister recited "a fine prayer and gave them an exhortation pronouncing all the blessings on those that would fight boldly for their country," a Massachusetts lieutenant recorded. The preacher cursed any who would act the role of coward. At the conclusion of his homily the men "gave three cheers which made a beautiful show."

⌒

On October 22, George Washington wrote to General Schuyler, advising him to keep the British "at bay till the rigour of the season would oblige them to raise the siege." Washington was wrestling with problems of his own. General Howe had transported regiments north into Westchester County, threatening to break into the American rear. The move forced Washington to withdraw most of his troops from the island of Manhattan.

With the addition of militia forces, Gates now had fourteen thousand men under his command. Nine thousand of them were stationed at Ticonderoga. Yet gunpowder remained in short supply and militiamen were notoriously unreliable. The general understood that a well-planned British attack could panic the garrison.

For now, General Carleton seemed reluctant to put the fort's defenders to the test. His timidity puzzled American officers. Gates had assigned Benedict Arnold to oversee the Jersey Redoubt and nearby fortifications. This would likely be the target of a British assault from the north. Arnold also served as commodore of the remaining vessels of the fleet. The ships stood ready to defend the narrow passage between Ticonderoga and Mount Independence.

Engineer Baldwin had directed men to float tree trunks along the lake and chain them together into a sturdy boom to protect the gap. The double lengths of logs would slow British vessels, leaving them exposed to fire from the shore batteries and the guns of the American warships. Workmen finished the boom in two days, then hammered planks across the logs to turn it into a light bridge between the two points.

✑

Every day before dawn, the morning gun sounded and the drummers beat reveille. The men sprang from their beds and ran to their alarm posts with loaded weapons. They stood ready until sunrise. Some men had been issued twelve-foot-long poles with iron points. Like the pikes of ancient days, the weapons would be effective in hand-to-hand combat should attackers mount the parapets.

Gates assured his men that they could only be defeated if the enemy surprised them. They could only be surprised if they neglected to "exert their utmost Vigilance whilst on Duty."

Dr. James Thacher, a surgeon's mate, noted that "every morning, our continental colors are advantageously displayed on the ramparts, and our cannon and spears are in readiness for action. . . . Both officers and men, are full of activity and vigilance."

Such a show could be effective, but far more crucial were the fifteen additional tons of gunpowder and three tons of lead to fashion bullets that General Schuyler was finally able to send to the fort. Soon after the shipment arrived, each man carried a full load of twenty-four rounds of ammunition in his cartridge box.

"Our Men work with life & spirits," Baldwin wrote, "which

shows a determined resolution to defend this place to the last extremity."

And so they waited. Every day, every minute, they expected the enemy to appear. Lieutenant Colonel Israel Shreve of New Jersey said his troops were "in good order waiting impatiently to see them, not in the least doubting that we shall defeat them."

Pennsylvania general Arthur St. Clair expressed a similar opinion. "Mr. Carleton has not yet made us a visit which surprises me very much," he wrote on October 25. "His passing the Lake and defeating our fleet was to very little purpose if he rests there." He noted that the delay had given the Americans time to prepare and to bring in additional militia. Although the weather had remained unusually fine, "this however I am certain of, General Winter cannot be very far off."

A successful end to the campaign was still far from certain, but things were looking up. "I don't know," St. Clair wrote, "but we may turn the tables."

∽

"As the enemy's attack will most probably be rash & sudden," read Gates's general orders to the troops on Sunday, October 27, the officers were to "be deliberate & cool in suffering their men to fire." They were to hold fire until the enemy had advanced to within fifty yards, not waste ammunition in "scattered, random" shooting.

The next morning, after two weeks of strain, an American guard boat fired a warning gun. Alarm shots sounded up and down the lines. Drummers beat the men to their posts. A force of British gunboats was approaching from the north.

This appeared to be the start of the offensive that the Americans had been expecting. No one knew whether it was the main thrust or a diversion to mask an attack from another direction.

Although the wind had swung around and was blowing lightly from the north, the enemy did not deploy their main war vessels. American eyes kept peering up the lake for the towering sails of the *Inflexible* and the *Thunderer*, whose guns could chew up the fortifications and heave shells over the fort's walls.

Expecting a landing above the Jersey Redoubt, General Gates ordered three regiments, more than six hundred men, to rush across the newly constructed bridge from Mount Independence to reinforce the position.

Yet no attack developed. The boats floated nearly a mile away for several hours. Sailors could be seen taking soundings of the depths of the lake. The men in the boats surveyed the American defenses through spyglasses. No troops landed.

When an enemy boat came within three-quarters of a mile, several cannon in the Americans' forward batteries opened up. A cannonball struck the bow of a British boat, blasting a spray of splinters and killing at least one of the sailors. The Americans watching from the lines shouted with delight. The British boats pulled back out of range. As Dr. Lewis Beebe put it, "One of their boats received a few merry shot from our batteries for coming too near us."

The wait went on. "The Army under Arms all Day," Colonel Wigglesworth wrote in his diary, "nothing happened at Night." The British boats departed.

The Americans later learned that General Carleton himself, along with his artillery commander General William Phillips, had occupied one of the boats. They had come down the lake to reconnoiter the patriots' strength. They observed the American artillery batteries on both sides of the lake, the thousands of musket barrels bristling from the tops of parapets, the regimental flags, the redoubts, and the boom blocking the channel. They saw enough.

⁓

Gates would not allow the men to let down their guard. On Friday, November 1, a British deserter reported that Carleton had ten thousand redcoats at the ready, along with another eight hundred Canadian and Indian volunteers. He was planning to attack any minute. The American general ordered his men to "have 3 Days provisions ready Cooked and to lie on their arms ready."

The next day, the men awoke to a world turned white. A raw wind stung cheeks and numbed fingers. Jahiel Stewart recorded in his journal that "this morning the snow was very hard." On Sunday, November 3, Stewart reported the death of Isaac Chapman, a member of his company. He also noted, "We hear the regulars has left Crown Point." Three weeks to the day since the enemy had demolished the American fleet, they were gone.

American troops were as astounded as they were thrilled. The reversal was especially satisfying to those veterans who had begun the season retreating from Canada, sick, beaten, humiliated, and utterly discouraged. They had rallied. Trained. Fortified. Armed themselves. Readied for battle. And now it was the enemy who had flinched, who were running away.

"Their retreat," a Pennsylvania soldier noted, "will have very near the same effect as a defeat." All their preparations, their construction of a mighty fleet, their massing of soldiers, "has ended in nothing more than destroying a number of our vessels."

The great threat of a northern invasion was over.

26

---

*Zeal for
the Service*

"THE REBEL FLEET UPON LAKE CHAMPLAIN HAS BEEN entirely defeated," Guy Carleton wrote to Lord George Germain on Monday, October 14, the day after the fight that culminated at Ferris Bay.

Back in Canada, soldiers of the British Army, who had heard the day of thunder from Valcour Island and the fainter cannonading two days later, waited expectantly for news. It arrived that same Monday as a canoe glided up to the shore and Sir Francis Clark, General Burgoyne's aide-de-camp, leapt out waving the red and white striped flag taken from the captured *Washington*. "Three huzzas, and the joy expressed by the whole, gave evident signs of their satisfaction."

Clark also carried Carleton's orders for the 1st Brigade, about three thousand men, to hurry south. The rest of the army, including the Hessians, would remain for the time being in their camps along the Richelieu. Rowers soon got hundreds of bateaux under way. The eager redcoats who filled the boats no longer had to worry about a rebel attack as they streamed south. They began to arrive at Crown Point on October 17.

Guy Carleton had good reason to be proud of himself. But even as he wrote to Germain in the warm glow of victory, he entertained a chill of doubt. "General Winter" was peeking over his shoulder. He warned the secretary that "the season is so far advanced that I cannot yet pretend to Your Lordship whether anything further can be done this year." To the puzzlement of the Americans, Carleton remained inactive at Crown Point over the next two weeks. Then he left. Why?

Like every officer in the British Army, Carleton was acutely aware of General James Abercrombie's grievous error in 1758 when he attacked the French lines at Ticonderoga without waiting for his artillery to come up. His men were "cut . . . like grass." Their ghosts whispered to Carleton. Faced with the prospect of launching his own attack on the fort, he was determined to avoid Abercrombie's rashness.

His intelligence about the state of the fort was imprecise. He knew efforts had been going on all summer to repair and improve the outer works. Scouts may have reported new redoubts and a fortified battery on the opposite side of the lake. Rumors indicated that General Gates had twenty thousand troops inside his lines, a significant exaggeration.

From his experience in Canada, Carleton knew that cold killed. A British officer noted that "after the fifteenth of November on account of the frost . . . Canada is as much shut out from all communications with the rest of the world as possible."

If defeating his opponent required a siege, the weather would become a fierce opponent. The Americans had burned the makeshift barracks at Crown Point; Carleton would have to begin from scratch to create shelter. On October 20, less than a week after his arrival, he wrote to General Howe, "I fear the want of time (the severe season is approaching fast) to put it in a proper state of defense . . . will force us back to Canada." Carleton reassured Howe, who was contending with George Washington's army at New York, "that our appearance on this side the lake will occasion a diversion which may be favourable to your operations."

Supply was another worry flitting around Carleton's mind. Any force in the southern reaches of the lake would be 115 miles from

St. Johns, with no roads by which to send food, ammunition, and needed equipment. Ice would soon block the water route, isolating any force left behind.

The events of recent days had an impact on Carleton's thinking. Supremely confident as he set sail with his powerful armada, he had seen his ships battered by a fanatical enemy who displayed surprising proficiency even in the technical elements of naval warfare. The American rebels had expended plenty of gunpowder and absorbed a pounding from British cannon, yet they had continued to fight. The staunch resistance of Arnold's forces could presage a similar doggedness at Ticonderoga.

❧

Any general can find reasons not to act. A more aggressive commander might have considered that the Americans were not the French professionals Abercrombie had faced. Might have seen that the field guns on the British naval vessels, especially the *Thunderer*, were a potent weapon for dislodging raw militiamen. Might have understood that General Gates's supply situation was little better than his own. Might have calculated that the raw American army could be susceptible to a violent onslaught. Might have punched through the boom with his powerful ships and hurried to Skenesborough, cutting American communications, grabbing supplies, and opening a path to Albany. These were possibilities that needed only imagination to bring them to life.

The commander of British artillery, Major General William Phillips, wrote that he wanted to "teach these rebels *war*." His view aligned with that of Germain and of King George himself. The way to put down the rebellion was to crush the Americans' will to fight by applying overwhelming force, not to temper chastisement with mercy. The time for reconciliation was over. A gaggle of so-called patriots was threatening the foundations of the British empire.

Guy Carleton felt he had done enough. "This success cannot be deemed less than a complete victory," he insisted. If it was not a "cause of public rejoicing," it was because his troops were fighting

Englishmen, not foreign enemies. After his lake victory, he had written to Burgoyne: "We should suppress all signs of triumph."

Carleton had made up his mind not to attack Ticonderoga within days of landing his army at Crown Point. Although he claimed he was "forced" into the decision, he may have welcomed the prospect of returning to sheltered winter quarters in Canada and starting the next year's campaign with well-rested troops, assured of his mastery of the lake.

By October 20, all the 1st Brigade soldiers, along with their commander, General Burgoyne, had arrived at Crown Point. Burgoyne was dismayed at Carleton's decision not to attack. He departed four days later on the *Washington*—British carpenters had quickly repaired the captured American row galley. He had received notice that his beloved wife had died, and he wanted to go home. Burgoyne would use the winter months to convince Germain and the king that his own plan of conquest would put an end to the rebellion during the 1777 season.

Before leaving, Burgoyne had advised Carleton to at least "throw a corps of Indians & light troops round the enemy's post." He assumed that Crown Point would be made "tenable for one brigade for the winter" and posts established along the lake to support the position. He felt that Carleton's strategy of retreat "puts us in danger, besides conveying a bad impression to the publick, of losing the fruits of our summer's labour."

General Phillips, who stayed in Crown Point, also expressed frustration at Carleton's "sloth." He complained that the commander was not sending scouts to probe the American lines. He thought it essential to "feel the pulse of the enemy." Citing deserters who reported the Americans at the fort were in a panic, Phillips felt it would take only a "strong feint" to stampede them.

"It is the humor here," Phillips grumbled, "to suppose that it is no disgrace to retire if it is not done in the face of the enemy." He was of the opinion "that, notwithstanding the success upon the lake, we terminate the campaign ill."

Opinion in the army was divided. Lieutenant William Digby asserted that "every officer in the army, if called upon, would acquit [Carleton] of acting imprudently in retiring from that place to winter in Canada." Certainly many officers were content to return to Canada rather than continue a wilderness fight during the looming winter.

The foray that the British made up the lake on October 28, which had set off an alarm in the American camp, had not been intended even as a feint. It simply gave Carleton a chance to observe the American defenses in person and let his men sound the depth of the water, all with a view of returning in the spring.

Colonel John Trumbull felt that "Ticonderoga must have had a very imposing aspect that day, when viewed from the lake." American general Arthur St. Clair noted that the British retreat was "an event which I look upon as of as great Consequence as if they had been defeated."

The result had come at a cost. Sixteen-year-old patriot John Greenwood, a fifer in the 26th Massachusetts Regiment, noted in his account of the war, "Out of the 500 men we had in our regiment upon entering Canada, but 100 were left when orders came, toward the close of November, for marching to Albany."

On their way north, the British sailed past Ferris Bay. They observed the grim flotsam of war. "Some of their dead," a soldier wrote, "were then floating on the brink of the water, just as the surf threw them; these were ordered to be directly buried."

The bay where the final act of the Battle of Valcour Island had been played out would afterward be known as Arnold's Bay. It is called so to this day, the only place named for him in the country he would betray.

⁓

In the immediate aftermath of the Americans' fierce naval battle on Lake Champlain, many thought the real victor of the northern campaign was Benedict Arnold. Benjamin Rush, the Philadelphia physician and statesman, said the American general had "conducted himself like a hero." He had "lost all save honor."

Richard Varick was sure that Arnold "will still humble the pride and arrogance of haughty Britons, and convince them that one defeat does not dispirit Americans." General Gates only wished that "the gallant behavior and steady good conduct of that excellent officer [had] been supported by a fleet in any degree equal to the enemy's."

British officers gave Arnold credit as well. James Dacres, who had been knocked unconscious on the deck of the *Carleton*, credited Arnold for the "defense he made against a superior enemy." Army lieutenant Digby noted that the American general had acted "with remarkable coolness and bravery . . . he is certainly a brave man."

Some Americans were less generous in their assessment. Veteran general William Maxwell wrote to the governor of New Jersey from Ticonderoga to express his sneering condescension toward Arnold. He stated that "our evil genius to the north, has, with a good deal of industry, got us clear of all our fine fleet." Incorrectly judging that "our fleet . . . was much the strongest," he upbraided Arnold for "bantering" the British, then mishandling the battle and the retreat up the lake.

Virginia congressman Richard Henry Lee called Arnold "fiery, hot and impetuous, but without discretion." Contrary to Maxwell, Lee thought the British "so much superior to his force" that Arnold was wrong not to run from them. David Waterbury's grumbling about Arnold, backed by his implication that his former friend had dishonorably abandoned him during the fight on the lake, added to the clouds that shadowed Arnold's reputation.

It was an ambiguous reaction to an ambiguous campaign. A clear-cut victory is reason to celebrate. The defensive strategy forced on the Americans, which required retreat and delay, did not inspire expressions of glory. But it was the only approach available and the best suited to the American landscape and circumstances in 1776.

༄

During that first week in November, the men at Ticonderoga walked about in a euphoria of relief. John Trumbull, who would go on to a career as an artist, noted stately pines "reflected in the pellucid surface of the lake, which lay like a beautiful mirror in the stillness." This "magnificent scene" had been there all along, unnoticed during the desperate campaign.

Men's thoughts turned homeward. "I am in good health & high spirits," Captain Edmund Munro wrote to his wife. "The nights are cold which puts me in mind of you in your warm bed many times in the night. The enemy have left us."

Along the shore, the water began to show a skim of transparent ice, foretelling the hungry winter to come. Toward the end of November, General Gates wrote to John Hancock, "Lake Champlain is closed with ice, as low as Three-Mile Point so all is secure in that quarter until the beginning of May."

General Schuyler dismissed the militia who had been called up after Valcour. They had served their purpose and could go home, relieving the army of a drain on provisions. Continental regiments whose enlistments were nearing expiration were given furloughs. Schuyler chose Pennsylvania colonel Anthony Wayne, "a capable, good officer," to command the garrison at Ticonderoga.

Only six regiments, a total of about twenty-eight hundred men, were to occupy the fortifications on both sides of the lake. This would be hard and dismal duty. As winter descended, Wayne labeled Ticonderoga "the last part of the world that God made." The penetrating cold made the struggle to keep warm the main occupation at the fort.

༄

At the other end of the Great Warpath the alarm only grew. Having captured New York City, the British forced Washington off the island of Manhattan. By late November, enemy forces were chasing his dwindling army across New Jersey. "I am wearied almost to death with the retrograde motions of things," the commander lamented.

A month after the British boarded bateaux to depart from Crown Point, Washington's men were climbing into boats to escape across the Delaware River to Pennsylvania. New Jersey militiamen had failed to support them, and many citizens of the state were signing loyalty oaths to the British crown in exchange for pardons. The developments left Washington "trembling for the fate of America."

Washington's difficulties were compounded by his own inexperience and shortcomings. His strategy had failed. He had repeatedly divided his forces, repeatedly attempted to occupy more territory than he had the strength to defend. By December, even members of his own staff were questioning his leadership. General Charles Lee wrote to Horatio Gates that "a certain great man is damnably deficient."

Washington had commanded more than twenty thousand men in New York City. Now the number of effective soldiers in Pennsylvania was down to three thousand, troops he described as "animated scarecrows." Many of his men had left when their enlistments expired on December 1, and most of the rest would be free to depart at the end of the month.

In the final weeks of 1776, the American cause teetered on the brink of extinction. It was then that the pamphleteer Thomas Paine, traveling with the troops fleeing across New Jersey, had penned his stirring call to arms, which he called *The American Crisis*. "These are the times," he wrote, "that try men's souls."

అ

On November 26, General Gates received an order from Washington to "hasten on with all the disposable troops, and join him behind the Delaware River." Washington needed soldiers and the force that had just finished their long campaign in the north was now free. General Schuyler canceled the furloughs he had granted to the Ticonderoga troops. On December 3, he reported to Congress: "I ordered seven [regiments] of the regular troops to join his Excellency General Washington. The last of those embarked yesterday at Albany under the command of General Gates." Although the undermanned units who boarded vessels on the Hudson River comprised only six hundred men, they represented a needed infusion of veterans.

General Gates advised Schuyler that Benedict Arnold was anxious to go home "after his very long absence, to see his family and settle his public accounts." The Connecticut general had been campaigning for more than a year and a half and had not seen his sister and three children in fifteen months. Even so, Gates noted, his "zeal for the service will outweigh all other considerations."

From Albany, the northern battalion sailed south to Newburgh on the Hudson River. Because the British now controlled New York City and the lower Hudson, the men had to disembark and march 150 miles across New Jersey and Pennsylvania to join Washington, who was camped opposite Trenton. The trek was a weary one for the soldiers. Private Greenwood, who had taken sick, remembered that "with no tents to shelter us from the snow and rain, we were obliged to get through it as well as we could."

The men trudged over mountainous terrain through the ugly weather, circling westward to avoid the British troops in New Jersey. According to Greenwood, they "proceeded, still without tents and some of our men without even shoes." They reached Bethlehem, Pennsylvania, on December 15. With fifty miles still to cover, Gates allowed the men a few days' rest.

Benedict Arnold rode ahead to Washington's camp, where he stayed three days. It was the first time the two men had been together since Washington sent Arnold over the Maine mountains to attack Quebec the previous September. There were few officers that the sorely vexed commander would rather have seen.

The Connecticut trader and the Virginia planter were both astute businessmen. Both had been fascinated by war at a young age. Physical, athletic men, both were noted for their remarkable equanimity under fire and their ability to inspire men by means of their courage and sympathy. Both had made mistakes and endured criticism. Both had found the initiative to go on.

Washington still believed in the "justice of our Cause" and was hopeful that the nation's "prospects will brighten." But he had confided to his brother, and probably told Arnold as well, "I think the game is pretty much up."

The general insisted on the strictest secrecy concerning a plan he had in mind. It's unlikely that he revealed it to his visitor. If he had, there is little doubt that Arnold would have praised its audacity and given it a rousing vote of confidence. In any event, the commander in chief must have been heartened by the resolve and energy of the young man who at the time stood above even Washington himself as the greatest military hero of the Revolution.

⁓

Word had arrived at headquarters that British general Henry Clinton had landed a force in New England, from which Washington had withdrawn most of his Continental troops to pursue his unsuccessful attempt to protect New York. On December 8, seven thousand redcoats had come ashore unopposed in Newport, Rhode Island, then a major seaport. His Excellency wanted Arnold to hurry to the scene and prevent Clinton from breaking out into the New England countryside.

Arnold had already ridden off on this mission when General Gates and his northern regiments came into the American camp. Gates was more convinced than ever that he himself should be serving as commanding general of the army. Pleading illness, he rode off to consult with his friends in Congress, who had decamped to Baltimore when the military crisis appeared to threaten Philadelphia.

On December 22, Washington called a council of war to discuss his plan. The events at Lake Champlain had canceled, for now, the threat of invasion from the north. The arrival of Gates's regiments had added punch to Washington's army. If the attack he had in mind was to happen, it would have to be carried out before the expiration of many of the soldiers' enlistments at the end of December. After long discussion, the men agreed on a date and a target. The Continental Army would attack. Washington would cross the Delaware on Christmas night.

⁓

Reports that General Clinton was inactive at Newport allowed Benedict Arnold time to visit his family on his way to Rhode Island.

As he rode through Hartford and Middletown and the small villages along the way, he was greeted by crowds waving flags and firing salutes from muskets and cannon. A country demoralized by the bad news from New York was eager to lionize the hero who had faced the enemy at Valcour Island.

When he reached New Haven, the celebration could hardly be contained. He had left the town just after the Revolution began and was returning draped in glory. Veterans of the Quebec march, men he had last seen as they prepared to storm the walls of that northern city, turned out to welcome him home. They had been exchanged for British captives and now greeted their commander with tears and cheers. John Lamb, who had lost an eye in the struggle, embraced him. Eleazar Oswald, who had helped him capture Ticonderoga, gripped his hand. The New Haven Foot Guards, the unit he had led to Boston, saluted him.

His sister, Hannah, was waiting with his three boys. Richard was eight now, Benedict seven, and little Henry, who had sent him kisses on Lake Champlain, was already four. The boys gloried in his fame. Hannah thanked God for his survival.

New Havenites rushed to the big house on Water Street to pay their respects to their renowned neighbor. Relatives came to greet the man who had restored the Arnold name to prominence. John Lamb stopped in to drink his commander's health and describe his frustration that, having organized an artillery regiment, he could get neither Congress nor the state of Connecticut to put up the money he needed to buy guns and equipment. Before he left for Rhode Island, Arnold wrote out a note for a thousand pounds of his own money to cover most of Lamb's expenses.

Arnold stayed home for a week, hardly enough time to recover from the aches of continual campaigning or to renew his bonds with his sons. He arrived in Providence and set himself to training hastily raised militia forces to face Clinton's professional troops.

∽

On Christmas night, George Washington led twenty-four hundred men across the icy Delaware River to surprise the Hessians occupying Trenton, New Jersey. Having endured blasts of snow and sleet along the way, the men opened up on the mercenaries with cannon, muskets, and righteous anger. Among those who joined the attack was young John Greenwood, who had fought in Canada, helped man the lines at Ticonderoga, and marched south after Valcour. The patriots routed the enemy and hurried almost nine hundred prisoners back across the river. They returned a week later to fight British reinforcements in Trenton and to defeat a battalion of redcoats in Princeton before seeking refuge in the highlands of central New Jersey.

The Trenton coup so shocked British general Howe that he withdrew from his forward posts, allowing the patriot cause to rekindle in western New Jersey and taking the pressure off the rebel capital at Philadelphia.

Before Washington moved, few in the patriot camp had much hope that the American cause could endure another campaign. After the stunning victories, he regained the faith of Congress, of his own troops, and of the country at large. It became clear that the Continental Army would survive to fight another day.

༄

Benedict Arnold wrote Washington from Providence, congratulating him and assuring him that the victory at Trenton was "a most happy stroke" that had "greatly raised the sinking spirits of the country." He informed the commander that in his sector the British had "no intention of penetrating the country at present." Clinton's men in Newport spent the winter near their fires.

On February 19, Congress promoted five men to major general, the highest rank in the army below Washington's own. Arnold searched in vain to find his own name on the list. The congressmen's failure to recognize his unstinting service was not an oversight and he knew it. This was a deliberate affront by venal politicians. The injustice struck him in his heart. "I sensibly feel the unmerited injury my countrymen have done me," he wrote to Gates.

George Washington wrote to Arnold, "I was surprised, when I did not see your name in the list of major generals." He recognized that such a slight could induce a man to resign his position. He loathed the prospect of losing his best fighting general, but all he could advise was that "your own feelings must be your guide."

Nathanael Greene, already a major general, warned John Adams about the politicians' interference: "I fear your late Promotions will give great disgust to many."

Arnold replied to Washington by pointing out that he had "sacrificed my interest, ease and happiness" in the country's cause. His reward was a deliberate and public snub that left him subordinate to men of lesser ability.

The hero of Valcour Island wondered whether he could continue to serve "with honor." He began to contemplate resigning his commission and returning to private life.

27

$\cdot$————$\cdot$————$\cdot$

Active, Judicious and Brave

IN 1776, THE PEOPLE OF AMERICA WERE DIVIDED. Patriots and loyalists gathered into opposing camps. Regional animosity, class resentment, and political disagreement fueled dissension in the army, in Congress, and in the population as a whole.

That year, the prospects of victory over the British seemed remote. American soldiers were inexperienced, resources limited, allies nowhere to be found. The British sent nearly fifty thousand hardened professional soldiers and a large portion of the Royal Navy across the sea to win the war in a single campaign. The effort gave the king's forces their best chance of success during what would increasingly seem an endless war.

Important victories and important defeats were still to come for the American cause. But more crucial than the outcome of a given battle was the persistence of the Continental Army. George Washington was a great general not because he won battles but because he kept the army in existence. Year by year, British will flagged. History would look back on 1776, on the northern army's valiant effort, and on Guy Carleton's failure to carry out his invasion, as a decisive phase in the war.

❦

Following the campaign that culminated at Valcour Island, General Carleton was glad for the chance to return to Canada and join his young wife and three children. Maria had come across the Atlantic bearing honors for his defense of the province during the previous winter. King George recognized that in saving Quebec City, Carleton had saved Canada. His majesty had made the general a Knight of the Bath—he was Sir Guy now.

On the last day of 1776, the elite of Quebec City attended a feast for sixty guests, followed by an elaborate public ball. It was a tribute to General Carleton's achievement: a year earlier they had been fighting for their lives as American rebels tried to storm the citadel walls.

But George Germain sent Carleton less welcome news in the spring of 1777. "I have had the Mortification to learn," he wrote, that reinforcement of George Washington's forces by troops from the north "enabled the rebels to break in with some degree of success upon parts of the winter Quarters that were taken up by the army under the Command of Sir Wm Howe."

Carleton thought the implication ludicrous. "I could never imagine why," he wrote back, "if an army to the southward found it necessary to finish their campaign and to go into winter quarters, your Lordship could possibly expect troops so far north to continue their operations lest Mr. Howe should be disturbed during the winter!"

Germain had never liked Carleton. He now informed the general that he would no longer command the invasion army. General John Burgoyne would take over and lead the regiments south as soon as the campaign season of 1777 opened. The governor was to attend to his civil duties in Canada. As Sir Guy saw it, Burgoyne would be scooping up the credit for the victories he had made possible.

❦

The strategy devised by Philip Schuyler, Horatio Gates, and Benedict Arnold had worked. The action at Valcour had saved Fort

Ticonderoga for the patriots. And there was truth in Germain's complaint to Carleton "that upon your repassing Lake Champlain, a very considerable Number of Insurgents . . . immediately marched from thence & joined the rebel Forces in the province of New York & Jersey." The American troops who had marched south, though relatively few, had added to both the spirit and strength of Washington's attack on Trenton and Princeton.

The events of 1777 followed directly from the campaign on Lake Champlain a year earlier. Alfred Thayer Mahan, the American naval officer and historian of the nineteenth century, emphasized the importance of the Valcour campaign. "The little American navy on Champlain was wiped out," he wrote, "but never had any force, big or small, lived to better purpose or died more gloriously, for it had saved the Lake for that year."

∽

In the middle of May 1777, Benedict Arnold arrived in Philadelphia to plead his case with Congress. The legislators had finally promoted him to major general—his leadership in fighting off a British raid on Danbury, Connecticut, in April had forced them to acknowledge his ability. But in doing so, they refused to restore his seniority. Stature in the Revolutionary era was based on precedence. A man who was promoted later would always be "younger" than those raised earlier. Arnold wanted the recognition he felt was due him.

Assured of his own ability, Arnold's egotism merged with his durable belief in the republican principle of advancement by merit rather than by connections. He assumed that the representatives of the people would support him.

He did not grasp with what jealousy members of Congress guarded their own power. The weakness of the new government and the representatives' dependence on the military to defeat the British made them sensitive to any challenge from army officers. Subordination to the civil authority must be absolute. George Washington deferred to Congress with a fine sense of diplomacy. Arnold was no diplomat.

To John Adams, the matter was trivial. Frustrated with the machinations and backbiting in the army, he said that the officers "worry one another like mastiffs, scrambling for rank and pay like apes for nuts."

While Arnold was making the rounds of congressional delegates trying to engineer the restoration of his seniority, he encountered Philip Schuyler, who was in Philadelphia on a similar mission. The New York Provisional Congress had reappointed the commander of the northern army a delegate to the Continental Congress. From that position, he was toiling to clear his own name.

Like Arnold, Schuyler had been criticized rather than praised for his successful effort to hold off the British invasion in 1776. Enemies accused him of everything from profiteering at public expense to being responsible for the debacle in Canada. Delegates from New England wanted Horatio Gates, a more populist general, to take over the Northern Department. They appointed Gates temporary commander while Schuyler was in Philadelphia. Gates, in turn, named Arthur St. Clair to take charge of Fort Ticonderoga. General Arnold, who had helped capture the fort and had devoted himself to defending it during most of the previous year, felt he should have been awarded the assignment. St. Clair was one of the five men whom Congress had promoted to major general over Arnold.

Schuyler advised Arnold about the need to play the complicated political game that shaped relations between civilian authorities and military officers. For the Albany aristocrat, it worked. He had convinced Congress to appoint a committee to review his conduct. On May 22, the legislature exonerated Schuyler by a five-to-four vote. At the end of the month he returned to Albany to resume his duties as northern commander.

Arnold had earlier criticized Congress, writing, "I think it betrays want of judgment and weakness to appoint officers and break or displace them on trifling occasions." It was, he asserted, something Congress did for their "sport or pastime." Expressing such sentiments was hardly the way to curry favor in the legislature.

The delegates did nothing further to mollify the zealous general.

On July 11, 1777, all his efforts frustrated, Arnold submitted his resignation. He was unaware that six days earlier, Arthur St. Clair had been forced to abandon Fort Ticonderoga to the British, and that General Burgoyne's powerful invasion army was moving southward toward the Hudson River.

George Washington had already suggested that Congress send Arnold north to help deal with the crisis. "If General Arnold has settled his affairs and can be spared from Philadelphia," the commander wrote, "I would recommend him for the business and that he should immediately set out for the Northern Department. He is active, judicious and brave, and an officer in whom the militia will repose great confidence." That Arnold was well acquainted with the territory went without saying. "I have no doubt," Washington concluded, "of his adding much to the Honors he has already acquired."

The question of his resignation was put aside. On July 15, Benedict Arnold rode north. Less than a month later, Congress voted sixteen to six not to restore his seniority.

ॐ

Since he enjoyed naval dominance of Lake Champlain in advance, Burgoyne had found the first part of the 1777 campaign easy. By avoiding Ticonderoga's main fortifications, cutting the post off from Lake George, and threatening to haul guns up Mount Defiance in the fort's rear, he induced in General St. Clair a fear that his troops were about to be surrounded. To save the army, he ordered his men to hurry across the bridge to Mount Independence and retreat without firing a shot.

Of the remaining boats of the American Champlain fleet, the galley *Trumbull* and the schooner *Liberty* were captured by the British. The fleeing rebels sailed the others—the sloop *Enterprise*, the schooner *Revenge*, and the gondola *New York*—to Skenesborough. Determined to leave nothing for the enemy, they burned them at their moorings before fleeing south.

Philip Schuyler, for the third year running, began the frantic effort of collecting the men, ammunition, and supplies needed to mount a military operation in the north. He started with only three thousand Continental soldiers and fifteen hundred militiamen to oppose Burgoyne's ten-thousand-man army of professionals. He ordered rearguard troops to fell trees in Burgoyne's path, to flood the road from Skenesborough to Fort Edward by diverting Wood Creek, to strip the region of food and fodder, and to harass the enemy's forward units.

By August, Burgoyne's fortunes had begun to turn. He sent a force of Hessians eastward to capture horses and fresh supplies at Bennington. A tough battalion of American militiamen beat the Germans decisively in the summer heat. At the same time, Benedict Arnold rode west to head off an enemy invasion down the Mohawk Valley. His efforts, along with a determined stance by patriot soldiers at Fort Stanwix, turned back the redcoats and their Indian allies.

On August 19, Congress finally named Horatio Gates commander of the northern army, the post he had long craved. New England militiamen, who had been reluctant to serve under Philip Schuyler, poured in to aid their favored general. Gates stationed his forces at Bemis Heights, a position overlooking the Hudson River outside the village of Saratoga, thirty miles north of Albany.

Two clashes, one on September 19 and the other on October 7, were collectively known as the Battle of Saratoga. During both, Gates commanded from within strong fortifications. In September, Benedict Arnold led forward the troops who thwarted the British attack. During the second fight he placed himself at the head of men he knew from his earlier campaigns and organized a ferocious assault against the enemy. Spurring his horse, he led troops in storming a critical British redoubt. While the attack broke the enemy's position, a musket ball shattered Arnold's left leg. Ten days later, Burgoyne surrendered his entire army to General Gates.

It was the last time Benedict Arnold would fight for the American cause.

28

---·◆·---

The Cause
of Liberty

THE BATTLE AT VALCOUR ISLAND, THE CULMINATION OF
the campaign in the north during the summer of 1776, was the ac-
complishment of three men whose reputations would be shadowed
by the clouds of history.

With the outbreak of war, Horatio Gates had volunteered his
considerable talents in military administration to the patriots opposing the crown. Although Gates, as historian Willard Randall
put it, "preferred the fort to the battlefield," he was able to trans-
form the beaten, sick, and discouraged army that had dragged itself out of Canada in the spring of 1776. Under his experienced
eye, they became a respectable fighting force, well entrenched in
fortifications at Ticonderoga. The feat, which took him only three
months, was one of the stellar achievements of the war.

Gates frequently stumbled over his own ambition. He was certain that inexperienced American officers could never match the
prowess of professionals like himself. He played a dirty game of
politics, currying favor with the influential and stealing credit from
the deserving.

But at Bemis Heights in 1777, Gates matched his performance
of the year before, once again bringing order to a hastily formed

conglomeration of Continentals and state militiamen. His "arrival raised us as if by magic," one soldier said. "We began to hope and then to act." Gates's efforts paid off at Ticonderoga, his plan worked at Saratoga. The delay he imposed on Carleton and the victory he won over Burgoyne revitalized American hopes and led to the entry of the French into the war against Britain. He was rightly designated a hero, and he deserved the gold medal that Congress voted him.

Unfortunately, Gates spent the next two years plotting ways to achieve his real goal of replacing Washington as commander of the army. In 1780, he returned to a field command as leader of forces trying to reverse the army's deteriorating situation in the South. At Camden, South Carolina, Gates's army was trounced in one of the worst defeats of the war. His personal headlong retreat, which he continued for three days, permanently stained his reputation. The hero of Saratoga became a "whipping boy" of the Revolution, a historian wrote, "his triumphs forgotten, only his mistakes recalled."

༄

Philip Schuyler represented much of what the ardent patriots of 1776 were fighting against: family privilege, aristocratic airs, and a moderate political stance that to some smelled of loyalty to the crown. Schuyler had enjoyed every advantage in life, and his good faith as a revolutionary was continually suspect. Many of his friends and relatives were loyalists.

Yet when the revolution came, he willingly put his land and wealth at risk to support the insurgency. It is unlikely that anyone else could have organized an army to march into Canada as quickly as Schuyler did in 1775. The fact that illness kept him from participating in the ill-conceived and doomed venture was hardly a moral failing.

During the crisis of 1776, Schuyler again used his wide business connections, intricate intelligence networks, and dogged energy to invigorate the northern army. He oversaw the construction of a fleet of war vessels in the wilderness, a force that was able to intimidate the British and contend for Lake Champlain. In a contest where logistics trumped any battle victory, the Albany aristocrat was the right man for the job. In addition, his skill at preserving the neutrality of the Native Americans who might have threatened the patriots from the rear was a crucial factor in withstanding the British onslaught that summer.

In 1777, even as he was organizing the resistance to Burgoyne's invasion, Schuyler was criticized—by Gates in particular—for the loss of Ticonderoga. After a court-martial cleared him of the charge, he resigned his army commission and spent the rest of his life actively involved in state and national politics, including a stint as senator in the first Congress under the new Constitution. He lent his prestige to the nation's formative secretary of the treasury, Alexander Hamilton, who married Schuyler's daughter Elizabeth at the family's Albany mansion in 1780.

Fighting men became heroes. Those whose specialties were supply and administration rarely rose to attention. In spite of his achievements, history has painted Philip Schuyler as a lukewarm patriot and a lackluster general. He deserves better.

◆

If the reputations of Gates and Schuyler fell under a shadow, that of Benedict Arnold plunged into the densest black hole in American history. Three years after Saratoga, Arnold stunned the nation. Having wrangled an appointment as commander of the critical fort at West Point, he conspired to hand over the post to the enemy. Had the plot not been uncovered at the last moment, it might have turned the course of the war and allowed the British to nullify America's independence. In making the attempt, Arnold blackened his honor, betrayed his comrades, and broke the heart of his friend George Washington.

So intense was the gravitational force of his treason that it sucked his reputation into a singularity of infamy. His name became a synonym for traitor. Generations of historians painted his entire career in shades of ignominy, only grudgingly acknowledging the bright spots during his first years serving the cause.

Many attempts have been made to solve the paradox that is

Benedict Arnold. The reasons for his change of heart have been the subject of endless conjecture. Certainly the carping of his enemies in the summer of 1776 and the refusal of Congress to recognize his achievement on Lake Champlain contributed to his apostasy. But the heroic feats of many officers went unacknowledged, and many were frustrated by the meanness and chicanery of politicians. Yet very few lost faith in the cause, none on the scale of the former apothecary.

Throughout his career, Arnold's great strength and fatal weakness was pride. Although his fortunes rose and fell, his self-esteem never wavered. It was the very American pride of the self-made man. It was also the unchecked pride of the autocrat. It was a confidence that inspired men to be confident, to follow him, to love him, and to hate him.

We like our heroes pure. It has always been hard to accept, as a historian put it in 1913, "that we owe the salvation of our country at a critical juncture to one of the blackest traitors in history." Great men can be tragically flawed and still accomplish great things. Do their flaws erase their greatness? Can we honor their achievements while at the same time condemning their treachery? An accurate view of history demands we must.

In many ways, the men who fought the Revolution, especially the officers who pulled an improbable victory from the defeat at Valcour Island, represented much of what was essential about Americans then and now. Like all of us, they were imperfect—inconstant, corrupt, sometimes beguiled by foolish notions of their own importance. Yet each of them did his part. We need to coldly acknowledge their faults, which stand as warnings. But we must also recognize their heroism. They were the men who fought and won a war to create a new order for the ages.

In a critical moment, Benedict Arnold stood as the best America had to offer. Not a man of great ideas like Jefferson. Not a man of outstanding rectitude like Washington. He was that quintessential American: a man of action, of initiative, of skill and boldness and overflowing enthusiasm. He was a man who believed deeply, who led others with daring, who displayed raw courage, and who bent his self-interest for as long as he could to the public purpose. He was the vital man at a pivotal moment in our history. His later fall from grace does not erase the brilliance of his achievement or the fact that his actions on Lake Champlain in the summer and fall of 1776 helped save the cause of liberty.

∽

Americans have fought many wars since the guns of the Revolution fell silent at Yorktown in 1781. Generals and politicians have basked in renown. Ordinary fighting men and innocent civilians have carried the burden. The idea of war can inspire glory—its reality is anguish, hardship, and loss.

In October 1776, ten-year-old Sally Kellogg heard the murderous cannonballs whiz over her head as she and her frightened family fled from Ferris Bay, stunned by the noise of the British guns, the firing from the shore, and the explosions of the American boats. The family made it as far as Bennington, leaving their home to be burned, their fields trampled.

The following year, Sally's father, Benjamin, joined the militia force that fought the Hessians outside Bennington and helped to thwart Burgoyne's invasion. In the aftermath, Sally saw the results of war on full display. She would remember all her life the scenes of blood and suffering. It was "a sight to behold. There was not a house but was stowed full of wounded."

The names of common soldiers who suffer grievous wounds or who give their lives in battle only rarely make it into the history books. But someone—a spouse, a parent, a brother, a friend—carries their memory inside a broken heart forever.

Benoni Simmons, the gunner whose left arm was shot off at the shoulder during the fighting on October 11, returned to serve his country in both the army and the navy. When he married in 1784, his wife, Nancy, said, "I'd rather be hugged by that one arm than all the rest of the arms in the world."

When, in the heat of the Valcour fighting, a 6-pounder cannon exploded on the gondola *New York*, the fragments tore apart the body of Lieutenant Thomas Rogers, killing him instantly. His blood gushed onto the deck. His horrified companions lifted his corpse over the gunwale and dropped it into the lake without ceremony. They continued the struggle. Rogers' friend and neighbor Jonas Holden was wounded in the explosion but would live to fight on during the war.

That autumn, the lieutenant's widow, Molly Rogers, nine months pregnant, waited in vain at their home in Westford, northwest of Boston, for her husband to return from the fight. Finally, Private Holden arrived at her door, bringing the dreaded, aching news.

Molly erected a stone inscribed with a memorial to her young hero. It stands in a Westford churchyard to this day:

> *He was Killed by the Splitting of a*
> *Cannon on the Lake Champlain*
> *On the 11th day of Oct'1776 in the*
> *Continental Army in the Serves of his*
> *Country and in the caus of*
> *Liberty Aged 26 years and 9 months.*

The Gondola Philadelphia, *in the National Museum of American History*

Afterword

By the time the Revolutionary War was over, all the boats of the small American fleet that saved the cause of liberty in 1776 were gone. The charred remains of the *Royal Savage* and of some of the vessels Arnold had led into Ferris Bay were eventually hauled out of the lake and picked over by relic hunters.

Only two of the boats were ever discovered intact. The gondola *Philadelphia*, sent to the bottom of the Valcour strait during the fighting on October 11, was brought up in 1936. Her guns remained aboard, one of them still loaded. A British 24-pounder cannonball was still wedged in the hole it had smashed through her hull. A cooking pot, a teacup, sailors' shoes, and human teeth were among the debris scattered across her deck.

In 1964, the *Philadelphia* found a permanent home at the Smithsonian's National Museum of American History. She remains on display there today, the oldest existing vessel of the United States Navy and one of the most evocative artifacts of the Revolutionary War. Visitors can stand beside her and see the guns that fired, look at the decks once stained with the blood of patriots.

In 1997, a survey of the bottom of Lake Champlain found another gunboat from the battle, the *Spitfire*, resting in the depths.

With enough interest and support, archeologists will one day bring her to the surface to join her sister ship as an emblem of our history.

The last guns to sound along the Great Warpath went silent following the War of 1812. The fort at Ticonderoga fell into ruins during the nineteenth century. The property was acquired by the Pell family, who restored the fort and opened it to visitors in 1909. Today operated by a private foundation, it stands as one of the premier historic sites in the country. Along with the ruins at Crown Point, it offers a palpable sense of the history that saturates the area. The Lake Champlain Maritime Museum in nearby Vergennes, Vermont, displays significant artifacts from the battle as well as a full-scale sailing replica of the *Philadelphia*.

While there are no remnants of the battle visible in the place where it was fought, Valcour Island, just south of the city of Plattsburgh, is still uninhabited and has changed little in the intervening centuries. The strait remains a memorial to the men who fought and died there, and whose bones lie scattered beneath the waves.

These places and objects are vivid reminders of the struggle that created the United States. The story that surrounds them gives us keen insights into the DNA of our nation—the courage, sacrifice, and sheer audacity of the men and women who were willing to take a stand and die for the idea that all are created equal, all endowed with unalienable rights.

Acknowledgments

I am fortunate to have had the help of many people on this project. I want to extend my gratitude to my editor, Elisabeth Dyssegaard, to my agent, Eric Lupfer, and to all the team members at St. Martin's Press for another great job.

Among those who have given generously of their time to help me get the story right are Arthur Cohn and Susan Evans McClure at the Lake Champlain Maritime Museum, Matthew Keagle at the Fort Ticonderoga Museum, Jennifer Jones at the Smithsonian's National Museum of American History, Ian Mumpton at the Schuyler Mansion, Eric Schnitzer at the Saratoga National Historic Park, and subject-matter experts David Glenn and Michael Barbieri. Eloise Beil at LCMM helped with illustrations.

I am also very appreciative for help and suggestions from James Kirby Martin, Edward Lengel, Terry Golway, James Nelson, Roger Williams, Norman Bollen, Brian Mack, David Brooks, David Osborn, Michael Callahan, Chris Jarrett, Lisa Percival, Helen Nerska, and Kyle Page.

For additional support and help, thanks to Jeff Brouws, Eric Snowdon, Bob Kelly, David Kettler, Mike Cass, Myron Gittell, Lee Waterman, Kate Avery, Jim Kelly, Nina Sheldon, Wendy Burton, Gail Terry, and especially, Joy Taylor.

Appendix:
The American
Champlain Fleet

1. Schooner Royal Savage
Length: 50 feet
Crew: 45
Guns: 10 (plus 12 swivels)

2. *Sloop* Enterprise *(hospital ship)*
Length: 45 feet
Crew: 50
Guns: 10 (plus 10 swivels)

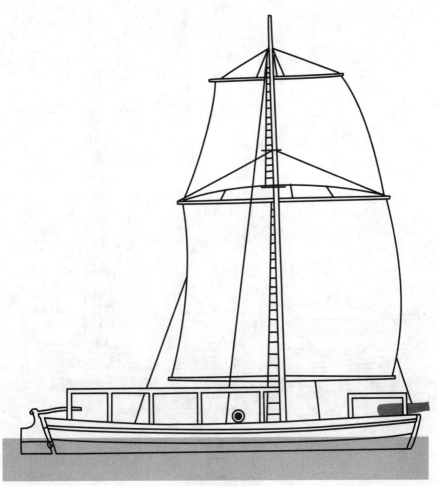

3. *Typical Gondola*
Length: 53 feet
Crew: 45
Guns: 3 (plus 8 swivels)

4. Typical Row Galley
Length: 72 feet
Crew: 70
Guns: 8–10 (plus 10 swivels)

5. *The* Philadelphia II *under oars*
Replica of the original Lake Champlain gondola
Launched: 1991

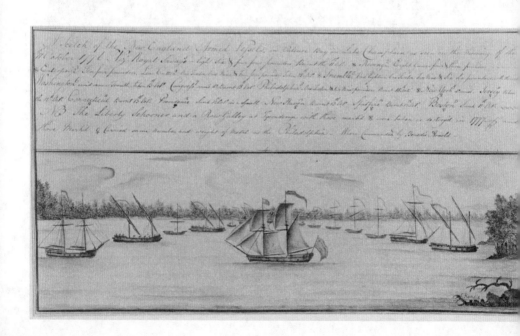

SOURCE NOTES

Some quotations have been altered from their original spelling and capitalization for readability.

1: The Last Man

5 "neglected by Congress": Cubbison, 120.

5 "in the most helter skelter manner": Randall, *Benedict Arnold*, 232.

5 "keep possession of this": Martin, 206.

6 "The junction of the Canadians": ibid., 218.

6 "had the effect of sending": Nelson, 216.

6 "Our days are days": Atkinson, 284.

6 "Had not the wind": Nelson, 217.

8 "The important day is come": AA, 4th Series, 4:1529.

8 "I am sorry you did not": Wilson, 125.

2: Superiority on the Lakes

10 "Was struck with amazement": Beebe, 335.

10 "with fluxes, fevers": Weir, 306.

10 "God seems to be": Beebe, 338.

12 "holding on as it made": Martin, 13.

12 "None but Almighty God": ibid., 63.

13 "in a ruinous condition": Carroll, 75.

14 "attractive in its simple": Gerlach, *Philip Schuyler*, 37.

14 "strong, fertile and cultivated": ibid., 157.

15 "indelicate . . . His language": Philbrick, 59.

15 "will turn out a great man": Wilson, 10.

16 "a gentleman of great independency": Bush, 11.

17 "readily lay down his power": Gerlach, *Philip Schuyler*, 2.

17 "good Sense must govern": ibid., 10.

18 "Our whole dependence": ibid., 142.

19 "broken and spiritless": AA, 5th Series, 4:1102.

20 "I wish you was a major general": Randall, *Benedict Arnold*, 242.

21 "I cannot hesitate": AA, 5th Series, 4:1216.

21 "if Congress intended": Schuyler, "Letter to George Washington, 1 July 1776." *Founders Online.*
21 "vest him with a superior": Nelson, 221.
21 "I am no Dictator here": Gates, "Letter to John Adams, 17 July 1776." *Founders Online.*

3: The Great Warpath
23 "The Great Warpath": Cohen, 2.
26 "a body of men not to exceed": Sellers, 27.
26 "in the name of the great": Randall, *Ethan Allen*, 309.
27 "not worth repairing": Nelson, 40.
27 "invested with numberless swarms": Brumwell, 41.
27 "said to be a Native": Bratten, 11.
28 "How uncertain is life": Randall, *Benedict Arnold*, 65.
28 "restoration of former harmony": Flexner, 51.

4: Canada
29 "for our own defense": Flexner, 53.
29 "Whether we should march": Hatch, 32.
29–30 "which may have a tendency": Fowler, 176.
30 "licentious fanatics": Everest, 15.
31 "not be disagreeable": Hatch, 34.
31 "America . . . will not oppress": Gerlach, *Philip Schuyler*, 284.
32 "If Job had been a general": Lossing, 1:411.
32 "lacked both energy and": Gerlach, *Proud Patriot*, 19.
33 "Had I been ten days sooner": Phillips, 470.
33 "Could I, with decency": Atkinson, 147.
34 "We have met with": Gerlach, *Proud Patriot*, 98.
34 "crawling after us": Fenn, 55.

5: Not an Army
36 "endeavor to pass the lakes": Atkinson, 295.
36 "will doubtless become masters": Miller, 165.

38 "Take Charge of the Carpenters": NDAR, 5:411.
38 "one of the Gundalows is so far": Nelson, 228.
39 "We'll be able to launch One": ibid., 230.
39 "We have, happily, such a naval": Miller, 165.
39 "Go on by Night as well": Bratten, 16.
39 "undutiful children": O'Shaughnessy, 174.
39 "sentimental manner of making war": ibid., 176.
40 "to finish the rebellion in one campaign": Ketchum, 67.
41 "rowed till I thought they would fall": Cubbison, 124.
42 "difficult to conceive a state": Trumbull, 28.
42 "It broke my heart": Cubbison, 124.
42 "the most descriptive pen": Laramie, 63.
42 "some few in tents": Trumbull, 28.
42 "had the dysentery, diarrhea, ague": Cubbison, 131.
43 "I can scarcely imagine a more": ibid., 132.
44 "the most effectual measures be taken": NDAR, 5:961.
45 "Under our present Circumstances": AA, 5th Series, 1:233.
45 "dispute every inch of the ground": Lossing, 2:117.
45 "Your relinquishing Crown Point": Fowler, 324.
45 "would only be heaping one hospital": ibid.
45 "deeply chagrinned": Lossing, 2:121.
46 "I trust neither courage": Randall, *Benedict Arnold*, 247.

6: Straining Every Nerve
48 "Generalship is now dealt out": Billias, 86.
48 "into our army designedly": Tucker, 21.
48 "indecorous, yet fascinating arts": Atkinson, 200.
48 "the smallpox is ten times": Lundberg et al., 16.

49 "a hen-house on a warm April morn":
   Willrich, 11.
49 "so loathsome and evil-smelling": Fenn,
   18.
50 "the camp is in a most sickly state":
   Robbins, 29.
50 "I stood still & beheld": Cubbison,
   159.
50 "jalap, ipecac, bark, salts": ibid., 160.
50 "good women to dry and cure": ibid.,
   162.
51 "I cannot die, do, sir, pray": Robbins, 39.
51 "by no manner inoculate": Cubbison,
   159.
51 "be immediately sent": ibid.
52 "straining every nerve to annihilate":
   Fenn, 58.
52 "low, dirty, griping, cowardly": Atkinson, 411.
53 "the unhappy dissensions": Lossing,
   2:105.
53 "General Gates . . . is putting": Nelson,
   66.
54 "fresh provision is become": Cubbison,
   172.
54 "No broiling, frying": ibid., 156.
55 "the Destroying Angel": Cubbison, 163.
55 "pointed out our own mortality": Beebe,
   337.
55 "the drummers to beat": Cubbison,
   163.
55 "All ye of far countries": ibid., 164.

7: Sometimes I Dream

56 "three sloops and two schooners": Nelson, 237.
56 "constantly report all": Cubbison, 184.
57 "wind and rain being severe": AA, 5th
   Series, 1:828.
57 "a presumptuous fellow": Bayley, 55.
57 "French Men being uneasy": AA, 5th
   Series, 1:828–29.
58 "appearing to Work": ibid., 829.
59 "threw their hats in the air": Rorison, 16.
59 "I broke out all over": BFTM 8 (1951):
   92.
59 "very weak and unfit": Cohen, 175.
60 "Nabbycrombie": Phillips, 280.

61 "snakes of every description": Greenwood, 79.
61 "I have the intire direction": Baldwin,
   62–63.

8: Fired on an Officer

64 "to be ready on any emergency":
   BFTM 6 (1941–43): 5.
65 "fired on an officer": AA, 5th Series,
   1:829.
65 "The Rebel Runaways": Barbieri.
65 "indecent, illiberal and scurrilous":
   Washington, "Letter to John Hancock. 20 August, 1776." *Founder's Archives.*
65 "abominable outrage": Barbieri.
66 "it was impossible": ibid.
66 "you are positively forbid": AA, 5th
   Series, 1:1202.
67 "be very glad to meet him": Stark, 491.

9: Life and Spirit

68 "We shall be happy, or miserable": Randall, *Benedict Arnold*, 252.
68 "a matter of the greatest importance":
   ibid., 256.
68 "assigned to General Arnold": Flexner,
   101.
68 "How happy must every good officer":
   Cubbison, 146.
68 "I labor continually": Nelson, 243.
69 "I think the Commodore": NDAR,
   5:1116.
69 "an able seaman": Cubbison, 219.
69 "must be very ill-attended to": Bratten,
   24.
69 "If the enemy gives us time": ibid., 25.
71 "General Arnold arrived here": Cubbison, 203.
72 "two or three hundred seamen": Randall, *Benedict Arnold*, 254.
72 "is just returned from Skenesboro": AA,
   5th Series, 1:649.
73 "many of the articles in my list": Nelson, 246.
74 "exorbitant rates": Atkinson, 414.
74 "Neither the love of money": Gerlach,
   Proud Patriot, 178.

74 "your love & Industry to serve": Nelson, 69.

74 "Captain Varick has been very": AA, 5th Series, 1:1033.

75 "unnecessary salutes": Cubbison, 169.

75 "It is immediately necessary": ibid., 170.

75 "not to be worn out": ibid.

75 "was blown into many": Baldwin, 65.

76 "We must have them": NDAR, 5:1198.

77 "the drafts from the Regiments": AA, 5th Series, 2:441.

77 "much forwarder than I expected": NDAR, 6:98.

77 "our fleet grows daily more": NDAR, 6:145.

10: Honor May Require

79 "the most immoral collection": Everest, 15.

79 "a sensible, judicious officer": AA, 4th Series, 5:1099.

80 "reproachful language": Martin, 213.

80 "undeserved reflection": Everest, 43.

82 "so far interested": ibid.

82 "is not the least interested": Duling.

82 "marked with contempt": AA, 5th Series, 1:1274.

82 "indecent reflections": AA, 5th Series, 1:1273.

82 "using profane oaths": Duling.

83 "the warmth of general Arnold's": Martin, 243.

83 "astonished at the calumnies": ibid.

83 "I cannot but think it extremely": AA, 5th Series, 2:224.

11: Princes of the Wilderness

85 "his mind is old": Gerlach, *Proud Patriot*, 53.

85 "Brothers, Sachems": Lossing, 2:107.

86 "very warm": Gerlach, *Proud Patriot*, 184.

86 "It is plain to me that": A. Taylor, 83.

86 "to employ in the Continental": Rindfleisch.

88 "they may with impunity": Bush, 29.

88 "broken the covenant chain": Graymont, 72.

88 "slip their hand into our pocket": ibid.

88 "not to take any part": Lossing, 2:109.

88 "We do not wish you": Graymont, 72.

88 "prudence, zeal, and temper": Gerlach, *Proud Patriot*, 106.

88 "impress on the Indians": A. Taylor, 91.

89 "observant of those in Company": Bloomfield, 84.

89 "exert themselves to great": ibid., 82.

89 "ancient enemy": Gerlach, *Proud Patriot*, 106.

90 "to make one weary of Life": ibid.

90 "acted directly contrary": Lossing, 2:109.

90 "You were very troublesome": ibid., 2:110.

91 "attend to the voice": ibid., 2:111.

91 "that the attempt to induce": ibid., 2:113.

92 "no inclination or purpose": AA, 4th Series, 2:842.

92 "in the time of Queder": AA, 5th Series, 1:1038.

12: Setting Sail

93 "Preventing the enemy's invasion": AA, 5th Series, 1:826.

94 "They were no sooner under": NDAR, 6:216.

94 "I know of no Orders": ibid., 6:215.

94 "You surely must be": ibid.

94 "It is my Orders": AA, 5th Series, 1:1277.

94 "and I dare say": NDAR, 6:223.

94 "although I believe him brave": AA, 5th Series, 1:1221–22.

94 "If it can be done": NDAR, 6:234.

95 "or someone else": ibid., 6:205.

95 "I don't think it prudent": AA, 5th Series, 1:988.

95 "very happy at his arrival": ibid., 1:1129.

96 "I am sorry to hear": Malcolm, 146.

97 "Fell Down the Lake": Wells, 270.

98 "Set a Watch": ibid., 271.

98 "the hard gale": NDAR, 6:371.

99 "rode out the Storm": ibid.

100 "most Genteel feast": Wells, 272.

13: Dare Cross the Lake

101 "We roused all hands up": Wells.

102 "made a precipitate retreat": Randall, *Benedict Arnold*, 272.

102 "it is my positive Order": NDAR, 6:95.

103 "I wish, on the Contrary": ibid., 6:96.

103 "the enemy will not dare": ibid., 6:654.

103 "soon to have it in my power": ibid.

104 "on the bows and sides": AA, 5th Series, 2:223.

104 "attacked by a Party of Savages": NDAR, 6:734.

105 "a very heavy cannonading": AA, 5th Series, 2:353.

105 "all hands at work at Daylight": Baldwin, 74.

105 "it is probable": AA, 5th Series, 2:263.

106 "We very distinctly heard": Digby, 142.

106 "I think we are very safe": NDAR, 6:760.

107 "attacked our lines": AA, 5th Series, 2:186.

107 "weaken and discourage": ibid., 2:265.

108 "When you ask for a frigate": Randall, *Benedict Arnold*, 260.

109 "The stile be altered": Nelson, 277.

109 "the wind south very strong": Wells, 277.

109 "a more windy night I scarce": ibid., 279.

109 "desired to be taken on board": NDAR, 6:925.

109 "three Cahoops": Wells, 279.

110 "the Enemy are Subtile": NDAR, 6:791.

110 "I make no doubt of their soon": ibid., 6:884.

14: A Considerable Naval Force

111 "two schooners taken": AA, 5th Series, 2:532.

112 "to give the foregoing": NDAR, 6:858.

112 "cautious of giving any": ibid., 6:884.

113 "planked to her wales": ibid., 6:858.

113 "I am inclined to think": ibid., 6:884.

115 "I only wish he had given": Bradley, 76.

116 "the most insolent": Atkinson, 279.

117 "calculated to carry": Bratten, 41.

119 "he has a rigid strictness": Digby, 156.

119 "winning manner": Howson, 109.

121 "we must risk and depend": Griffith, 322.

15: Prepared for the Enemy

122 "We are moored in a small bay": NDAR, 6:1032.

122 "pleased to find you": ibid., 6:1237.

123 "We have continual gales": AA, 5th Series, 2:834.

124 "A great part of my seamen": ibid.

125 "We are as well-prepared": NDAR, 6:926.

125 "most enjoyable entertainment": Wells, 280.

127 "fired about one mile": Martin, 263.

127 "made the best Shots": Wells, 281.

128 "who will be of no service": NDAR, 6:735.

128 "talk of crossing the lake soon": ibid., 6:884.

129 "Ansel Fox was Cabbd twelve": Wells, 279.

129 "I am surprised": AA, 5th Series, 2:834.

129 "We have but very indifferent": NDAR, 6:735.

130 "I beg that at least": AA, 5th Series, 2:481.

130 "The men on board the fleet": Cubbison, 220.

130 "the powder, lead and flints": AA, 5th Series, 2:481.

130 "every article that you Demanded": NDAR, 6:1116–17.

130 "hear in time that Lord Howe": ibid., 6:982.

131 "blessed in ignorance": Randall, *Benedict Arnold*, 261.

131 "As far as courage goes": Martin, 267.

131 "If you ever live to return": Philbrick, 40.

131 "Pray my dear": Randall, *Benedict Arnold*, 25.

132 "disabled in the use of understanding": Murphy, 20.

132 "To the great Disposer": Martin, 268.

132 "sends a kiss to Pa": ibid., 267.

16: No Landlubbers

133 "every report to your prejudice": Martin, 258.

133 "approve the behavior": ibid.

134 "When the enemy drives": AA, 5th Series, 1:1267.

134 "I am greatly at a loss": NDAR, 6:926.

134 "no doubt the enemy will soon": ibid., 6:961.

134 "I wish the Workmen": ibid., 6:926.

135 "not half finished or rigged": AA, 5th Series, 2:834.

135 "Economy is the word": AA, 2:556.

135 "I hope to be excused": Bratten, 53.

136 "memorandum of articles": NDAR, 6:1082.

137 "one moment sooner": AA, 5th Series, 2:861.

17: A Noble Sight

139 "No considerable time": NDAR, 6:763.

140 "It was no uncommon thing": Hadden, 539–40.

142 "We were all provided": Digby, 150.

142 "We lay on our arms": NDAR, 6:1111.

143 "It certainly was a noble": Laramie, 60.

143 "As the *Inflexible* is of the party": Bratten, 41.

18: Make Ready

148 "hazarding himself on an element": Digby, 157.

149 "Put out cookfires": Randall, *Benedict Arnold*, 301.

149 "at 5 o'clock in the morning": NDAR, 6:1259.

150 "it was reported to General Carleton": Eelking, 70.

150 "without discovering any traces": Randall, *Benedict Arnold*, 303.

150 "On the 10th in the evening": Lundberg et al., 32.

150 "had information": NDAR, 9:49.

151 "Mr. Arnold had a fleet": Nelson, 291.

154 "To our great mortification": ibid., 294.

154 "You formed no plan": NDAR, 9:49.

19: Engage

156 "full of pranks and plays": Randall, *Benedict Arnold*, 27.

157 "The guard boat came in": Wells, 283.

157 "We had alarm": Wickman, 92.

157 "six sail of the Enemy Being": Darley, 110.

159 "lie where we should be surrounded": Philbrick, 45.

159 "I gave it as my opinion": AA, 5th Series, 2:1224.

160 "Carleton the Haughty": Randall, *Benedict Arnold*, 292.

160 "At ½ past nine": Darley, 113–14.

160 "river Valcour": ibid., 137.

161 "At 10 saw a strange sail": Pippenger, "A New Eyewitness."

162 "After we had got beyond": NDAR, 6:1272.

163 "Acquainted me that I could": Pippenger, "A New Eyewitness."

163 "was without order or regularity": Hadden, 22.

164 "we saw the *Royal Savage*": Pippenger, "A New Eyewitness."

164 "some bad management": NDAR, 6:1235.

164–65 "sheared Her bowsprit": Pippenger, "A New Eyewitness."

20: The Battle Was Very Hot

167 "At this time the Gunboats": Pippenger, "A New Eyewitness."

167 "One of her masts was wounded": NDAR, 6:1235.

167 "and four of the Enemies vessels": Hadden, 22.

168 "the Regulars boarded her": Wickman, 92.

168 "gondolas, one after another": Darley, 132.

169 "were obliged to tack": Nelson, 299.
169 "We had a narrow passage": NDAR, 6:1272.
169 "Few vessels can attack us": AA, 5th Series, 591.
169 "At half past twelve": AA, 5th Series, 3:253.
170 "obliged . . . to point": ibid.
170 "with the most uncommon": Darley, 138.
171 "the Com'r in Chief was on": Hadden, 32.
171 "one of the most distant": Digby, 156.
171 "yourself in the *Maria*": NDAR, 9:49–51.
172 "During the affair": Cubbison, 239.
172 "The wind was so unfavorable": Darley, 156.
173 "the rebels directed their": Cubbison, 249.
173 "the good service done": NDAR, 6:1258.
173 "tho' under the Enemies whole fire": Hadden, 23.
174 "lucky flaw": Pippenger, "A New Eyewitness."
174 "the *Carleton* schooner": NDAR, 6:1275.
174 "nearly into the middle of": Flexner, 108.
175 "being low in the Water": NDAR, 7:123.
175 "immediately received the Enemies": Hadden, 23.
175 "she was suffering": Cubbison, 238.
176 "We Cut her Rigging": Wickman, 92.

21: With Great Fury

178 "The Enemy Fleet attacked": Darley, III.
179 "he was our fighting general": I. Arnold, 29.
179 "we suffered much": Nelson, 277.
180 "Seeing all hesitate": Cubbison, 238.
182 "till we brought our brod": Darley, 152.
184 "Our decks were stain'd": ibid.
184 "his flesh and brains": ibid., 106.
184 "I was aboard of the hospital": Wickman, 92.

184 "entered on board of the Galley": Gaspee Virtual Archives.
184 "The Doctors cut off": Wickman, 92.
185 "by cords on their caps": Cubbison, 239.
186 "hulled a Number of Times": NDAR, 6:1235.
186 "shivered it almost to pieces": Nelson, 302.
186 "The battle lasted eight": Wells, 284.
186 "There ensued a most terrible": Darley, 114.
187 "tested its 24-pound cannons": Cubbison, 239–40.
187 "Five broadsides silenced": S. Taylor, 39.
188 "A boat Came a Long side": Darley, III.

22: Extreme Obscurity

190 "upon the whole the British Fleet": Hadden, 31.
191 "The *Congress* and *Washington*": AA, 5th Series, 3:1038.
192 "Every vessels ammunition": NDAR, 6:1235.
192 "enemy greatly superior": Allen, 172.
192 "It was thought prudent": ibid.
194 "We run a ground": Wickman, 92.
194 "row'd out clear": Darley, 114.
195 "a rage": Flexner, 110.
195 "gave us the slip": NDAR, 6:1257.
195 "expecting in the morning": ibid., 6:1274.
195 "between us and the shore": Darley, 135.
195 "anchor in a line as near": Bellico, 135.
196 "Just as she was going away": Pippenger, "A New Eyewitness."
196 "by which means the rear": Randall, *Benedict Arnold*, 313.
196 "having received a small supply": Hadden, 24.
197 "wideawake and on the alert": Darley, 133.
197 "this retreat did great honor to": Hadden, 24.
197 "the great diligence": NDAR, 6:1274.

197 "To our utter astonishment": Darley, 138.

198 "The signal was made to sail": Pippenger, "A New Eyewitness."

198 "under double reeft topsails": ibid.

198 "wind was so hard against us": Bellico, 155.

198 "been retarded as well as us": NDAR, 6:1274.

199 "Most of the fleet": AA, 5th Series, 3:217.

199 "The Enemy came hard": Wells, 284.

200 "so torn to pieces": Bratten, 68.

23: In Shattered Condition

201 "to wait for the fleet": Bellico, 156.

201 "that the Enemy had pursued": Nelson, 312.

202 "Weighed anchor with a fresh": NDAR, 6:1389.

203 "taking one of them for the Enemy": Pippenger, "A New Eyewitness."

203 "In the morning on Sunday": Darley, 115.

204 "Enemy's Fleet were very": NDAR, 6:1079.

204 "I do not think the retreat": Darley, 150.

204 "After a chase of seven hours": Pippenger, "A New Eyewitness."

205 "Began to grow calm": NDAR, 7:1295.

206 "I received for answer": ibid.

206 "When I came to Split Rock": AA, 5th Series, 2:1224.

206 "a Going three feet": NDAR, 7:1296.

207 "I found no Vessel to Make": ibid., 7:1295.

24: The End of the Fight

208 "We manned all our oars": Wickman, 94.

208 "I soon discovered": Darley, 115.

209 "closely pursued": ibid., 112.

209 "At twelve o'clock": Darley, 138.

209 "but did no damage except": ibid.

209 "a greater distance when abreast": NDAR, 9:50.

209 "kept up an incessant fire": AA, 5th Series, 2:1080.

210 "The sails, rigging, and hull": ibid.

210 "Still gaining ground on": Pippenger, "A New Eyewitness."

211 "the Daniel Boone": Hopkins, 116.

213 "we saw the shipping": Cubbison, 244.

213 "They were so black": Atkinson, 422.

214 "The galley *Congress* Sustained": Darley, 112.

214 "The British fleet arrived": Cubbison, 246.

214 "chiefly gloried in the dangerous": Flexner, 113.

214 "We shoved out into the Lake": Nelson, 318.

215 "The enemy kept up": Cubbison, 246.

215 "by a bridle way through": ibid.

215 "very luckily escaped": AA, 5th Series, 2:1080.

216 "in the greatest distress": Baldwin, 81.

216 "exceedingly fatigued": AA, 5th Series, 2:1080.

25: Want of Time

217 "by a smart cannonading": Robbins, 44.

217 "information that our fleet": Baldwin, 80.

218 "Visited the wounded": Robbins, 44.

218 "boast a victory": AA, 5th Series, 2:1192.

218 "It has pleased Providence": NDAR, 6:1277.

218 "Such magnanimous behavior": Cubbison, 250.

219 "A number of row boats approached": Trumbull, 35.

219 "regretted that it had not": ibid.

220 "appeared to me": ibid., 36.

220 "I thought we were all friends": NDAR, 7:1295.

220 "well acquainted with their": AA, 5th Series, 3:527.

220 "will be succeeded immediately": AA, 5th Series, 3:575.

220 "which I am sorry": NDAR, 6:1276.

221 "Our situation is critical": Atkinson, 424.

221 "to certify that the bearer": Lundberg et al., 45.

221 "which was taken for one": Corbett, 216.

222 "whole body of the enemy": Nelson, 322.

222 "Carleton said he would be": Baldwin, 82.

222 "These poor emaciated worthy": Cubbison, 256.

222 "a fine prayer and gave them": ibid.

222 "at bay till the rigour of the season": AA, 5th Series, 2:1186.

223 "exert their utmost": Anonymous, *Orderly Book*, 12.

223 "every morning, our continental": Thacher, 64.

223 "Our Men work with life": Baldwin, 82.

224 "in good order waiting": Cubbison, 250.

224 "Mr. Carleton has not yet": ibid., 257.

224 "As the enemy's attack": ibid.

225 "One of their boats received": ibid., 261.

225 "The Army under Arms all Day": Pippenger, "Finding Edward."

225 "have 3 Days provisions": Nelson, 325.

226 "This morning the snow": Wickman, 97.

226 "Their retreat": Laramie, 85.

26: Zeal for the Service

227 "The Rebel fleet upon": AA, 5th Series, 2:1040.

227 "Three huzzas, and the joy": Nelson, 323.

228 "the season is so far": NDAR, 6:1258.

228 "cut . . . like grass": Ferling, 20.

228 "after the fifteenth of November": Johnson, 278.

228 "I fear the want of time": Bellico, 161.

228 "that our appearance": NDAR, 6:1336.

229 "teach these rebels *war*": Cubbison, 263.

229 "This success cannot": Cohen, 167.

230 "throw a corps of Indians": Cubbison, 264.

230 "sloth": ibid., 263.

230 "It is the humor here": ibid., 264.

230 "every officer in the army": Nelson, 335.

231 "Ticonderoga must have had": Trumbull, 36.

231 "an event which I look upon": Cubbison, 267.

231 "Out of the 500 men": Greenwood, 373.

231 "Some of their dead": Bellico, 162.

231 "conducted himself like a hero": Martin, 287.

231 "will still humble the pride": Brumwell, 73.

232 "the gallant behavior": Martin, 287.

232 "defense he made against": I. Arnold, 120.

232 "with remarkable coolness": Digby, 164.

232 "our evil genius to the north": AA, 5th Series, 2:1134.

232 "fiery, hot and impetuous": ibid., 320.

232–33 "reflected in the pellucid": Trumbull, 37.

233 "I am in good health": Atkinson, 425.

233 "Lake Champlain is closed": AA, 5th Series, 3:873.

233 "a capable, good officer": Cubbison, 268.

233 "the last part of the world God": ibid.

233 "I am wearied almost to death:" D. Palmer, 144.

234 "trembling for the fate": Chernow, *Washington*, 269.

234 "a certain great man": Ferling, 171.

234 "animated scarecrows": ibid., 165.

234 "hasten on with all": Trumbull, 35.

234 "regular troops to join": AA, 5th Series, 3:1062.

235 "after his very long absence": ibid., 3:875.

235 "with no tents to shelter": Greenwood, 373.

235 "proceeded, still without": ibid.

235 "justice of our Cause": Ferling, 167.

238 "a most happy stroke": B. Arnold, "Letter to George Washington, 13 January 1777." *Founders Online.*

238 "I sensibly feel": Randall, *Benedict Arnold*, 331.

239 "I was surprised, when I did": ibid., 330.

239 "I fear your late Promotions": Procknow.

239 "sacrificed my interest": Randall, *Benedict Arnold*, 329.

27: Active, Judicious and Brave

241 "I have had the Mortification": Nelson, 336.

241 "I could never imagine": Bradley, 168.

242 "that upon your repassing": Nelson, 336.

242 "The little American navy": Mahan, 25.

243 "worry one another like": McCullough, *John Adams*, 169.

243 "I think it betrays want": Martin, 311.

244 "If General Arnold has": I. Arnold, 138.

28: The Cause of Liberty

246 "preferred the fort": Randall, *Benedict Arnold*, 319.

247 "arrival raised us": Billias, 90.

247 "whipping boy": Penrose et al., 7.

249 "that we owe the salvation": Brumwell, 76.

250 "a sight to behold": Anonymous, "Women in the American."

250 "I'd rather be hugged": Concannon.

251 *"He was Killed by the Splitting"*: Lundberg et al., 142.

Bibliography

Abbreviations used:

NDAR—*Naval Documents of the American Revolution*, edited by William J. Morgan. Washington, DC: U.S. Government Printing Office, various dates.

AA—*American Archives*, edited by Peter Force. Washington, DC: M. St. Clair Clarke and P. Force, 1853.

BFTM—*Bulletin of the Fort Ticonderoga Museum.*

༄

Allen, Gardner W. *A Naval History of the American Revolution.* New York: Houghton Mifflin, 1913.

Anonymous. *Orderly Book of the Northern Army, at Ticonderoga and Mt. Independence from October 17th, 1776, to January 8th, 1777.* Albany, NY: J. Munsell, 1859.

———. "Women in the American Revolution." *American Battlefield Trust.* https://www.battlefields.org/learn/articles/women-american-revolution (accessed March 19, 2020).

Arnold, Benedict. "Letter to George Washington, 13 January 1777." *Founders Online.* https://founders.archives.gov/documents/Washington/03-08-02-0060 (accessed March 19, 2020).

Arnold, Isaac N. *The Life of Benedict Arnold: His Patriotism and His Treason.* Chicago: Jansen, McClurg, 1880.

Atkinson, Rick. *The British Are Coming: The War for America, Lexington to Princeton, 1775–1777.* New York: Henry Holt, 2019.

Baldwin, Jeduthan. *The Revolutionary Diary of Col. Jeduthan Baldwin.* Bangor, ME: The De Burians, 1906.

Barbieri, Michael. "Infamous Skulkers: The Shooting of Brigadier General Patrick Gordon." *Journal of the American Revolution*, September 11, 2013. https://allthingsliberty

.com/2013/09/infamous-skulkers-shooting-brigadier-general-patrick-gordon (accessed March 19, 2020).

Bayley, Frye. "Colonel Frye Bayley's Reminiscences." *Proceedings of the Vermont Historical Society, 1923–1925.* Bellows Falls: Vermont Historical Society, 1926.

Beebe, Lewis. *Journal of Dr. Lewis Beebe.* New York: New York Times, 1971.

Bellesiles, Michael A., ed. *Lethal Imagination: Violence and Brutality in American History.* New York: New York University Press, 1999.

Bellico, Russell P. *Sails and Steam in the Mountains: A Maritime and Military History of Lake George and Lake Champlain.* Fleischmanns, NY: Purple Mountain Press, 1992.

Berleth, Richard J. *Bloody Mohawk: The French and Indian War and American Revolution on New York's Frontier.* Hensonville, NY: Black Dome Press, 2010.

Billias, George A., ed. *George Washington's Generals.* Westport, CT: Greenwood Press, 1967.

Bird, Harrison. *Navies in the Mountains: The Battles on the Waters of Lake Champlain and Lake George, 1609–1814.* New York: Oxford University Press, 1962.

Black, Jeremy. *Crisis of Empire: Britain and America in the Eighteenth Century.* New York: Continuum, 2008.

———. ed. *Warfare in Europe 1650–1792.* Burlington, VT: Ashgate, 2005.

Bloomfield, Joseph. *Citizen Soldier: The Revolutionary War Journal of Joseph Bloomfield.* Edited by Mark E. Lender and James K. Martin. Yardley, PA: Westholme Publishing, 2018.

Boot, Max. *Invisible Armies: An Epic History of Guerrilla Warfare from Ancient Times to the Present.* New York: Liveright, 2013.

Bradley, A. G. *Lord Dorchester.* Toronto: Morang, 1907.

Brandt, Clare. *The Man in the Mirror: A Life of Benedict Arnold.* New York: Random House, 1994.

Bratten, John R. *The Gondola Philadelphia and the Battle of Lake Champlain.* College Station: Texas A&M University Press, 2002.

Brumwell, Stephen. *Turncoat: Benedict Arnold and the Crisis of American Liberty.* New Haven, CT: Yale University Press, 2018.

Buchanan, John. *The Road to Valley Forge: How Washington Built the Army That Won the Revolution.* Hoboken, NJ: John Wiley & Sons, 2004.

Bush, Martin H. *Revolutionary Enigma: A Re-appraisal of General Philip Schuyler of New York.* Port Washington, NY: I. J. Friedman, 1969.

Calloway, Colin G. *The Indian World of George Washington: The First President, the First Americans, and the Birth of the Nation.* New York: Oxford University Press, 2018.

Carroll, Charles. *Journal of Charles Carroll of Carrollton.* Baltimore: Maryland Historical Society, 1876.

Chapelle, Howard I. *The History of American Sailing Ships.* New York: W. W. Norton, 1935.

Chernow, Ron. *Alexander Hamilton.* New York: Penguin Press, 2004.

———. *Washington: A Life.* New York: Penguin Press, 2010.

Cohen, Eliot A. *Conquered into Liberty: Two Centuries of Battles Along the Great Warpath That Made the American Way of War.* New York: Free Press, 2011.

Concannon, John. "Benoni Simmons: Long-Serving Hero of the American Revolution." *Journal of the American Revolution,* October 8, 2019. https://allthingsliberty.com/2019/10/benoni-simmons-long-serving-hero-of-the-american-revolution (accessed March 19, 2020).

Corbett, Theodore. *No Turning Point: The Saratoga Campaign in Perspective.* Norman: University of Oklahoma Press, 2012.

Cubbison, Douglas R. T*he American Northern Theater Army in 1776: The Ruin and Reconstruction of the Continental Force.* Jefferson, NC: McFarland, 2010.

Cumming, William Patterson. *The Fate of a Nation: The American Revolution Through Contemporary Eyes.* London: Phaidon, 1975.

Darley, Stephen. *The Battle of Valcour Island: The Participants and Vessels of Benedict Arnold's 1776 Defense of Lake Champlain.* North Haven, CT: Darley, 2013.

Desjardin, Thomas A. *Through a Howling Wilderness: Benedict Arnold's March to Quebec, 1775.* New York: St. Martin's Press, 2006.

Digby, William. *The British Invasion from the North.* Albany, NY: Joel Munsell's Sons, 1887.

Duffy, Christopher. *The Military Experience in the Age of Reason.* London: Routledge & Kegan Paul, 1987.

Duling, Ennis. "Arnold, Hazen and the Mysterious Major Scott." *Journal of the American Revolution,* February 23, 2016. https://allthingsliberty.com/2016/02/arnold-hazen-and-the-mysterious-major-scott (accessed March 19, 2020).

Eelking, Max von. *Memoirs, Letters, and Journals of Major General Riedesel.* New York: New York Times, 1969.

Everest, Allan S. *Moses Hazen and the Canadian Refugees in the American Revolution.* Syracuse, NY: Syracuse University Press, 1976.

Fenn, Elizabeth A. *Pox Americana: The Great Smallpox Epidemic of 1775–82.* New York: Hill and Wang, 2001.

Ferling, John E. *Almost a Miracle: The American Victory in the War of Independence.* New York: Oxford University Press, 2007.

Fischer, David Hackett. *Champlain's Dream.* New York: Simon & Schuster, 2008.

Fleming, Thomas J. *1776, Year of Illusions.* New York: W. W. Norton, 1975.

Flexner, James Thomas. *The Traitor and the Spy: Benedict Arnold and John André.* New York: Harcourt Brace, 1953.

Force, Peter, ed. *American Archives.* Washington, DC: M. St. Clair Clarke and P. Force, 1853.

Fowler, William M., Jr. *Rebels Under Sail: The American Navy During the Revolution.* New York: Charles Scribner's Sons, 1976.

Frazier, Patrick. *The Mohicans of Stockbridge.* Lincoln: University of Nebraska Press, 1992.

Gaspee Virtual Archives. "Benoni Simmons." http://gaspee.org/BenoniSimmons.html (accessed March 19, 2020).

Gates, Horatio. "Letter to John Adams, 17 July 1776." *Founders Online.* https://founders.archives.gov/documents/Adams/06-04-02-0168 (accessed March 18, 2020).

Gerlach, Don R. *Philip Schuyler and the American Revolution in New York, 1733–1777.* Lincoln: University of Nebraska Press, 1964.

———. *Proud Patriot: Philip Schuyler and the War of Independence, 1775–1783.* Syracuse, NY: Syracuse University Press, 1987.

Goldenberg, Joseph A. *Shipbuilding In Colonial America.* Charlottesville: University Press of Virginia, 1976.

Graymont, Barbara. *The Iroquois in the American Revolution.* Syracuse, NY: Syracuse University Press, 1972.

Greenwood, John. *The Revolutionary Services of John Greenwood of Boston and New York.* New York: Divine Press, 1922.

Griffith, Samuel B. *The War for American Independence: From 1760 to the Surrender at Yorktown in 1781.* Urbana: University of Illinois Press, 2002.

Hadden, James. *A Journal Kept in Canada and upon Burgoyne's Campaign in 1776 and 1777.* Albany, NY: Joel Munson's Sons, 1884.

Hamilton, Edward P. *Fort Ticonderoga, Key to a Continent.* Boston: Little, Brown, 1964.

Hatch, Robert M. *Thrust for Canada: The American Invasion of 1775–1776.* Boston: Houghton Mifflin, 1979.

Hopkins, Timothy. *The Kelloggs in the Old World and the New, Volume 1.* San Francisco: Sunset Press and Photo Engraving, 1903.

Howson, Gerald. *Burgoyne of Saratoga: A Biography.* New York: Times Books, 1978.

Johnson, James M., ed. *Key to the Northern Country: The Hudson River Valley in the American Revolution.* Albany, NY: Excelsior Editions, 2013.

Ketchum, Richard M. *Saratoga: Turning Point of America's Revolutionary War.* New York: Henry Holt, 1999.

Laramie, Michael G. *By Wind and Iron: Naval Campaigns in the Champlain Valley, 1665–1815.* Yardley, PA: Westholme, 2015.

Lewis, Michael. *The Navy of Britain: A Historical Portrait.* London: G. Allen and Unwin, 1948.

Lossing, Benson John. *The Life and Times of Philip Schuyler.* 2 vols. New York: Mason Brothers, 1860.

Lundberg, Philip K., et al. *A Tale of Three Gunboats: Lake Champlain's Revolutionary War Heritage.* Washington, DC: Smithsonian Institution, 2017.

Mahan, A. T. *The Major Operations of the Navies in the War of American Independence.* Boston: Little, Brown, 1913.

Malcolm, Joyce Lee. *The Tragedy of Benedict Arnold: An American.* New York: Pegasus Books, 2018.

Malone, Patrick M. *The Skulking Way of War: Technology and Tactics Among the New England Indians.* Lanham, MD: Madison Books, 1991.

Martin, James Kirby. *Benedict Arnold, Revolutionary Hero: An American Warrior Reconsidered.* New York: New York University Press, 1997.

McCullough, David G. *John Adams.* New York: Simon & Schuster, 2001.

———. *1776.* New York: Simon & Schuster, 2005.

McNeill, William H. *The Pursuit of Power: Technology, Armed Force, and Society Since A.D. 1000.* Chicago: University of Chicago Press, 1982.

Miller, Nathan. *Sea of Glory: A Naval History of the American Revolution.* Annapolis, MD: Naval Institute Press, 1992.

Morgan, William J., ed. *Naval Documents of the American Revolution.* Washington, DC: U.S. Government Printing Office, various dates.

Murphy, Jim. *The Real Benedict Arnold.* New York: Clarion Books, 2007.

Nelson, James L. *Benedict Arnold's Navy: The Ragtag Fleet That Lost the Battle of Lake Champlain but Won the American Revolution.* Camden, ME: International Marine/ McGraw-Hill, 2006.

Nelson, Paul David. *General Horatio Gates: A Biography.* Baton Rouge: Louisiana State University Press, 1976.

O'Shaughnessy, Andrew J. *The Men Who Lost America: British Leadership, the American Revolution, and the Fate of the Empire.* New Haven, CT: Yale University Press, 2013.

O'Toole, Fintan. *White Savage: William Johnson and the Invention of America.* London: Faber, 2005.

Palmer, Dave R. *George Washington's Military Genius.* Washington, DC: Regnery, 2012.

Palmer, Peter S. *Battle of Valcour on Lake Champlain, October 11th, 1776.* Plattsburgh, NY: Lake Shore Press, 1876.

Parkman, Francis. *Historic Handbook of the Northern Tour.* Boston: Little, Brown, 1885.

Penrose, Charles, et al. *Horatio Gates Reconsidered: An Address at Yaddo Mansion, Saratoga Springs.* n.p.: La Crosse County Historical Society, 1866.

Philbrick, Nathaniel. *Valiant Ambition: George Washington, Benedict Arnold, and the Fate of the American Revolution.* New York: Viking, 2016.

Phillips, Kevin. *1775: A Good Year for Revolution.* New York: Viking, 2012.

Pippenger, C. E. "A New Eyewitness Account of Valcour Island Resolves the Pringle Controversy." *Journal of the American Revolution,* October 13, 2016. https://allthingsliberty .com/2016/10/new-eyewitness-account-valcour-island-resolves-pringle-controversy (accessed March 19, 2020).

———. "Finding Edward Wigglesworth's Lost Diary." *Journal of the American Revolution,* October 11, 2018. https://allthingsliberty.com/2018/10/finding-edward-wigglesworths -lost-diary (accessed March 19, 2020).

Procknow, Gene. "Personal Honor and Promotion Among Revolutionary Generals and Congress." *Journal of the American Revolution,* January 23, 2018. https://allthingsliberty .com/2018/01/personal-honor-promotion-among-revolutionary-generals-congress (accessed March 19, 2020).

Randall, Willard S. *Benedict Arnold: Patriot and Traitor.* New York: Morrow, 1990.

———. *Ethan Allen: His Life and Times.* New York: W. W. Norton, 2011.

Rindfleisch, Bryan. "The Stockbridge-Mohican Community, 1775–1783." *Journal of the American Revolution,* February 3, 2016. https://allthingsliberty.com/2016/02/the -stockbridge-mohican-community-1775-1783 (accessed March 19, 2020).

Robbins, Ammi R. *Journal of the Rev. Ammi R. Robbins, a Chaplain in the American Army, in the Northern Campaign of 1776.* New Haven, CT: B. L. Hamlen, 1850.

Rorison, Arda B. *Major-General Arthur St. Clair: A Brief Sketch.* New York: n.p., 1910.

Ross, John F. *War on the Run: The Epic Story of Robert Rogers and the Conquest of America's First Frontier.* New York: Bantam Books, 2009.

Rossie, Jonathan G. *The Politics of Command in the American Revolution.* Syracuse, NY: Syracuse University Press, 1975.

Schecter, Barnet. *The Battle for New York: The City at the Heart of the American Revolution.* New York: Walker, 2002.

Schuyler, Philip. "Letter to George Washington, 1 July 1776." *Founders Online.* https:// founders.archives.gov/documents/Washington/03-05-02-0115 (accessed March 18, 2020).

Sellers, Charles Coleman. *Benedict Arnold, the Proud Warrior.* New York: Milton, Balch, 1930.

Shy, John W. *A People Numerous and Armed: Reflections on the Military Struggle for American Independence.* Ann Arbor: University of Michigan Press, 1990.

Smith, Justin Harvey. *Our Struggle for the Fourteenth Colony: Canada, and the American Revolution.* New York: G. P. Putnam's Sons, 1907.

Spring, Matthew H. *With Zeal and with Bayonets Only: The British Army on Campaign in North America, 1775–1783.* Norman: University of Oklahoma Press, 2008.

Stark, Caleb. *Memoir and Official Correspondence of Gen. John Stark.* Concord, NH: E. C. Eastman, 1877.

Taylor, Alan. *The Divided Ground: Indians, Settlers and the Northern Borderland of the American Revolution.* New York: Alfred A. Knopf, 2006.

Taylor, Stephen. *Commander: The Life and Exploits of Britain's Greatest Frigate Captain.* New York: W. W. Norton, 2012.

Thacher, James. *Military Journal During the American Revolutionary War.* Mineola, NY: Dover Publications, 2019.

Trumbull, John. *The Autobiography of Colonel John Trumbull, Patriot-Artist.* New Haven, CT: Yale University Press, 1970.

Tucker, Jonathan B. *Scourge: The Once and Future Threat of Smallpox.* New York: Atlantic Monthly Press, 2001.

Van de Water, Frederic Franklyn. *Lake Champlain and Lake George.* New York: Bobbs-Merrill, 1946.

Washington, George. "Letter to John Hancock, August 20, 1776." *Founder's Online.* https://founders.archives.gov/documents/Washington/03-06-02-0082 (accessed March 19, 2020).

Weir, Jeffrey M. "A Challenge to the Cause: Smallpox Inoculation in the Era of American Independence, 1764–1781." Ph.D. dissertation, George Mason University, 2014.

Wells, Bayze. *Jounal of Bayze Wells of Farmington.* Hartford: Connecticut Historical Society, 1899.

Wickman, Donald, ed. "A Most Unsettled Time on Lake Champlain: The October 1776 Journal of Jahiel Stewart." *Vermont History* 64 (Spring 1996): 89–98.

Willis, Sam. *The Struggle for Sea Power: A Naval History of the American Revolution.* New York: W. W. Norton, 2016.

Willrich, Michael. *Pox: An American History.* New York: Penguin Press, 2011.

Wilson, Barry. *Benedict Arnold: A Traitor in Our Midst.* Montreal: McGill-Queen's University Press, 2001.

Wood, William. *The Father of British Canada: A Chronicle of Carleton.* Toronto: Glasgow, Brook, 1935.

Index